Revised

Cooperation in the Classroom

David W. Johnson

Roger T. Johnson

Edythe Johnson Holubec

Interaction Book Company

7208 Cornelia Drive

Edina, Minnesota 55435

(612) 831-9500

This book is dedicated to the thousands of teachers who have taken training in cooperative learning and created classroom environments where students care about each other and each other's learning.

ISBN: 0-939603-04-7

Table Of Contents

Preface

How students interact with each other as they learn has been a relatively ignored variable in teaching despite its powerful effects on a wide range of instructional outcomes. Learning situations may be structured so that students compete with each other, ignore each other and work independently, or work together cooperatively. The extensive research comparing these student-student interaction patterns clearly suggests that cooperation among students produces higher achievement, greater motivation to learn, more positive relationships among students, greater acceptance of differences, higher self-esteem, and a number of other outcomes than do competition or working individualistically. At the same time, teachers have been taught and encouraged to prevent students from helping each other, talking to each other, or encouraging each other. Rather, teachers have been taught to ensure that students work alone.

This book is about structuring learning situations cooperatively, so that students work together. Cooperative learning is an old idea. Shifting the emphasis from working alone to caring about whether classmates are learning is a relatively simple idea. Implementing it is not. This book contains a set of practical strategies for structuring cooperative learning groups and specific suggestions for teaching collaborative skills to students. Gaining a high level of expertise in implementing cooperative learning strategies is not easy. It will take some training, perseverence, and support. The training that has been planned to go with these chapters should provide a good start, but it may take a year or two before cooperative learning becomes an integrated and natural part of your teaching. Persisting until you can use cooperative learning procedures and strategies at a routine-use level will benefit your students in numerous ways. It is well worth your efforts.

If students are to learn and master the procedures and skills required for working cooperatively with others, they must do so in the classroom. First they must have the opportunity to do so. This is much more than simply placing them in groups. Teachers must carefully structure learning situations cooperatively. Doing so requires implementing the five basic elements of a well-structured cooperative lesson (i.e., positive interdependence, face-to-face promotive interaction, individual accountability, social skills, and group processing). Having the opportunity to cooperate with classmates does not guarantee that students will be competent in doing so. Teachers must instruct students in how to provide the leadership, communication, trust, decision-making, and conflict management required for learning groups to be effective. This book includes many practical strategies as well as specific suggestions for teaching cooperative procedures and skills to students. Doing so will not be easy. It will take training, perseverence, and support. The training that has been planned to go with this book will provide a good start, but it may take a year or two of actual experience in the classroom before teaching students cooperative procedures and skills becomes a natural part of your teaching. The results for your students are well worth your efforts.

It has taken us nearly 25 years to build the theory, research, and practical experience required to write this book. In the 1960s we began reviewing the research, conducting our initial research studies, and training teachers in the classroom use of cooperation. Since then our work has proliferated. Previous writings on cooperative learning include **Learning Together and Alone** (Johnson & Johnson, 1975, 1987) and **Circles of Learning** (Johnson, Johnson, & Holubec, 1986). Related work on interpersonal skills may be found in our books such as **Reaching Out** (Johnson, 1986) and **Joining Together** (Johnson & F. Johnson, 1987). Recently we have published **Creative Conflict** (Johnson & Johnson, 1987b) a book on the classroom use of conflict to teach students how to manage conflicts within cooperative learning groups constructively. Yet the concept of cooperative learning is much, much older than our work. Our roots reach back to Morton Deutsch and then to Kurt Lewin. We wish to acknowledge our indebtedness to the work of both of these social psychologists.

Many teachers have taught us procedures for implementing cooperative learning and have field tested our ideas in their classrooms with considerable success. We have been in their classrooms and we have sometimes taught beside them. We appreciate their ideas and celebrate their successes. In addition, we have had many talented and productive graduate students who have conducted research studies that have made significant contributions to our understanding of cooperation. We feel privileged to have worked with them.

Our debt to Judy Bartlett is unmeasurable. Her talents, her dedication, and her work beyond the call of duty have all contributed to the completion of this book. We are continually impressed with and are grateful for her work. She also believes in cooperative learning and often works beyond the call of duty to ensure that it is shared with students in the classroom. We wish to thank Thomas Grummett and Nancy Valin for most of the drawings in this book.

COOPERATION
in the CLASSROOM

Introduction To Course

What Is Described

In this introduction the following are described:

1. Overview and objectives of the course.

2. Description of base groups.

3. Implementation assignments.

4. Expectations for participants.

5. Base group assignments.

6. Grading procedures.

7. Case study.

8. Journal.

9. Recommended readings.

Overview Of Course

Each time teachers prepare for a lesson, they must make decisions about the teaching strategies they will use. Teachers may structure lessons so that:

1. Students are in a win-lose struggle to see who is best.

2. Students learn on their own, individually, without interacting with classmates.

3. Students work in pairs or small groups to help each other master the assigned material.

An essential instructional skill that all teachers need is knowing how and when to structure students' learning goals competitively, individualistically, and cooperatively.

Despite the long tradition of using cooperative learning in U.S. education, competitive and individualistic learning has dominated schools for the past 50 years. Cooperation is now being rediscovered. The considerable research validating the effectiveness of cooperative learning has been organized and synthesized. Dozens of new research studies are being conducted each year. Clear procedures for teachers to follow in structuring cooperation among students have been developed, field tested, and perfected. The myths supporting the overuse and inappropriate use of individualistic and competitive learning are being dispelled.

The intent of this course is to communicate the nature of cooperative learning and the procedures for utilizing cooperative learning. More specifically, **the key messages of this course are:**

1. Whenever a learning task is assigned, a clear goal structure should be given so that students know what behaviors are appropriate. There are three goal structures: cooperative, competitive, and individualistic.

2. Cooperative, competitive, and individualistic learning are all important and should be used, but the dominant goal structure in the class should be cooperative.

3. The basic elements of cooperative learning are positive interdependence, individual accountability, face-to-face interaction, cooperative skills, and group processing.

4. The relative superiority of cooperative over competitive and individualistic learning in promoting high achievement and cognitive and social development has been demonstrated by hundreds of research studies. Many teachers,

administrators, students, and parents are unaware of the amount of evidence available.

5. The teacher's role in structuring learning situations cooperatively involves clearly specifying the objectives for the lesson, placing students in productive learning groups and providing appropriate materials, clearly explaining the cooperative goal structure, monitoring students as they work, and evaluating students' performance. The students should always be aware that they "sink or swim together" in a cooperative learning situation.

6. For cooperative learning groups to be productive, students must be able to engage in the needed collaborative skills. Teaching cooperative skills can be done simultaneously with teaching academic material.

7. Any lesson can be taught cooperatively. Any curriculum unit can be organized around cooperative lessons.

8. The implementation of cooperative learning needs to be coupled with the implementation of colleagial support groups among teachers. Both the success of implementation efforts and the quality of life within most schools depend on teachers and other staff members cooperating with each other. Colleagial relationships take as careful structuring and monitoring as does cooperative learning.

In this introduction the expectations for readers who are implementing cooperative learning into their classrooms are discussed. The nature of the base groups within which the book is read is covered. Finally, grading procedures and requirements are discussed.

Description of Base Groups

During this course you will be a part of a base group consisting of four participants. These base groups will stay the same during the entire course. **The base group functions as a support group for the participants that:**

1. Gives support and encouragement for personally mastering the cooperative learning procedures and skills emphasized in the course and provides feedback on how well they are being learned.

2. Gives support and encouragement for implementing the cooperative learning procedures within their classrooms and for teaching students the social skills required to cooperate effectively.

3. Provides an arena for trying out the cooperative learning procedures and skills emphasized within the course and thus serves as an example of building a cooperative group.

4. Provides a structure for managing course evaluation.

You have three major responsibilities:

1. Master and implement in your classrooms the cooperative learning procedures and skills emphasized in the course.

2. Ensure that all members of your base group master and implement the cooperative learning procedures and skills emphasized in the course.

3. Ensure that all members of the class master and implement the cooperative learning procedures and skills emphasized in the course. In other words, if your group is successful, find another group to help until all members of the class are successful.

Each week the work of all members of your base group will be evaluated. Your group will be assigned a file box in which you will place your completed implementation assignments each week and turn them in to the instructor. The following week, at the beginning of the session, your group will be given your file box with the evaluated implementation assignments in it for your review. The score you receive for your work will be the total score of all members of your base group. If all base groups complete the weekly assignment at a 100 percent level, every participant will receive 10 bonus points.

You are expected to contribute actively to the class discussions, work to maintain effective working relationships with other participants, complete all implementation assignments, assist classmates in completing their implementation assignments, express your ideas and do not change your mind unless you are persuaded by logic or information to do so, and indicate your agreement with your base group's work by signing the weekly contract.

Implementation Assignments

Each week you will plan in your base group how to apply to your classroom and school what you have learned. This implementation assignment functions as a learning contract with your base group. In planning how to implement what you have learned, it is important to be as specific as possible about implementation plans and to keep a careful record of your implementation efforts. There are three forms connected with the implementation assignments: the cooperative learning contract, cooperative learning progress report, and cooperative lessons log sheet.

Expectations For Participants

1. **Attend and actively participate in all class sessions.** Attending each session is only half the battle. Each participant needs to be active and not only concerned about his or her own work, but also concerned about the work of the other people in the class. Expect to be actively working during most of the session and to be able to improve your skill in working with others during the course.

2. **Do all the weekly implementation assignments.** The weekly Implementation Assignments are the heart of the course and are designed to be practical in getting cooperative learning started in your classroom. Keep in mind that each class session begins with a chance to share what you have done with the implementation assignment and to hear what the others in your base group have done. They are counting on you to bring back your results.

3. **Read the material in <u>Cooperation in the Classroom</u> with care.** Each chapter of **Cooperation in the Classroom** contains reading material that should be read with care. It is sometimes helpful to underline or highlight important points, write questions in the margin, and add your own thoughts to what is written.

4. **Plan and teach at least one cooperative lesson each week.** Except perhaps for the first week, you should try as many cooperative learning procedures and lessons as you can. Planning and implementing at least one lesson each week is the way that this course will become powerful for you. Part of the sharing in the base groups will center on what is happening in the teaching of cooperatively structured lessons and the use of cooperative learning strategies and skills.

5. **Plan and teach at least five specific cooperative skills over the course.** One of the most interesting and productive parts of the course is to teach students to be more effective in the way they cooperate with one another. The cooperative skills include basic behaviors like using quiet voices and staying with your group, to more complex leadership and communication skills like disagreeing while confirming other's competence. There are many reasons why teaching students cooperative skills is important. One of them is that students' efforts to work together become even more effective and, therefore, achievement continues to grow.

6. **Monitor the behaviors of your students with care while they are working cooperatively with special attention to at least two key students.** While it is important to monitor all students who are working cooperatively, you should pick out two particular students in whom you have a high interest. Perhaps it will be a student who is handicapped in some way, a very bright student, or a student who had real difficulty in working with others. Whoever you pick, you should regularly monitor him or her several times while he or she works in

cooperative learning groups and keep track of your observations for a Case Study (see Case Study Outline following this section).

7. **Keep a journal analyzing your implementation of cooperative learning.** From this journal will be developed assumptions about cooperative learning and your most frequently used cooperative learning strategies.

8. **Develop a colleagial relationship with at least one person in your school who is interested in what you are doing and perhaps even willing to try some cooperative lessons.** There is good evidence that people who innovate in their classrooms need the support of at least one colleague to persevere. Think about your staff and select at least one colleague who would be interested in cooperative learning and would interact with you about what you are doing. If you are participating in the training as part of a team from the same school, you may still want to think about keeping other colleagues informed and interested.

9. **Take an active and supportive interest in the work of the other members of your base group and assist them in accomplishing the course requirements.** The base group is only one of several groups you will be a part of during this course, but it is important. At the beginning of each session the base group will meet and share their experience from the week before. They are expected to provide encouragement for each other and assist each group member to get the most from this course. The assignments will be reviewed by the base group and direct communication with the instructor is provided by the base group file folder (a folder where implementation assignments are stored and instructor feedback is written).

10. **Enjoy yourself and help those around you enjoy themselves during the course sessions.**

Base Group Assignments

There are five assignments that are done individually but are edited, reviewed, and compiled by the base group. Before a participant's assignments can be turned in, they must be reviewed and edited by the other members of the participant's base group. The other group members then sign the assignment to guarantee that it meets the criteria for acceptable performance. The assignments are:

1. Each member is responsible for conducting at least 15 cooperative lessons (one per week). The favorite cooperative lesson is written up and handed in. The format for the lesson plan is provided in Chapter 2.

2. Each member writes up two case studies of students in his or her class. The format of the case studies is described in detail later in the chapter.

3. Each member keeps a personal journal. It is described in detail later in the chapter.

4. Each member teaches at least five lessons aimed at instructing students in the skills they need to cooperate constructively. The best one is selected, written up with some care, and turned in. The format for the lesson plan is provided in Chapter 5.

5. Each member describes how one curriculum area has been modified to include primarily cooperative lessons. The base group responsibility is to assist each group member to work through one or more curriculum areas and prepare a plan to be reviewed and turned in by the base group.

Keeping A Journal

As you read this book you will be asked to keep a journal in which you record what you are learning about cooperative learning. A **journal** is a personal collection of writing and thoughts that have value for the writer. It has to be kept up on a regular basis. Entries are evaluated by whether they are valuable to the author, have some possibilities for sharing with others, and reflect significant thinking. Such a journal will be of great interest to you after you have finished this course. You may also wish to include specific information you have learned about the social psychology of cooperative learning. **The purposes of the journal are:**

1. To keep track of the activities related to this course (what you are doing to make the material useful in your teaching).

2. To answer in writing some of the questions that are important for a clear understanding of the book's content (these will often be suggested, but others can be selected by you).

3. To collect thoughts that are related to the book's content (the best thinking often occurs when you are driving to or from school, about to go to sleep at night, and so forth).

4. To collect newspaper and magazine articles and references that are relevant to the topics covered in each chapter.

5. To keep summaries of conversations and anecdotal material that are unique, interesting or illustrate things related to cooperative learning.

6. To collect interesting thoughts, articles, and conversations not especially related to cooperative learning, but important to you.

(Note: If you publish your journal as did John Holt, Hugh Prather, and others, all we ask is a modest 10 percent of the royalties.)

The journal is an important part of this book. It is not an easy part. The entries should be important to you in your effort to make this course useful, and since this is a cooperative course, useful to your fellow participants. The journal will not be turned in (some of the material you may not want to share), but it is expected that parts of your journal will be shared with others in this class. You may be surprised how writing sharpens and organizes your thoughts.

Case Study Outline

One of the base group assignments is to write a narrative case study of a student's experiences with cooperative learning. Here is a suggested outline for such a case study. Non-teachers may prefer to write about a colleague, teacher, or group they are a member of. Please include in your narrative the following information:

1. Your name, school, grade, and/or subject area, district, and the class you are taking.

2. Dates of the time span covered in the case study.

3. Diagnosis of the problem, or student entry characteristics (identified handicapping condition if any, achievement level, social skill development level, and so forth). Include an explanation of why you chose to study this student.

4. Goals and objectives for the student (specific changes you would like to see as a result of this student's experiences).

5. Interventions used (activities, procedures, and materials employed to help the student meet the goals and objectives). Include ideas for the teacher, the student, and the student's learning partners.

6. Evaluation of the student's progress (any test scores, changes observed, interventions that worked, and revised objectives if appropriate).

Grading Policies

To earn a grade of "A," all participants must:

1. Meet the expectations for participants.

2. Complete all Base Group Assignments satisfactorily.

3. Satisfactorily complete an individual project consisting of:

a. A number of curriculum units utilizing cooperative learning procedures and skills.

b. An introduction that discusses the related theory and research.

The individual project should be at least 10 pages in length and have appropriate academic charm (good form, typed or written with real care, and complete with bibliography and any appropriate appendices).

Nature Of This Book And How To Use It

This is not a book you can read with detachment. It is written to involve you with its contents. By reading this book you will not only be able to learn the theoretical and empirical knowledge now available on cooperative learning, but you will also learn to apply this knowledge in practical ways within your classroom and school. Often in the past, practitioners concerned with cooperative learning did not pay attention to the research literature, and cooperation researchers neglected to specify how their findings could be applied. Thus, the knowledge about effective use of cooperation was often divided. In this book we directly apply existing theory and research to the learning and application of effective cooperative learning procedures and skills. In other words, this book combines theory, research, and practical application to the classroom. In using this book, diagnose your present knowledge and skills, actively participate in the exercises, reflect on your experiences, read the chapters carefully, discuss the relevant theory and research provided, and integrate the information and experiences into your teaching repertoire. In doing so, you will bridge the gap between theory and practice. You should then plan how to continue your skill- and knowledge-building activities after you have finished this book. Most important of all, you should systematically plan how to implement the material covered in each chapter into your classroom.

THE COOPERATIVE UMBRELL

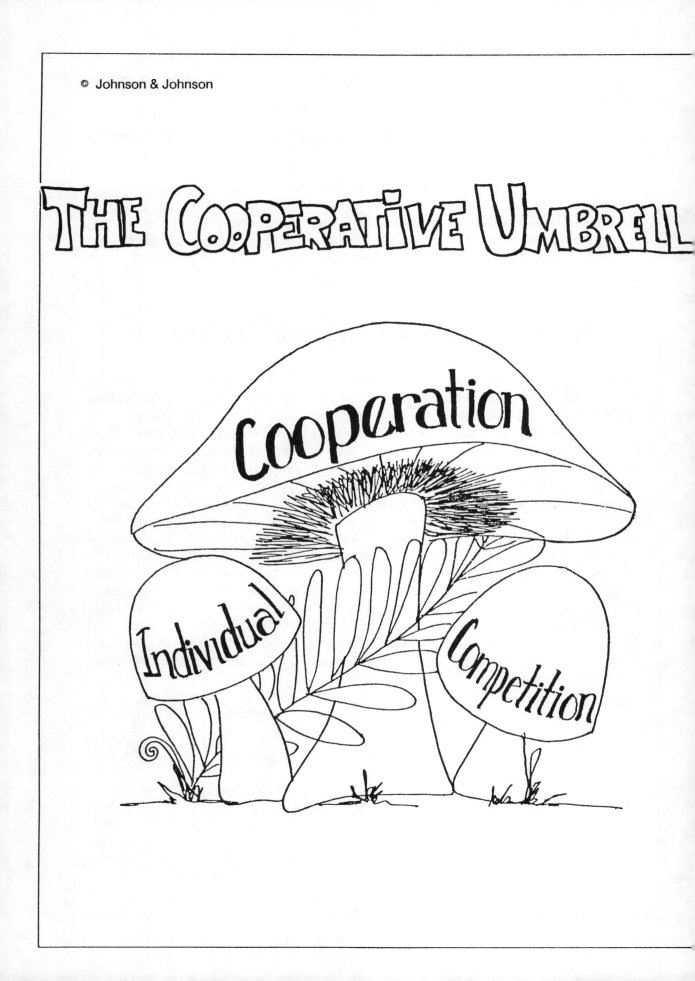

Chapter 1

What Is Cooperative Learning?

Table Of Contents

Introduction

On July 15, 1982, Don Bennett, a Seattle businessman, was the first amputee ever to climb Mount Rainier (reported in Kouzes & Posner, 1987). He climbed 14,410 feet on one leg and two crutches. It took him five days. When asked to state the most important lesson he learned from doing so, without hesitation he said, "You can't do it alone."

Teachers (and students) are coming to a similar conclusion. In every classroom, no matter what the subject area or age of the students, teachers may structure lessons so that students:

1. Work collaboratively in small groups, ensuring that all members master the assigned material.

2. Engage in a win-lose struggle to see who is best.

3. Work independently on their own learning goals at their own pace and in their own space to achieve a preset criterion of excellence.

When faced with the choice, more and more teachers are realizing that students "can't do it alone." We are currently leaving an era of competitive and individualistic learning. The "me" classrooms and "do your own thing" seatwork are fading. We are entering an era of interdependence and mutuality in schools. **The current trend is for "we" classrooms and "we are all in this together" learning.** In contrast to fads, which are generated from the top down, trends are generated from the bottom up and, like horses, they are easier to ride in the direction they are already going. This book is about the trend, being set by teachers and administrators from all parts of our country, toward utilizing cooperative learning procedures in classrooms from preschools to graduate schools.

After half a century of relative neglect, cooperative learning procedures are increasingly being used throughout public and private schools and colleges. The intent of this book is to provide teachers with the knowledge required for beginning the journey of gaining expertise in using cooperative learning. In order to do so, teachers must:

1. Conceptually understand what cooperative learning is and how it differs from competitive and individualistic learning (Chapter 1).

2. Conceptually understand the essential components that differentiate cooperative learning from "traditional classroom grouping" and "individualistic efforts with talking" (Chapter 1). Three of the most important and complex components are positive interdependence, the teaching of social skills, and group processing (Chapters 4, 5, and 6).

3. Conceptually understand the teacher's role in using cooperative learning (Chapter 2).

4. Be able to plan and teach cooperative lessons.

5. Be personally committed to gaining expertise in using cooperative learning. This commitment must be rationale in the sense that it is built on knowledge of the theory and research supporting the use of cooperative learning (Chapter 3).

6. Be part of a colleagial support group made up of teachers who are working hard to gain expertise in the use of cooperative learning within their classrooms (Chapter 7).

Cooperative learning is a basic instructional strategy that should be implemented in every grade level and subject area. In this chapter the basic nature of cooperative learning is defined and contrasted with competitive and individualistic learning. A brief history of cooperative learning is presented. The basic elements of cooperation and how it differs from traditional classroom grouping are discussed. In Chapter 2 the specific procedures teachers use in implementing cooperative learning will be covered.

Student-Student Interaction

Jim is sitting in the classroom, doing nothing. His book is open--to the wrong page. His sheet of printed questions has disappeared. He does not care. He is 17 years old. His classmates ignore him. Within a competitive class Jim is considered a loser to be shunned. Within an individualistic class Jim is considered irrelevant to one's own striving for personal success.

When students are required to **compete** with each other for grades, they work against each other to achieve a goal that only one or a few students can attain. Students are graded on a norm- referenced basis, which requires them to work faster and more accurately than their peers. In doing so, they strive to be better than classmates ("Who can beat Jim in math?"), work to deprive others ("You win, Jim loses."), to celebrate classmates' failures ("Jim did not do his homework, that puts you ahead."), view resources such as grades as limited ("Remember, in a class of 30, only 5 people can get an A."), recognize their negatively linked fate (the more you gain, the less for me; the more I gain, the less for you), and believe that the more competent and hard working individuals become "haves" and the less

competent and deserving individuals become the "have nots" (only the strong prosper). In **competitive situations** there is a negative interdependence among goal achievements; students perceive that they can obtain their goals if and only if the other students in the class fail to obtain their goals (Deutsch, 1962; Johnson & Johnson, 1987). Unfortunately, most students perceive school as predominantly a competitive enterprise. They either work hard in school to do better than the other students, or they take it easy because they do not believe they have a chance to win.

When students are required to work **individualistically** on their own, they work by themselves to accomplish learning goals unrelated to those of the other students. Individual goals are assigned each day, students' efforts are evaluated on a criteria- referenced basis. Each student has his or her own set of materials and works at his or her own speed, ignoring the other students in the class. Students are expected and encouraged to focus on their strict self-interest ("How well can I do?"), valuing only their own efforts and own success ("If I study hard, I may get a high grade."), and ignoring as irrelevant the success or failure of others ("Whether Jim studies or not does not affect me"). In **individualistic learning situations**, students' goal achievements are independent; students perceive that the achievement of their learning goals is unrelated to what other students do (Deutsch, 1962; Johnson & Johnson, 1987).

Consider again the case of Jim, who is sitting in the classroom doing nothing. The teacher assigns all students to cooperative learning groups. Jim finds himself sitting with three class mates. "Jim, where is your paper?" they immediately ask. "Don't know," Jim replied. "Here are the questions," the group members reply, "let's go over them and make sure you know the answers. Don't worry. We'll help you." **Cooperation** is working together to accomplish shared goals. Within cooperative activities individuals seek outcomes that are beneficial to themselves **and** beneficial to all other group members. **Cooperative learning** is the instructional use of small groups so that students work together to maximize their own and each other's learning. The idea is simple. Class members are split into groups of from two to five members after receiving instruction from the teacher. They then work through the assignment until all group members have successfully understood and completed it. Cooperative efforts result in participants striving for mutual benefit so that all group members benefit from one's efforts ("Jim, your success benefits me and my success benefits you."), recognizing that all group members share a common fate ("We all sink or swim together here."), recognizing that one's performance is mutually caused by oneself and one's colleagues ("We can not do it without you, Jim."), and feeling proud and jointly celebrating when a group member is recognized for achievement ("Jim, you got an B! That is terrific!"). In cooperative learning situations there is a positive interdependence among students' goal attainments; students perceive that they can reach their learning goals if and only if the other students in the learning group also reach their goals (Deutsch, 1962; Johnson & Johnson, 1987).

In summary, students' learning goals may be structured to promote cooperative, competitive, or no interdependence among students as they strive to accomplish their learning goals. In every classroom, instructional activities are aimed at accomplishing goals and are conducted under a goal structure. A **learning goal** is a desired future state of demonstrating competence or mastery in the subject area being studied, such as conceptual understanding of math processes, facility in the proper use of a language, or mastering the procedures of inquiry. The **goal structure** specifies the ways in which students will interact with each other and the teacher during the instructional session. Each goal structure has its place. In the ideal classroom, all students would learn how to work collaboratively with others, compete for fun and enjoyment, and work autonomously on their own. The teacher decides which goal structure to implement within each lesson. If cooperation is the only way students learn in school, they may never learn to compete appropriately for fun or have the opportunity to follow a learning trail on their own (Johnson & Johnson, 1987, 1988). Thus, competitive and individualistic work should supplement cooperative learning when it is appropriate.

Cooperative learning is the most important of the three types of learning situations, yet currently it is the least used. Current evidence indicates that class sessions are structured cooperatively only for 7 to 20 percent of the time (Anderson, 1984; Goodlad, 1983; D. Johnson & Johnson, 1976; R. Johnson, 1976; R. Johnson, Johnson, & Bryant, 1973; Schumaker, Sheldon-Wildgen, & Sherman, 1980). On the other hand, what we know about effective instruction indicates that cooperative learning should be used when we want students to learn more, like school better, like each other better, like themselves better, and learn more effective social skills. It is clear from the research that classrooms should be dominated by cooperation among students. In the next sections of this chapter, therefore, we shall give a brief history of cooperative learning, define its essential components, and note the differences between cooperative learning and traditional small group instruction.

History Of Cooperative Learning

> "Two are better than one, because they have a good reward for *their toil. For if they fall, one will lift up his fellow; but woe to him who is alone when he falls and has not another to lift him up...And though a man might prevail against one who is alone, two will withstand him. A threefold cord is not quickly broken.*"

Ecclesiastics 4:9-12

Cooperative learning is an old idea. The capacity to work cooperatively has been a major contributor to the survival of our species. The Talmud clearly states that in order to learn one must have a learning partner. As early as the first century, Quintilian argued that students could benefit from teaching one another. **Johann Amos Comenius** (1592-1679) believed that students would benefit both by teaching and being taught by other students. In the late 1700's **Joseph Lancaster** and Andrew Bell made extensive use of cooperative learning groups in England, and the idea was brought to America when a Lancastrian school was opened in New York City in 1806. Within the **Common School Movement** in the United States in the early 1800's there was a strong emphasis on cooperative learning. Certainly, the use of cooperative learning is not new to American education. There have been periods in which cooperative learning had strong advocates and was widely used to promote the educational goals of that time.

One of the most successful advocates of cooperative learning was **Colonel Francis Parker**. In the last three decades of the 19th Century, Colonel Parker brought to his advocacy of cooperative learning enthusiasm, idealism, practicality, and an intense devotion to freedom, democracy, and individuality in the public schools. His fame and success rested on the vivid and regenerating spirit that he brought into the schoolroom and on his power to create a classroom atmosphere that was truly cooperative and democratic. When he was superintendent of the public schools at Quincy, Massachusetts (1875-1880), he averaged more than 30,000 visitors a year to examine his use of cooperative learning procedures.

Parker's instructional methods of promoting coopera- tion among students dominated American education through the turn of the century. Following Parker, **John Dewey** promoted the use of cooperative learning groups as part of his famous project method in instruc- tion. In the late 1930's, however, interpersonal com- petition began to be emphasized in public schools.

In the 1940's **Morton Deutsch**, building on the theorizing of **Kurt Lewin**, proposed a theory of cooperative and competitive situations that has served as the primary foundation on which subsequent re- search on and discussion of cooperative learning has been based. Our own research is directly based on Deutsch's work. There are several groups of re- searchers and practitioners scattered throughout the United States and Canada and in several other countries engaged in the study and implemen- tation of cooperative learning lessons, curriculums, strategies, and procedures.

Not All Group Learning Is Cooperative Learning

In a classroom the teacher is trying out learning groups. "This is a mess," she thinks. In one group students are bickering over who is going to do the writing. In another group a member sits quietly, too shy to participate. Two members of a third group are talking about football while the third member works on the assignment. "My students do not know how to work cooperatively," the teacher concludes.

What is a teacher to do in such a situation? Simply placing students in groups and telling them to work together does not mean that they know how to cooperate or that they will do so even if they know. Sitting students near each other and telling them that they are a group in and of itself does not produce cooperation or the higher achievement and other outcomes typically found in cooperative learning groups.

There are many ways in which the efforts of traditional learning groups may go wrong. Group members sometimes seek a free ride on others' work by "leaving it to Roger" to complete the group's tasks. Students who are stuck with doing all the work sometimes decrease their efforts to avoid being suckers. High ability group members may take over the important leadership roles in ways that benefit themselves at the expense of the lower achieving group members so that the rich-get-richer. In a traditional learning group, for example, the more able group member may give all the explanations of what is being learned. Since the amount of time spent explaining correlates highly with the amount learned, the more able member learns a great deal while the less able members flounder as a captive audience. Group work may break down because of divisive conflicts and power struggles. Dysfunctional divisions of labor may be formulated ("I'm the thinkist and you're the typist"). Inappropriate dependence on authority may exist. Group members may gang up against a task. Pressures to conform may suppress individual efforts. There are multiple ways that groups may fail.

The barriers to effective group learning are avoided when it is properly structured cooperatively. Effective cooperative learning occurs when you ensure that the essential components are structured within each cooperative lesson.

Essential Components of Cooperative Learning

In Roy Smith's Junior High School English class in Hingham, Massachusetts, students are given the assignment of writing thesis essays on a story, **The Choice**, which discusses the experience of a time traveler who goes into the future and returns. The class is divided into groups of four, with high-, medium-, and low-achieving students and both male and female students in each group. Seven instructional tasks are assigned over a four day unit:

1. A prereading discussion on what should be taken on a time-travel trip into the future, what should be found out, and what should be told to others on one's return.

2. Each student writes a letter/proposal requesting funding for a time-travel into the future.

3. Group members edit each other's letters/proposals and gives suggestions for improvement and mark any errors that need correcting. All revised letters/proposals are handed in with the signatures of the group members who edited them.

4. Each member reads the story, **The Choice**, and makes a tentative interpretation of its meaning.

5. Group members discuss the story and reach consensus on the answers to seven questions about its content.

6. Each student writes a composition, taking the position that the decision made by Williams was correct or incorrect and presenting a convincing rationale as to why his or her position is valid.

7. Group members edit two other members' compositions. Careful editing for spelling, punctuation, and the components of thesis essays is emphasized. All revised compositions are handed in with the signatures of the group members who edited them.

Within this lesson **positive interdependence** is structured by having each group start out with 100 points, and subtracting 5 points for every spelling or punctuation error and every failure to include the essential components of thesis essays. The group is given 20 bonus points if every member clearly articulates an interpretation of the story and supports it with valid reasoning. **Individual accountability** is ensured by requiring each student to write the letter/proposal and essay and revise them to meet the standards of his or her groupmates. The **cooperative skill** of criticizing ideas without criticizing the person is explained by the teacher and practiced by the students. Finally, the group spends some time during the final class session **processing** how well they worked together and what they could do in the future to be an even more effective group member. This lesson illustrates the essential components of cooperative learning.

Many educators who believe that they are using cooperative learning are, in fact, missing its essence. There is a crucial difference between simply putting students into groups to learn and in structuring cooperation among students.

Cooperation is **not** having students sit side-by-side at the same table to talk with each other as they do their individual assignments. Cooperation is **not** assigning a report to a group of students where one student does all the work and the others put their names on the product as well. Cooperation is much more than being physically near other students, discussing material with other students, helping other students, or sharing material among students, although each of these is important in cooperative learning. There are five essential components that must be included for small group learning to be truly cooperative.

Positive Interdependence

"All for one and one for all."

Alexandre Dumas

Within a football game, the quarterback who throws the pass and the receiver who catches the pass are positively interdependent. The success of one depends on the success of the other. It takes two to complete a pass. One player cannot succeed without the other. Both have to perform competently if their mutual success is to be assured. They sink or swim together.

The first requirement for an effectively structured cooperative lesson is that students believe that they "sink or swim together." Within cooperative learning situations students have two responsibilities: learn the assigned material and ensure that all members of their group learn the assigned material. The technical term for that dual responsibility is positive interdependence. **Positive interdependence** exists when students perceive that they are linked with groupmates in a way so that they cannot succeed unless their groupmates do (and vice versa) and/or that they must coordinate their efforts with the efforts of their groupmates to complete a task. Positive interdependence promotes a situation in which students see that their work benefits groupmates and vice versa, and students work together in small groups to maximize the learning of all members by sharing their resources, providing mutual support, and celebrating their joint success.

When positive interdependence is clearly understood, it highlights:

1. Each group member's efforts are required and indispensable for group success (i.e., there can be no "free-riders").

2. Each group member has a unique contribution to make to the joint effort because of his or her resources and/or role and task responsibilities.

There are a number of ways of structuring positive interdependence within a learning group (goal, reward, resource, and role interdependence). To ensure that students believe "they sink or swim together" and care about how much each other learns, you (the teacher) have to structure a clear **group or mutual goal** such as "learn the assigned material and make sure that all members of your group learn the assigned material." The group goal always has to be part of the lesson. To supplement goal interdependence, you may wish to add **joint rewards** (if all members of the group score 90 percent correct or better on the test, each will receive 5 bonus points), **divided resources** (giving each group member a part of the total information required to complete an assignment), and **complementary roles** (reader, checker, encourager, elaborator).

Face-To-Face Promotive Interaction

> *"In an industrial organization it's group effort that counts. There's really no room for stars in an industrial organization. You need talented people, but they can't do it alone. They have to have help."*

John F. Donnelly, President, Donnelly Mirrors

The second component is **face-to-face promotive interaction** among group members. Cooperative learning requires face-to-face interaction among students within which they promote each other's learning and success. There is no magic in positive interdependence in and of itself. It is the interaction patterns and verbal interchange among students promoted by the positive interdependence that affect education outcomes.

Within cooperative lessons, you need to maximize the opportunity for students to promote each other's success by helping, assisting, supporting, encouraging, and praising each other's efforts to learn. Such promotive interaction has a number of effects. **First**, there are cognitive activities and interpersonal dynamics that only occur when students explain to each other how the answers to assignments are derived. This includes orally explaining how to solve problems, discussing the nature of the concepts being learned, teaching one's knowledge to groupmates, and explaining how present learning is connected with past learning. **Second**, it is within face-to-face interaction that the opportunity for a wide variety of social influences and patterns emerge. Helping and assisting take place. Accountability to peers, influencing each other's reasoning and conclusions, social modeling, social support, and interpersonal rewards all increase as the face-to-face interaction among group members increase. **Third**, the verbal and nonverbal responses of other group members provide important feedback concerning each other's performance. **Fourth**, it provides an opportunity for peers to pressure unmotivated group members to achieve. **Fifth**, it is the interaction involved in completing the work that allows students to get to know each other as persons, which in turn forms the basis for caring and committed relationships among members.

To obtain meaningful face-to-face interaction, the size of groups needs to be small (from 2 to 6 members), as the perception that one's participation and efforts are needed increases as the size of the group decreases. On the other hand, as the size of the group increases the amount of pressure peers may place on unmotivated group members increases. Whatever the size, the effects of social interaction cannot be achieved through nonsocial substitutes such as instructions and materials.

Individual Accountability / Personal Responsibility

"What children can do together today, they can do alone tomorrow."

Vygotsky

Among the early settlers of Massachusetts there was a saying, "If you do not work, you do not eat." The third essential component of cooperative learning is **individual accountability**, which exists when the performance of each individual student is assessed and the results given back to the group and the individual. It is important that the group knows who needs more assistance, support, and encouragement in completing the assignment. It is also important that group members know that they cannot "hitch-hike" on the work of others.

To ensure that each student is individually accountable to do his or her fair share of the group's work, you need to:

1. Assess how much effort each member is contributing to the group's work.

2. Provide feedback to groups and individual students.

3. Help groups avoid redundant efforts by members.

4. Ensure that every member is responsible for the final outcome.

When it is difficult to identify members' contributions, when members' contributions are redundant, and when members are not responsible for the final group outcome, members are likely to loaf and seek a free ride. The smaller the size of the group, furthermore, the greater the individual accountability may be.

The purpose of cooperative learning groups is to make each member a stronger individual. Individual accountability is the key to ensuring that all group members are in fact strengthened by learning cooperatively. After participating in a cooperative lesson, group members should be better able to complete similar tasks by themselves. There is a pattern to classroom learning. First, students learn how to solve the problem or use the strategy in a cooperative group, then secondly, they perform it alone. Common ways to structure individual accountability include giving an individual test to each student, randomly selecting one student's product to represent the entire group, having students teach what they have learned to someone else, and have students explain what they know to the group.

Interpersonal And Small Group Skills

"I will pay more for the ability to deal with people than any other ability under the sun."

John D. Rockefeller

The fourth essential component of cooperative learning is the appropriate use of **interpersonal and small group skills.** Placing socially unskilled individuals in a group and telling them to cooperate does not guarantee that they are able to do so effectively. We are not born instinctively knowing how to interact effectively with others. Interpersonal and group skills do not magically appear when they are needed. Persons must be taught the social skills required for high quality collaboration and be motivated to use them if cooperative groups are to be productive. In order to coordinate efforts to achieve mutual goals, students must (1) get to know and trust each other, (2) communicate accurately and unambiguously, (3) accept and support each other, and (4) resolve conflicts constructively (Johnson, 1986, 1987; Johnson & F. Johnson, 1987). Interpersonal and small group skills form the basic nexus among students, and if students are to work together productively and cope with the stresses and strains of doing so, they must have a modicum of these skills.

Group Processing

The fifth essential component of cooperative learning is **group processing**, which exists when group members discuss how well they are achieving their goals and maintaining

Table 1.1 What Is the Difference?

Cooperative Learning Groups	Traditional Learning Groups
Positive interdependence	No interdependence
Individual accountability	No individual accountability
Heterogenous membership	Homogeneous membership
Shared leadership	One appointed leader
Responsible for each other	Responsible only for self
Task & maintenace emphasized	Only task emphasized
Social skills directly taught	Social skills assumed & ignored
Teacher observes & intervenes	Teacher ignores groups
Group processing occurs	No group processing

effective working relationships. Effective group work is influenced by whether or not groups reflect on (i.e., process) how well they are functioning. A **process** is an identifiable sequence of events taking place over time, and **process goals** refer to the sequence of events instrumental in achieving outcome goals. **Group processing** may be defined as reflecting on a group session to (a) describe what member actions were helpful and unhelpful and (b) make decisions about what actions to continue or change. The purpose of group processing is to clarify and improve the effectiveness of the members in contributing to the collaborative efforts to achieve the group's goals. Groups need to describe what member actions were helpful and unhelpful in completing the group's work and make decisions about what behaviors to continue or change. Such processing (1) enables learning groups to focus on maintaining good working relationships among members, (2) facilitates the learning of cooperative skills, (3) ensures that members receive feedback on their participation, (4) ensures that students think on the meta-cognitive as well as the cognitive level, and (5) provides the means to celebrate the success of the group and reinforce the positive behaviors of group members. Some of the keys to successful processing are allowing sufficient time for it to take place, emphasizing positive feedback, making the processing specific rather than vague, maintaining student involvement in processing, reminding students to use their cooperative skills while they process, and communicating clear expectations as to the purpose of processing.

Besides having each learning group process, teachers may lead whole-class processing. When cooperative learning groups are used, the teacher observes the groups, analyzes the problems they have working together, and gives feedback to each group on how well they are working together. An important aspect of both small-group and whole-class processing is group and class celebrations. It is feeling successful, appreciated, and respected that builds commitment to learning and a sense of self- efficacy.

Approaches To Cooperative Learning

There are two different but interrelated approaches to training teachers to use cooperative learning: conceptual and direct. The **direct approach** involves training teachers how to use a specific cooperative activity (such as group-building activities like "favorite sports and hobbies," "pets I wish I had," and "team juggling"), how to teach a specific cooperative lesson (such as an English lesson on punctuation or a math lesson on long division), how to apply a specific cooperative strategy (such as arranging reading assignments like a jig-saw puzzle or having students work together to complete a group project), and how to use a curriculum package based on cooperative learning (such as Teams Games Tournaments). Some of the most powerful strategies include the jigsaw method developed by Elliot Aronson and his colleagues (Aronson, 1978), the coop/coop strategy developed by Spencer Kagan (Kagan, 1988), the group project method developed by the Sharans (Sharan & Sharan, 1976), math groups-of-four developed by Marilyn Burns (Burns, 1987), tribes developed by Jeanne Gibbs (1987), and many more.

The **conceptual approach** involves training teachers how to apply an overall conceptual system to build cooperative activities, lessons, and strategies. The conceptual approach is based on a theoretical framework that provides general principles on how to structure cooperative learning activities in a teacher's specific subject area, curricula, students, and setting. Using the general principles teachers can analyze their current curriculums, students, and instructional goals and design appropriate cooperative lessons. The advantage of conceptual principles is that they can be used in any classroom from preschool to graduate school. The particulars can be adapted for differences in age, ability, and background of students. The two conceptual approaches to cooperative learning have been developed by Elizabeth Cohen (1986) and the authors of this book (Johnson & Johnson, 1975/1991; Johnson, Johnson, & Holubec, 1986/1990). Cohen bases her conceptual principles on expectation-states theory while we base our conceptual principles on the theory of cooperation and competition Morton Deutsch derived from Kurt Lewin's field theory.

Just as many cooperative learning activities may be generated from one strategy, many strategies may be generated from a set of conceptual principles. The conceptual approach subsumes the direct approach to cooperative learning. Once teachers have mastered the basic conceptual principles of how to use the five essential components to structure learning cooperatively, a variety of strategies, lessons, and activities may be generated and utilized within any one lesson. Becoming competent in applying the essential elements is a requirement for obtaining real expertise in using cooperative learning.

Long-Term Goals And Developing Expertise

To be an expert in cooperative learning you have to use it long enough to:

1. Be able to take any lesson in any subject area and structure it cooperatively.

2. Use cooperative learning at the routine-use level.

3. Use cooperative learning at least 60 percent of the time.

Gaining and maintaining such expertise is a long-term process requiring up to two years or more of hard work. Learning how to structure learning situations cooperatively requires procedural learning (very similar to learning how to perform brain surgery, how to fly an airplane, or how to play tennis) and being a member of an ongoing colleagial support group.

Reading books for a recognition-level or even a total-recall-level of learning about cooperative learning is not enough. You not only have to read material such as this book, but you must actually perform the procedures involved in using cooperative learning. **Procedural learning** exists when you study cooperative learning to:

1. Learn conceptually what cooperative learning is.

2. Translate your conceptual understanding of cooperative learning into a set of operational procedures appropriate for your students and subjects taught.

3. Teach cooperatively structured lessons regularly.

4. Eliminate errors in using cooperative learning so that you move through the initial awkward and mechanical stages of skill mastery.

5. Attain a routine-use, automated level of use of cooperative learning.

Procedural learning differs from simply learning facts and acquiring knowledge. It relies heavily on feedback about performance and modifying your implementation until the errors of performance are eliminated. Usually your efforts will fail to match the ideal of what you wish to accomplish for a considerable length of time until cooperative learning is overlearned at a routine-use, automated level. **Failure is part of the process of gaining expertise. Success,** however, **is inevitable when failure is followed by persistent practice, feedback, and reflection on how to use cooperative learning more competently.** To gain expertise you need a colleagial support group made up of peers you like and trust. Gaining expertise takes learning partners who are willing to trust each other, talk frankly about their teaching, and observe each other's performance over a prolonged period of time to help each other identify and eliminate the errors being made in implementing cooperative learning. Unless you are willing to reveal your lack of expertise to obtain accurate feedback from trusted colleagues, teaching expertise cannot be gained. In other words, procedural learning requires cooperation among colleagues. Colleagial support groups are discussed in detail in Chapter 7.

Getting Started with Cooperative Groups

To begin using cooperative learning groups there are a number of stages teachers may go through. Once a teacher has made a decision to try cooperative learning, there may be an initial rather awkward use within which the lessons may not go well because both the students and the teacher are new to a system of using cooperative groups for instructional purposes. There are a number of "start up" issues such as teaching students the cooperative skills they need to work together effectively, and training students in how to move into and out of groups quickly and quietly. Once both the teacher and the students become used to the system of cooperative learning, then a stage of mechanically using cooperative learning procedures may set in. Teachers follow the general procedures for implementing cooperative learning in a step-by-step fashion, planning each lesson, and reviewing recommended procedures before each lesson. It may take teachers a year to reach this stage. Finally, when the cooperative learning strategies are fully integrated into the teachers' repertoires, teachers reach the routine-use level in which lessons may be automatically structured for cooperative learning situations without conscious thought or planning. The concurrent focus on academic and collaborative skills takes place spontaneously. It may take teachers two years to reach this stage. Some advice that may be helpful is:

1. Do not try to move this fast. Start with a single lesson. Move to conducting at least one cooperative lesson per week and then to modifying a curriculum unit to be primarily cooperative.

2. Persevere! Do not stop growing in your use of cooperative learning even though some students are not very skillful and no one else in your school seems to care. Lay out a long-range plan and stay with it. Especially persevere with students who have a hard time collaborating with peers.

3. Seek support from one or more colleagues and engage in joint sharing of successes, problems, new ideas, and curriculum modification.

4. Plan carefully for the start of each school year so that cooperative learning is emphasized right away.

Within this book practical advice is presented in order to help teachers move from the initial to routine stages of using cooperative learning strategies.

Starting Up Advice

An advantage of cooperative learning is that students become more directly involved in their learning and thereby learn more and enjoy it more. Specifically, students get immediate feedback on how well they learned, teach their peers, see learning strategies modeled, and verbalize what they learn. A disadvantage of group work is that many students don't know how to work effectively in groups, so problems arise. To minimize these problems, try the following.

1. Make up the groups yourself. Each group should have a high, medium, and low-achieving student in it, with a mix of sexes, cultural groups, and motivation levels in order to be most powerful. Do not put students with their friends unless you have a good reason. If students protest their group membership, explain that you will make new groups later on, so they won't always be with the same people.

2. Seat students close to their group members. This makes it quick and easy for you to get them in and out of their groups.

3. Start out with small groups. Groups sized two or three are best until students become skillful in including everyone. Then proceed carefully to four if you wish.

4. Integrate cooperative learning into your curriculum. Anything one can do, two can do better. Have them drill each other in pairs over material taught. Review for tests in trios. On some assignments, have them do the work individually first, then decide on group answers. They can certify each other's papers for accuracy, then you can pick one paper to grade. Three students can discuss chapter questions and turn in one paper for the group. The more oral discussion and summarizing of material the students do, the more they will learn.

5. Assign each student a job or role. Possibilities include **Reader, Recorder, Checker** (makes certain everyone knows and can explain the answers by having group members summarize), **Encourager** (encourages full participation by asking silent members what they think or what they have to add), and **Praiser** (praises good ideas or helpful group members).

6. Make your expectations of group behavior clear. "I expect to see everyone staying with the group, contributing ideas, listening carefully to other group members, making certain everyone is included in the work, and making certain everyone understands and agrees."

7. Observe and question while students are working. Ask any student you don't think is helping his or her groupmates to explain an answer. Make it clear to the group that it is responsible for making sure all group members participate and know the answers. Expect that some groups will finish before other groups; check over their work and have them correct any glaring errors, then let them review, talk quietly, study, or read until the other groups are finished.

8. After each session, have each group answer: "What did we do well today in working together? What could we do even better tomorrow?" Let them know what you saw them do. Be positive and reward positive behaviors.

Some Quick Cooperative Starters

Although we have found few limits to the number of ways cooperative learning groups can be used, here are some ideas to get you started.

1. **Turn to Your Neighbor**: Three to five minutes. Ask the students to turn to a neighbor and ask something about the lesson: to explain a concept you've just taught; to explain

the assignment; to explain how to do what you've just taught; to summarize the three most important points of the discussion, or whatever fits the lesson.

2. **Reading Groups**: Students read material together and answer the questions. One person is the **Reader**, another the **Recorder**, and the third the **Checker** (who checks to make certain everyone understands and agrees with the answers. They must come up with three possible answers to each question and circle their favorite one. When finished, they sign the paper to certify that they all understand and agree on the answers.

3. **Jigsaw**: Each person reads and studies part of a selection, then teaches what he or she has learned to the other members of the group. Each then quizzes the group members until satisfied that everyone knows his or her part thoroughly.

4. **Focus Trios**: Before a film, lecture, or reading, have students summarize together what they already know about the subject and come up with questions they have about it. Afterwards, the trios answer questions, discuss new information, and formulate new questions.

5. **Drill Partners**: Have students drill each other on the facts they need to know until they are certain both partners know and can remember them all. This works for spelling, vocabulary, math, grammar, test review, etc. Give bonus points on the test if all members score above a certain percentage.

6. **Reading Buddies**: In lower grades, have students read their stories to each other, getting help with words and discussing content with their partners. In upper grades, have students tell about their books and read their favorite parts to each other.

7. **Worksheet Checkmates**: Have two students, each with different jobs, do one worksheet. The **Reader** reads, then suggests an answer; the **Writer** either agrees or comes up with another answer. When they both understand and agree on an answer, the Writer can write it.

8. **Homework Checkers**: Have students compare homework answers, discuss any they have not answered similarly, then correct their papers and add the reason they changed an answer. They make certain everyone's answers agree, then staple the papers together. You grade one paper from each group and give group members that grade.

9. **Test Reviewers**: Have students prepare each other for a test. They get bonus points if every group member scores above a preset level.

10. **Composition Pairs**: Student A explains what s/he plans to write to Student B, while Student B takes notes or makes an outline. Together they plan the opening or thesis statement. Then Student B explains while Student A writes. They exchange outlines, and use them in writing their papers.

11. **Board Workers**: Students go together to the chalkboard. One can be the **Answer Suggester,** one the **Checker** to see if everyone agrees, and one the **Writer**.

12. **Problem Solvers**: Give groups a problem to solve. Each student must contribute to part of the solution. Groups can decide who does what, but they must show where all members contributed. Or, they can decide together, but each must be able to explain how to solve the problem.

13. **Computer Groups**: Students work together on the computer. They must agree on the input before it is typed in. One person is the **Keyboard Operator,** another the **Monitor Reader,** a third the **Verifier** (who collects opinions on the input from the other two and makes the final decision). Roles are rotated daily so everyone gets experience at all three jobs.

14. **Book Report Pairs**: Students interview each other on the books they read, then they report on their partner's book.

15. **Writing Response Groups**: Students read and respond to each other's papers three times:

    a. They mark what they like with a star and put a question mark anywhere there is something they don't understand or think is weak. Then they discuss the paper as a whole with the writer.

    b. They mark problems with grammar, usage, punctuation, spelling, or format and discuss it with the author.

    c. They proofread the final draft and point out any errors for the author to correct.

Teachers can assign questions for students to answer about their group members' papers to help them focus on certain problems or skills.

16. **Skill Teachers/Concept Clarifiers**: Students work with each other on skills (like identifying adjectives in sentences or showing proof in algebra) and/or concepts (like "ecology" or "economics") until both can do or explain it easily.

17. **Group Reports**: Students research a topic together. Each one is responsible for checking at least one different source and writing at least three notecards of information. They write the report together; each person is responsible for seeing that his/her information is included. For oral reports, each must take a part and help each other rehearse until they are all at ease.

18. **Summary Pairs**: Have students alternate reading and orally summarizing paragraphs. One reads and summarizes while the other checks the paragraph for accuracy and adds anything left out. They alternate roles with each paragraph.

19. **Elaborating and Relating Pairs**: Have students elaborate on what they are reading and learning by relating it to what they already know about the subject. This can be done before and after reading a selection, listening to a lecture, or seeing a film.

20. **Playwrights**: Students write a play together, perhaps about a time period recently studied, practice, and perform it for the class.

Back to the Basics

The importance of cooperative learning goes beyond maximizing outcomes such as achievement, positive attitudes toward subject areas, and the ability to think critically, although these are worthwhile outcomes. Knowledge and skills are of no use if the student cannot apply them in cooperative interaction with other people. Being able to perform technical skills such as reading, speaking, listening, writing, computing, and problem-solving are valuable but of little use if the person cannot apply those skills in cooperative interaction with other people. It does no good to train an engineer, secretary, accountant, teacher, or mechanic if the person does not have the cooperative skills needed to apply the knowledge and technical skills in cooperative relationships on the job.

Much of what students learn in school is worthless in the real world. Schools teach that work means performing tasks largely by oneself, helping and assisting others is cheating, technical competencies are the other thing that matters, attendance and punctuality are secondary to test scores, motivation is up to the teacher, success depends on performance on individual tests, and promotions are received no matter how little one works. In the real world of work, things are altogether different. Most employers do not expect people to sit in rows and compete with colleagues without interacting with them. The heart of most jobs, especially the higher-paying more interesting jobs, is teamwork, which involves getting others to cooperate, leading others, coping with complex power and influence issues, and helping solve people's problems in working with each other. Teamwork, communication, effective coordination, and divisions of labor characterize most real-life settings. It is time for schools to leave the ivory tower of working alone and sitting in rows to see who is best and more realistically reflect the realities of adult life.

Students increasingly live in a world characterized by interdependence, pluralism, conflict, and rapid change. Because of technological, economic, ecological, and political interdependence, the solution of most problems cannot be achieved by one country alone. The major problems faced by individuals (e.g., contamination of the environment, warming of the atmosphere, world hunger, international terrorism, nuclear war) are increasing ones that cannot be solved by actions taken only at the national level. Our students will live in a complex, interconnected world in which cultures collide every minute and dependencies limit the flexibility of individuals and nations. The internationalization of problems will increase so that there will be no clear division between domestic and international problems. Students need to learn the competencies involved in managing interdependence, resolving conflicts within cooperative systems made up of parties from different countries and cultures, and personally adapting to rapid change.

Quality of life depends on having close friends who last a lifetime, building and maintaining a loving family, being a responsible parent, caring about others, and contributing to the well-being of the world. These are things that make life worthwhile. Grades in school do not predict which students will have a high quality of life after they are graduated. The ability to work cooperatively with others does. The ability of students to work collaboratively with others is the keystone to building and maintaining the caring and committed relationships that largely determine quality of life.

Despite the importance of cooperative learning experiences, there are critics who challenge its use. They wish to know if the claims of advocates are really valid. In the next chapter, therefore, we shall review briefly the voluminous body of research that has validated the instructional use of cooperation.

Final Note

During one very difficult trek across an ice field in Don Bennett's hop to the top of Mount Rainer, his daughter stayed by his side for four hours and with each new hop told him (Kouzes & Posner, 1987), "You can do it, Dad. You're the best dad in the world. You can do it, Dad." There was no way Bennett would quit hopping to the top with his daughter yelling words of love and encouragement in his ear. The encouragement of his daughter kept him going, strengthening his commitment to make it to the top. The classroom is similar. With members of their cooperative group cheering them on, students amaze themselves and their teachers with what they can achieve.

Implementation Assignment 1

1. Read Introduction and Chapters 1 and 2.

2. Write down your feelings about competing, working individualistically, and cooperating with others. Think back over the years. What memories are most vivid about competing, cooperating, and working individualistically.

3. Examine the subject areas, curriculums, and lessons you teach and decide on ten places where cooperative learning may be (or is being) fruitfully used in your classroom. Carefully read the section on quick cooperative starters for ideas.

⸺⸙⸽[Cooperative Learning Contract]⸽⸚⸺

MAJOR LEARNINGS	IMPLEMENTATION PLANS

Date _____   Date of Progress Report Meeting _____

Participant's Signature _____

Signatures of Other Group Members _____

_____   _____   _____

⤑⟦ Cooperative Learning Progress Report ⟧⟨⤐

NAME _____ SCHOOL _____

AGE LEVEL _____ SUBJECT _____

DAY and DATE	DESCRIPTION OF TASKS and ACTIVITIES PERFORMED	SUCCESSES EXPERIENCED	PROBLEMS ENCOUNTERED

Description of critical or interesting incidents:

1:26

⧫[Cooperative Learning Log Sheet]⧫

WEEK	LESSONS PLANNED AND/OR TAUGHT	COLLAB. SKILL STRESSED	PLANNED WITH	OBSERVED BY	GIVEN AWAY TO
1					
2					
3					
4					
5					
6					
7					
8					
9					
10					
11					
12					
13					
14					
15					
GRP					
TOTAL					

EXERCISE

MATERIALS

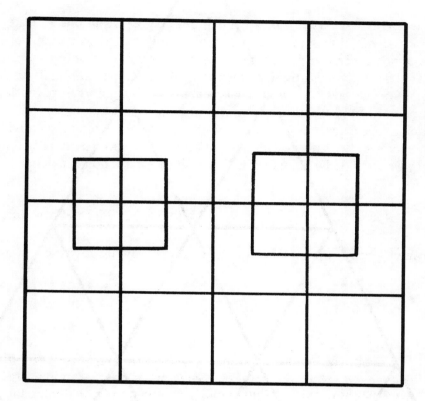

How Did I Feel?

What Did I Notice?

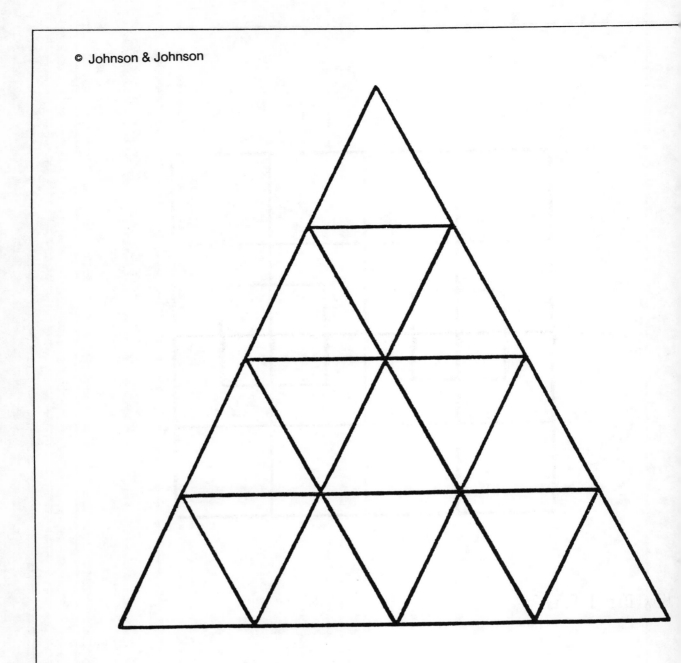

HOW DID I FEEL?

WHAT DID I NOTICE?

1:30

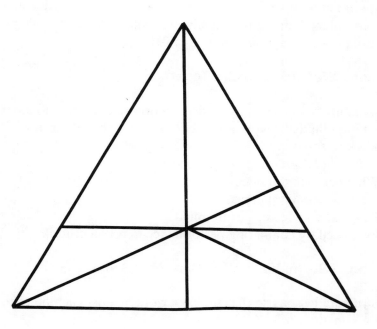

HOW DID I FEEL?

WHAT DID I NOTICE?

DEFINITIONS

A learning **goal** is a desired future state of competence or mastery in the subject area being studied. A **goal structure** specifies the type of interdependence among students as they strive to accomplish their learning goals. Interdependence may be positive (cooperation), negative (competition), or none (individualistic efforts).

Cooperation: We Sink Or Swim Together

Teachers structure lessons so that students work together to maximize their own and each other's learning. Students work together to achieve shared goals.

- Work in small, often heterogeneous groups
- Strive for all group members' success
- What benefits self benefits others
- Joint success is celebrated
- Rewards are viewed as unlimited
- Evaluated by comparing performance to preset criteria

Competition: I Swim, You Sink; I Sink, You Swim

Teachers structure lessons so that students work against each other to achieve a goal only one or a few can attain.

- Work alone
- Strive to be better than classmates
- What benefits self deprives others
- Own success and others' failure is celebrated
- Rewards are limited
- Graded on a curve or ranked from "best" to "worst"

Individualistic: We Are Each In This Alone

Students work by themselves to accomplish learning goals unrelated to those of other students.

- Work alone
- Strive for own success
- What benefits self does not affect others
- Own success is celebrated
- Rewards are viewed as unlimited
- Evaluated by comparing performance to preset criteria

 # asic Elements Of Cooperative Learning

Positive Interdependence

Students perceive that they need each other in order to complete the group's task ("sink or swim together"). Teachers may structure positive interdependence by establishing **mutual goals** (learn and make sure all other group members learn), **joint rewards** (if all group members achieve above the criteria, each will receive bonus points), **shared resources** (one paper for each group or each member receives part of the required information), and **assigned roles** (summarizer, encourager of participation, elaborator).

Face-to-Face Promotive Interaction

Students promote each other's learning by helping, sharing, and encouraging efforts to learn. Students explain, discuss, and teach what they know to classmates. Teachers structure the groups so that students sit knee-to-knee and talk through each aspect of the assignment.

Individual Accountability

Each student's performance is frequently assessed and the results are given to the group and the individual. Teachers may structure individual accountability by giving an individual test to each student or randomly selecting one group member to give the answer.

Interpersonal And Small Group Skills

Groups cannot function effectively if students do not have and use the needed social skills. Teachers teach these skills as purposefully and precisely as academic skills. Collaborative skills include leadership, decision-making, trust-building, communication, and conflict-management skills.

Group Processing

Groups need specific time to discuss how well they are achieving their goals and maintaining effective working relationships among members. Teachers structure group processing by assigning such tasks as (a) list at least three member actions that helped the group be successful and (b) list one action that could be added to make the group even more successful tomorrow. Teachers also monitor the groups and give feedback on how well the groups are working together to the groups and the class as a whole.

✧❀✧ **Basic Elements Of Cooperation** ✧❀✧

Task: Learn the five basic elements of a well-structured cooperative lesson so that you never forget them for as long as you live. For each element:
1. Read the paragraph defining it.
2. Restate its definition in your own words and write it down.
3. Rate from 1-to-10 the extent to which your group experienced the element while you completed the previous cooperative task.
4. Write down at least two things your instructor did to ensure that the element was structured into the previous cooperative task.

Cooperative: Ensure that all members complete the assignment by coming to agreement on the answers and ensuring that everyone can explain each answer. To assist in doing so, each member takes one of the following roles: Reader, Recorder, Checker.

Expected Criteria For Success: Everyone must be able to name and explain the basic elements.

Individual Accountability: One member from your group will be randomly chosen to name and explain the basic elements.

Expected Behaviors: Active participating, checking, encouraging, and elaborating by all members.

Intergroup Cooperation: Whenever it is helpful, check procedures, answers, and strategies with another group.

Your Definition	Rating	Ways It Was Structured

∽ Cooperative Learning Lesson Structures ∾

During the training sessions you will participate in a number of cooperative lessons. These lessons are generic in that they can be used daily (or at least several times a week). The cooperative lesson structures modeled in this training may be used repeatedly with any curriculum in any subject area. They are content free. During the training sessions each of these cooperative lesson structures will be modeled. They will then be explained. Your **tasks** are to:

1. Attend to the structure of the activities as well as the content.

2. For each cooperative learning structure complete the chart given below.

3. Plan how to use each cooperative learning structure in your classes. Translate each structure to make it useable with your students, curricula, and circumstances.

4. Use each cooperative lesson structure and adapt and fine-tune it until it produces the results you wish.

What I Liked About It	What To Watch Out For	What I Did To Help It Work

Problem Solving Lesson

Task: Solve the problem(s) correctly.

Cooperative: One set of answers from the group, everyone has to agree, everyone has to be able to explain the strategies used to solve each problem.

Expected Criteria For Success: Everyone must be able to explain the strategies used to solve each problem.

Individual Accountability: One member from your group will be randomly chosen to explain (a) the answer and (b) how to solve each problem. Alternatively, use the simultaneous responding procedure of having each group member explain the group's answers to a member of another group.

Expected Behaviors: Active participating, checking, encouraging, and elaborating by all members.

Intergroup Cooperation: Whenever it is helpful, check procedures, answers, and strategies with another group.

Assignment

Rewrite the above assignment for a math lesson in your classroom.
If you are not a math teacher,
modify the lesson into a problem-solving lesson in your subject area.
Script out exactly what you will say to your class.

Concept Induction

Concept formation may be done inductively by instructing students to figure out why the examples have been placed in the different boxes. A procedure for doing so is as follows:

1. Draw two (or three) boxes on the chalkboard. Label them Box 1, Box 2, or Box 3.
2. Place one item in each box.
3. Instruct students to use the **formulate, explain, listen, create** procedure to discuss how the items are different.
4. Place another item in each box and repeat. Tell students not to say outloud to another group or the class how the items are different. Each pair must discover it.
5. Once a pair "has it," the members are to make a definition for each box. They then create new examples that may be placed in the boxes.

Tasks: Analyze the examples the teacher places in each box. Identify the concept represented by each box. Then create new examples that may be placed in the boxes.

Cooperative: Students turn to the person next to them and create an answer they can agree on. Students:
1. **Formulate** an individual answer.
2. **Share** their answer with their partner.
3. **Listen** carefully to their partner's answer.
4. **Create** a new answer that is superior to their initial formulations through the processes of association, building on each other's thoughts, and synthesizing.

Expected Criteria For Success: Each student must be able to identify the concept represented by each box.

Individual Accountability: One member from the pair will be randomly chosen to explain the answer.

Expected Behaviors: Explaining, listening, synthesizing by all members.

Assignment

Think of a concept you will teach in the near future. Script out exactly what you will say to your class in using the **Concept Induction** procedure.

? **What Is It?**

Tasks: Analyze the examples the instructor places in each box. Identify the concept represented by each box. Assign each example given below to a box. Then create new examples that may be placed in each box.

Cooperative: Turn to the person next to you and create a joint answer.
1. **Formulate** an individual answer.
2. **Share** your answer with your partner.
3. **Listen** carefully to your partner's answer.
4. **Create** a new answer that is superior to your initial formulations through the processes of association, building on each other's thoughts, and synthesizing.

Expected Criteria For Success: Each person must be able to identify the concept represented by each box.

Individual Accountability: One member from the pair will be randomly chosen to explain the answer.

Expected Behaviors: Explaining, listening, synthesizing by all members.

Examples

1. Strive for everyone's success.
2. Strive to be better than others.
3. Strive for own success only.
4. What benefits self does not affect others.
5. Joint success is celebrated.
6. What benefits self benefits others.
7. Only own success is celebrated.
8. Motivated to help and assist others.
9. What benefits self deprives/hurts others.
10. Motivated only to maximize own productivity.
11. Own success and other's failure is celebrated.
12. Motivated to ensure that no one else does better than oneself.

Box 1

1.

2.

3.

4.

5.

6.

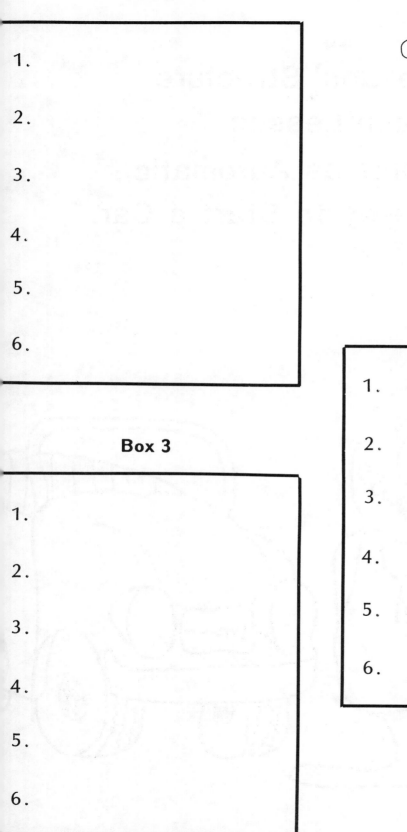

Box 2

1.

2.

3.

4.

5.

6.

Box 3

1.

2.

3.

4.

5.

6.

Setting the Goal Structure
for Each Lesson
Has to Become as Automatic
as Turning the Key to Start a Car.

Chapter 2

The Teacher's Role In Cooperative Learning

Table Of Contents

Introduction

At this point you know what cooperative learning is and how it is different from competitive and individualistic learning. **The essence of cooperative learning is positive interdependence where students recognize that "we are in this together, sink or swim."** In addition, cooperative learning situations are characterized by individual accountability where every student is accountable for both learning the assigned material and helping other group members learn, face-to-face interaction among students, students appropriately using interpersonal and group skills, and students processing how effectively their learning group has functioned.

When Roger was teaching fourth grade in Jefferson County, Colorado, one of his favorite science lessons was to ask the class to determine how long a candle burns in a quart jar. He assigned students to groups of two, making the pairs as heterogeneous as he could. Each pair was given one candle and one quart jar. He gave the instructional task of timing how long the candle would burn. Students then lit their candle, placed the quart jar over it, and clocked how long the candle burns. They were expected to share the materials and praise each other's work. The answers from the pairs are then announced. Roger then gave the pairs the task of generating a number of answers to the question, "How many factors make a difference in how long the candle burns in the jar?" The answers from the pairs were written on the board. The pairs were then assigned the task of repeating the experiment in ways that tested which of the suggested factors did in fact make a difference in how long the candle burned. The next day students individually took a quiz on the factors affecting the time a candle would burn in a quart jar and their scores were summed together to determine a joint score. They spent some time discussing the helpful actions of each member and what they could do to be even more effective in the future.

In this lesson **positive interdependence** was structured by requiring one answer from the pair and by the assignment of one set of materials to each group. There was constant **face-to-face interaction** between pair members. **Individual accountability** was structured by the individual quiz given after the experiments were carried out. The **collaborative skills** emphasized included sharing materials and ideas and praising. The pairs **processed** how effectively they functioned.

Science experiments are only one of the many places cooperative learning may be used. Cooperative learning is appropriate for any instructional task. The more conceptual the task, the more problem solving and decision making that are required, and the more creative the answers need to be, the greater the superiority of cooperative over competitive and individualistic learning. Whenever the learning goals are highly important, the task is complex or conceptual, problem solving is desired, divergent thinking or creativity is desired, quality of performance is expected, higher level reasoning strategies and critical thinking are needed, long-term retention is desired, or when the social development of students is one of the major instructional goals--cooperative learning should be used.

Within cooperative learning situations, the teacher, besides being a technical/subject-matter expert, is a classroom manager and consultant to promote effective group functioning. The teacher structures the learning groups, teaches the basic concepts and strategies, and then monitors the functioning of the learning groups and intervenes to teach collaborative skills and provide task assistance when it is needed. Students are taught to look to their peers for assistance, feedback, reinforcement, and support. Students are expected to interact with each other, share ideas and materials, support and encourage academic achievement, orally explain and elaborate the concepts being learned, and hold each other accountable for learning. A criterion-referenced evaluation system is used.

There is more to the teacher's role in structuring cooperative learning situations, however, than structuring cooperation among students. The teacher's role includes five major sets of strategies:

1. Clearly specifying the objectives for the lesson.

2. Making certain decisions about placing students in learning groups before the lesson is taught.

3. Clearly explaining the task and goal structure to the students.

4. Monitoring the effectiveness of the cooperative learning groups and intervening to provide task assistance (such as answering questions and teaching task skills) or to increase students' interpersonal and group skills.

5. Evaluating the students' achievement and helping students discuss how well they collaborated with each other.

The following eighteen steps elaborate these strategies and detail a procedure for structuring cooperative learning. Specific examples of lessons may be found in Johnson, Johnson, and Holubec (1987). There are also two films available demonstrating the use of cooperative learning procedures (**Belonging**, **Circles of Learning**).

Part 1: Formulating Objectives And Making Decisions

Specifying the Instructional Objectives

There are two types of objectives that a teacher needs to specify before the lesson begins. The **academic objective** needs to be specified at the correct level for the students and matched to the right level of instruction according to a conceptual or task analysis. The **collaborative skills objective** details what collaborative skills are going to be emphasized during the lesson. A common error many teachers make is to specify only academic objectives and to ignore the collaborative skills objectives needed to train students to cooperate with each other.

Deciding on the Size of the Group

Once the objectives of the lesson are clear, the teacher must decide which size of learning group is optimal. Cooperative learning groups tend to range in size from 2 to 6. A number of factors should be considered in selecting the size of a cooperative learning group:

1. **As the size of the learning group increases, the range of abilities, expertise, skills, and the number of minds available for acquiring and processing information increase.** The more group members you have, the more chance to have someone who has special knowledge helpful to the group and the more willing hands and talents are available to do the task.

2. **The larger the group, the more skillful group members must be in providing everyone with a chance to speak, coordinating the actions of group members, reaching consensus, ensuring explanation and elaboration of the material being learned, keeping all members on task, and maintaining good working relationships.** Within a pair students have to manage two interactions. Within a group of three there are six interactions to manage. Within a group of four there are twelve interactions to manage. As the size of the group increases, the interpersonal and small

group skills required to manage the interactions among group members become far more complex and sophisticated. Very few students have the social skills needed for effective group functioning even for small groups. A common mistake made by many teachers is to have students work in groups of four, five, and six members before the students have the skills to do so competently.

3. **The materials available or the specific nature of the task may dictate a group size.**

4. **The shorter the period of time available, the smaller the learning group should be.** If there is only a brief period of time available for the lesson, then smaller groups will be more effective because they take less time to get organized, they operate faster, and there is more "air time" per member.

Our best advice to beginning teachers is to start with pairs or threesomes. When students become more experienced and skillful they will be able to manage larger groups. Six may be the upper limit for a cooperative learning group. More members would be cumbersome even for very socially skilled students. In one classroom we recently observed the teacher had divided the class into "committees" of eight. In the typical committee some students were being left out, others were passive, and some were engaged in a conversation with only one or two other members. Cooperative learning groups have to be small enough that everyone is engaged in mutual discussion while achieving the group's goals. So be cautious about group size. Some students will not be ready for a group as large as four.

Assigning Students to Learning Groups

There are many different ways to assign students to learning groups. The following sections contain some suggestions for grouping students.

Stratified Random

1. *Rank order students from highest to lowest in terms of a pretest on the unit, a recent past test, past grades, or your best guess as a teacher.*

2. *Select the first group by choosing the highest student, the lowest student, and the two middle achievers. Assign them to the group unless they are all of one sex, they do not reflect the ethnic composition of the class, they are worst enemies, or they are best*

friends. *If any of these are true, move up or down one student from the middle to readjust.*

3. *Select the remaining groups by repeating the above procedure with the reduced list. If there are students left over, make one or two groups of three members.*

The same procedure may be used for assigning students to groups of three or two members.

Numbering

Divide the number of students in the class by the size of the group you wish to use (30 students divided by 3 = 10). Have students number off by the result (e.g., 10). Then have the students with the same number find each other.

Teachers may include handing out materials that have a number or symbol on them and ask students to find their classmates with the same number or symbol. Teachers may also pass out cards with a number or symbol on them to assign students to learning groups.

There are many variations to this procedure. Teachers may place a list of words on the board, such as a list of colors, animals, countries, rocks, or plants, and have students "word off." You need the same number of words as groups you wish to assign students to.

Roger's favorite variation is to count off in a different language (e.g., English, Spanish, French, Hungarian) each time students are assigned to groups. His rule is that any language may only be used one time during a semester or year.

Reducing Isolation

1. *Ask students to list three peers with whom they would like to work.*

2. *Identify the isolated students who are not chosen by any other of their classmates.*

3. *Build a group of skillful and supportive students around each isolated student.*

Math Method

There are endless variations to the math method of assigning students to groups. The basic structure is to give each student a math problem and ask students whose problems have the same answer to group together. This may vary from simple addition in the first grade to complex equations in high school classes. Thus, to form a group of three, the following three equations may be distributed throughout the class (3 + 3 = _; 4 + 2 = _; 5 + 1 = _).

States and Capitols

To assign students to groups of two or four the following procedure may be used. Divide the number of students in the class by two (30 divided by 2 = 15). Pick a geographic area of the U.S. and write out on cards the names of 15 states. Then on another set of cards write out the names of their capitol cities. Shuffle the cards and pass them out to students. Then have the students find the classmate who has the matching state or capitol. To form groups of four, have two adjacent states and their capitols combine.

Historical Characters

Give each student a card with the name of an historical character. S/he can then find the other members of their group on the basis of the historical period in which the characters lived. Variations include grouping according to the occupation of the person, country they came from, or significant event or accomplishment.

Geographical Areas

List a number of countries or states and have students group themselves according to most preferred to visit. Variations include grouping according to least preferred to visit, similar in terms of climate, similar in geological features, and so forth.

Literature Characters

Give students individual cards with the names of characters in the literature they recently have read. Ask them to group with the characters from the same story, play, or poem. Examples include Romeo and Juliet; Captain Hook, Peter Pan and Wendy; and Hansel, Gretel, Ginger-Bread-House Witch, and Step-Mother.

Preferences

Have students write their favorite sport to participate in on a slip of paper. Then have them find groupmates who like to participate in the same sport. Variations include favorite food, celebrity, skill, car, president, animal, vegetable, fairy tale character, and so forth.

Helpful Hints

1. *Explain to the class that before the year is over, everyone will work in a group with everyone else and, therefore, if you are not in a group with someone you would like to be, do not worry about it. The next group will be different.*

2. *Ask the students to help ensure that the groups are heterogeneous in terms of sex, ethnicity, and ability. In order to build constructive relationships between majority and minority students, between handicapped and nonhandicapped students, and even between male and female students, use heterogeneous cooperative learning groups with a variety of students within each learning group.*

3. *Before the students start to move into their groups say, "I would like you to take responsibility to make sure that everyone is included in a group. Before you begin the group task, look around the room. If you see someone who is not in a group, invite them to join your group or another group that has fewer members.*

For additional methods for assigning students to groups as well as a variety of team-building and warm-up activities see R. Johnson and Johnson (1985).

Assigning Students to Groups

Teachers often ask four basic questions about assigning students to groups:

1. **Should students be placed in learning groups homogeneous or heterogeneous in member ability?** There are times when cooperative learning groups homogeneous in ability may be used to master specific skills or to achieve certain instructional objectives. Generally, however, we recommend that teachers maximize the heterogeneity of students, placing high-, medium-, and low-ability students within the same learning group. More elaborative thinking, more frequent giving and receiving of explanations, and greater perspective taking in discussing material seems to occur in heterogeneous groups, all of which increase the depth of understanding, the quality of reasoning, and the accuracy of long-term retention.

2. **Should nontask-oriented students be placed in learning groups with task-oriented peers or be separated?** To keep nonacademically-oriented students on task it often helps to place them in a cooperative learning group with task-oriented peers.

3. **Should students select whom they want to work with or should the teacher assign students to groups?** Teacher-made groups often have the best mix since teachers can put together optimal combinations of students. Random assignment, such as having students "count off" is another possibility for getting a good mix of students in each group. Having students select their own groups is often not very successful. Student-selected groups often are homogeneous with high-achieving students working with other high-achieving students, white students working with other white students, minority students working with other minority students, and males working with other males. Often there is less on-task behavior in student-selected than in teacher-selected groups. A useful modification of the "select your own group" method is to have students list whom they would like to work with and then place them in a learning group with one person they choose and one or two or more students that the teacher selected.

4. **How long should the groups stay together?** Actually, there is no formula or simple answer to this question. Some teachers keep cooperative learning groups together for an entire year or semester. Other teachers like to keep a learning group together only long enough to complete a unit or chapter. In some schools student attendance is so unpredictable that teachers form new groups every day. Sooner or later, however, every student should work with every other classmate. An elementary setting allows students to be in several different learning groups during the day. Our best advice is to allow groups to remain stable long enough for them to be successful. Breaking up groups that are having trouble functioning effectively is often counterproductive as the students do not learn the skills they need to resolve problems in collaborating with each other.

There is merit in having students work with everyone in their class during a semester or school year. Building a strong positive feeling of collaboration across an entire class and giving students opportunities to practice the skills needed to begin new groups can add much to a school year. **Never underestimate the power of heterogeneous cooperative learning groups in promoting high quality, rich, and involved learning.**

Arranging the Room

How the teacher arranges the room is a symbolic message of what is appropriate behavior and it can facilitate the learning groups within the classroom. Members of a learning group should sit close enough to each other that they can share materials, maintain eye contact with all group members, and talk to each other quietly without disrupting the other learning groups. Circles are usually best. The teacher should have a clear access lane to every group. Common mistakes that teachers make in arranging a room are to (1) place students at a rectangular table where they cannot have eye contact with all the other members or (2) move several desks together, which may place students too far apart to communicate quietly with each other and share materials. Within each learning group students need to be able to see all relevant task materials, see each other, converse with each other without raising their voices, and exchange ideas and materials in a comfortable atmosphere. The groups need to be far enough apart so that they do not interfere with each other's learning. "Knee-to-knee and eye-to-eye"--the closer the better.

Planning the Instructional Materials to Promote Interdependence

Materials need to be distributed among group members so that all members participate and achieve. When a group is mature and experienced and group members have a high level of collaborative skills, the teacher may not have to arrange materials in any specific way. When a group is new or when members are not very skilled, however, teachers may wish to distribute materials in carefully planned ways to communicate that the assignment is to be a joint (not an individual) effort and that the students are in a "sink or swim together" learning situation. Three of the ways of doing so are:

1. **Materials Interdependence**: Give only one copy of the materials to the group. The students will then have to work together in order to be successful. This is especially effective the first few times the group meets. After students are accustomed to collaborating with each other, teachers will wish each student to have an individual copy of the materials.

2. **Information Interdependence**: Group members may each be given different books or resource materials to be synthesized. Or the materials may be arranged like a jigsaw puzzle so that each student has part of the materials needed to complete the task. Such procedures require that every member participate in order for the group to be successful.

3. **Interdependence from Outside Enemies**:
   Materials may be structured into a tournament
   format with intergroup competition as the basis
   to promote a perception of interdependence
   among group members. Such a procedure was
   introduced by Devries and Edwards (1973). In
   the teams-games-tournament format students are
   divided into heterogeneous cooperative learning
   teams to prepare members for a tournament in
   which they compete with the other teams. During the intergroup competition the
   students individually compete against members of about the same ability level from
   other teams. The team whose members do the best in the competition is pronounced
   the winner by the teacher.

All of these procedures may not be needed simultaneously. They are alternative methods
of ensuring that students perceive that they are involved in a "sink or swim together" learning
situation and behave collaboratively.

Assigning Roles to Ensure Interdependence

Positive interdependence may also be arranged through the assignment of complementary
and interconnected roles to group members. Each group member is assigned a responsibility
that the group needs to work effectively. Such roles include a **summarizer** (who restates
the group's major conclusions or answers), a **checker** (who ensures that all group members
can explicitly explain how to arrive at an answer or conclusion), an **accuracy coach** (who
corrects any mistakes in another member's explanations or summaries), a **relater/elabora-
tion seeker** (who asks members to relate current concepts and strategies to material studied
previously), a **researcher-runner** (who gets needed materials for the group and communi-
cates with the other learning groups and the teacher), a **recorder** to write down the group's
decisions and edit the group's report, an **encourager** to reinforce members' contributions,
and an **observer** to keep track of how well the group is collaborating. Assigning such roles
is an effective method of teaching students collaborative skills and fostering positive
interdependence.

Part 2: Structuring The Task And Interdependence

Explaining the Academic Task

Teachers explain the academic task so that students are clear about the assignment and understand the objectives of the lesson. Direct teaching of concepts, principles, and strategies may take place at this point. Teachers may wish to answer any questions students have about the concepts or facts they are to learn or apply in the lesson. Teachers need to consider several aspects of explaining an academic assignment to students:

1. **Set the task so that students are clear about the assignment.** Most teachers have considerable practice with this already. Instructions that are clear and specific are crucial in warding off student frustration. One advantage of cooperative learning groups is that they can handle more ambiguous tasks (when they are appropriate) than can students working alone. In cooperative learning groups students who do not understand what they are to do will ask their group for clarification before asking the teacher.

2. **Explain the objectives of the lesson and relate the concepts and information to be studied to students' past experience and learning to ensure maximum transfer and retention.** Explaining the intended outcomes of the lesson increases the likelihood that students will focus on the relevant concepts and information throughout the lesson.

3. **Define relevant concepts, explain procedures students should follow, and give examples to help students understand what they are to learn and do in completing the assignment.** To promote positive transfer of learning, point out the critical elements that separate this lesson from past learnings.

4. **Ask the class specific questions to check the students' understanding of the assignment.** Such questioning ensures thorough two-way communication, that the assignment has been given effectively, and that the students are ready to begin completing it.

Structuring Positive Goal Interdependence

Communicate to students that they have a group goal and must work collaboratively. We cannot overemphasize the importance of communicating to students that they are in a "sink or swim together" learning situation. In a cooperative learning group students are responsible for learning the assigned material, making sure that all other group members learn the assigned material, and making sure that all other class members successfully learn the assigned material, in that order. Teachers can do this in several ways.

1. **Ask the group to produce a single product, report, or paper.** Each group member should sign the paper to indicate that he or she agrees with the answers and can explain why the answers are appropriate. Each student must know the material. When a group is producing only one product it is especially important to stress individual accountability. Teachers may pick a student at random from each group to explain the rationale for their answers.

2. **Provide group rewards**. Bonus points and a total group score are ways to give students the "sink or swim together" message. An example is a spelling group where members work with each other during the week to make sure that all members learn their words correctly. They then take the test individually and are rewarded on the basis of the total number of words spelled correctly by all group members. Math lessons can be structured so that students work in cooperative learning groups, take a test individually, receive their individual score, and be given bonus points on the basis of how many group members reach a preset level of excellence. Some teachers have students work in cooperative learning groups, give individual tests, give students individual grades on the basis of their scores, and then reward groups where all members reach a preset criteria of excellence with free-time or extra recess.

Positive interdependence creates peer encouragement and support for learning. Such positive peer pressure influences underachieving students to become academically involved. Members of cooperative learning groups should give interrelated messages, "Do your work--we're counting on you!" and "How can I help you to do better?"

Structuring Individual Accountability

The purpose of a cooperative group is to maximize the learning of each member. A group is not truly cooperative if members are "slackers" who let others do all the work. To ensure that all members learn and that groups know which members to provide with encouragement and help, teachers need to assess frequently the level of performance of each group member. Practice tests, randomly selecting members to explain answers, having members edit each other's work, teach what they know to someone else, use what they have learned on a different problem, and randomly picking one paper from the group to grade, are ways to structure individual accountability.

Structuring Intergroup Cooperation

The positive outcomes found within a cooperative learning group can be extended throughout a whole class by structuring intergroup cooperation. Bonus points may be given if all members of a class reach a preset criteria of excellence. When a group finishes its work, the teacher should encourage the members to go help other groups complete the assignment.

Explaining Criteria for Success

Evaluation within cooperatively structured lessons needs to be criterion-referenced. Criterion must be established for acceptable work (rather than grading on a curve). Thus, at the beginning of the lesson teachers should clearly explain the criterion by which the students' work will be evaluated. The criterion for success must be structured so that students may reach it without penalizing other students and so that groups may reach it without penalizing other groups. For some learning groups all members can be working to reach the same criterion. For other learning groups different members may be evaluated according to different criteria. The criterion should be tailored to be challenging and realistic for each individual group member. In a spelling group, for example, some members may not be able to learn as many as 20 words and their number can be reduced accordingly. **Teachers may structure a second level of cooperation by not only keeping track of how well each group and its members are performing, but also by setting criterion for the whole class to reach.** Thus, the number of words the total class spells correctly can be recorded from week to week with an appropriate criterion being set to promote class-wide collaboration and encouragement. Criteria are important to give students information about what "doing well" is on assigned tasks, but they do not always have to be as formal as counting the number correct. On some assignments, simply completing the task may be adequate for a criterion. Or simply doing better this week than one did last week may be set as a criterion of excellence.

Specifying Desired Behaviors

The word **cooperation** has many different connotations and uses. Teachers will need to define cooperation operationally by specifying the behaviors that are appropriate and desirable within the learning groups. There are beginning behaviors, such as "stay with your group and do not wander around the room," "use quiet voices," "take turns," and "use each other's names." When groups begin to function effectively, expected behaviors may include:

1. Having each member explain how to get the answer.

2. Asking each member to relate what is being learned to previous learnings.

3. Checking to make sure everyone in the group understands the material and agrees with the answers.

4. Encouraging everyone to participate.

5. Listening accurately to what other group members are saying.

6. Not changing your mind unless you are logically persuaded (majority rule does not promote learning).

7. Criticizing ideas, not people.

Teachers should not make the list of expected behaviors too long. One or two behaviors to emphasize for a few lessons is enough. Students need to know what behavior is appropriate and desirable within a cooperative learning group, but they should not be subjected to information overload.

© Johnson & Johnson

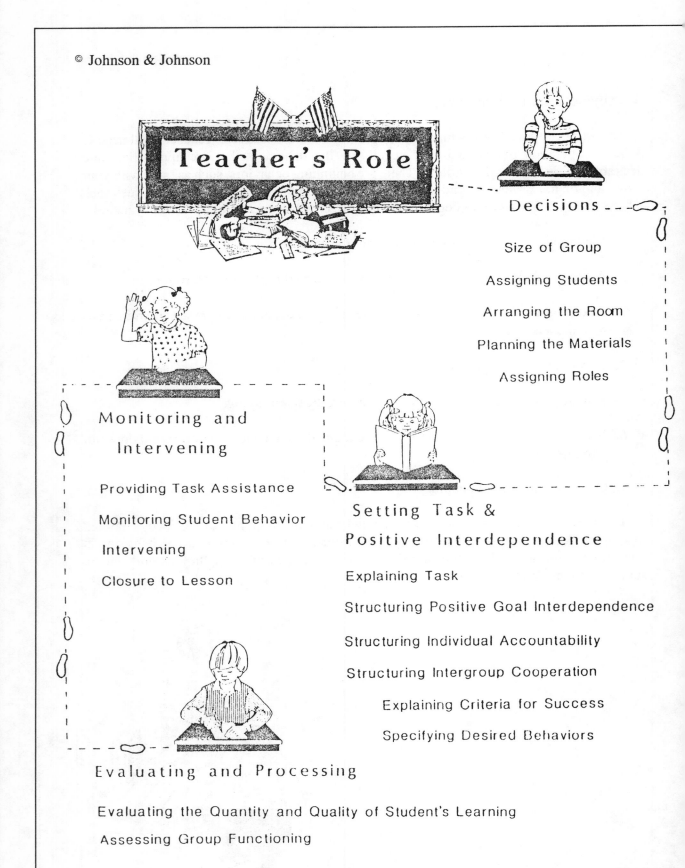

Teacher's Role

Decisions

Size of Group

Assigning Students

Arranging the Room

Planning the Materials

Assigning Roles

Monitoring and Intervening

Providing Task Assistance

Monitoring Student Behavior

Intervening

Closure to Lesson

Setting Task & Positive Interdependence

Explaining Task

Structuring Positive Goal Interdependence

Structuring Individual Accountability

Structuring Intergroup Cooperation

Explaining Criteria for Success

Specifying Desired Behaviors

Evaluating and Processing

Evaluating the Quantity and Quality of Student's Learning

Assessing Group Functioning

Part 3: Monitoring, Intervening and Evaluating

Monitoring Students' Behavior

The teacher's job begins in earnest when the cooperative learning groups start working. Resist that urge to go get a cup of coffee or grade some papers. Just because the teacher instructs students to cooperate and places them in learning groups does not mean that they will always do so. So, much of the teacher's time in cooperative learning situations should be spent observing group members in order to see what problems they are having in completing the assignment and in working collaboratively. A variety of observation instruments and procedures that can be used for these purposes can be found in Johnson and F. Johnson (1991), Johnson, Johnson, and Holubec (1990).

Whenever possible, teachers should use a formal observation sheet where they count the number of times they observe appropriate behaviors being used by students. The more concrete the data, the more useful it is to the teacher and to students. Teachers should not try to count too many different behaviors at one time, especially when they first start formal observation. At first they may want just to keep track of who talks in each group to get a participation pattern for the groups. We have a chapter describing systematic observation of cooperative groups in **Learning Together and Alone** (1991) and our current list of behaviors (though rather long) includes: contributing ideas, asking questions, expressing feelings, active listening, expressing support and acceptance (toward ideas), expressing warmth and liking (toward group members and group), encouraging all members to participate, summarizing, checking for understanding, relieving tension by joking, and giving direction to group's work. All the behaviors we look for are positive behaviors which are to be praised when they are appropriately present and are a cause for discussion when they are missing. It is also a good idea for the teacher to collect notes on specific student behaviors so that the frequency data is extended. Especially useful are skillful interchanges that can be shared with students later as objective praise and perhaps with parents in conferences or telephone conversations.

Student observers can be used to get even more extensive data on each group's functioning. For very young students the system must be kept very simple, perhaps only "Who talks?" Many teachers have had good success with student observers, even in kindergarten. One of the more important things to do is for the teacher to make sure that the class is given adequate instructions (and perhaps practice) on gathering the observation data and sharing it with the group. The observer is in the best position to learn about the skills of working in a group. We can remember one first grade teacher who had a student who talked all the time (even to himself while working alone). He tended to dominate any group he was in. When she introduced student observers to the class she made him an observer. One important rule for observers was not to interfere in the task but to gather data without talking. He was gathering data on who talks and he did a good job, noticing that one student had done quite a bit of talking in the group while another had talked very little. The next day when he was a group member, and there was another observer, he was seen starting to talk, clamping his hand over his mouth and glancing at the observer. He knew what was being observed for and he didn't want to be the only one with marks. The teacher said he may have listened for the first time in the year. So the observer often benefits in learning about group skills.

When teachers are worried about losing the lesson content (observers, however, often know quite a bit about the lesson) then they can have the group as a last review take the observer through the material and see if they can get her signature on the paper as well. Often important changes are made during this review.

It is not necessary to use student observers all the time and we would not recommend their use until cooperative learning groups are used a few times. It is enough for teachers just to structure the groups to be cooperative in the beginning without having to worry about structuring student observers, too. Whether student observers are used or not, however, teachers should always do some observing and spend some time monitoring the groups. Sometimes a simple checklist is helpful in addition to a systematic observation form. Some questions to ask on the checklist might be:

1. Do students understand the task?

2. Have students accepted the positive interdependence and the individual accountability?

3. Are students working toward the criteria, and are those criteria for success appropriate?

4. Are students practicing the specified behaviors, or not?

Providing Task Assistance

In monitoring the groups as they work, teachers will wish to clarify instructions, review important procedures and strategies for completing the assignment, answer questions, and teach task skills as necessary. In discussing the concepts and information to be learned, teachers will wish to use the language or terms relevant to the learning. Instead of saying, "Yes, that is right," teachers will wish to say something more specific to the assignment, such as, "Yes, that is one way to find the main idea of a paragraph." The use of the more specific statement reinforces the desired learning and promotes positive transfer by helping the students associate a term with their learning.

Intervening to Teach Collaborative Skills

While monitoring the learning groups teachers will also find students who do not have the necessary collaborative skills and groups where problems in collaborating have arisen. **In these cases the teacher will wish to intervene to suggest more effective procedures for working together and more effective behaviors for students to engage in.** Teachers may also wish to intervene and reinforce particularly effective and skillful behaviors that they notice. At times the teacher becomes a consultant to a group in order to help it function more effectively. When it is obvious that group members lack certain social skills they need in order to cooperate with each other, the teacher will want to intervene in order to help the members learn the collaborative skills. The social skills required for productive group work are discussed in Chapter 5. Activities that may be used in teaching them are covered in Johnson and F. Johnson (1991) and Johnson (1990, 1991).

Teachers should not intervene any more than is absolutely necessary in the groups. Most of us as teachers are geared to jumping in and solving problems for students to get them back on track. With a little patience we would find that cooperative groups can often work their way through their own problems (task and maintenance) and acquire not only a solution, but also a method of solving similar problems in the future. Choosing when to intervene and when not to is part of the art of teaching and with some restraint, teachers can usually trust their intuition. Even when intervening, teachers can turn the problem back to the group to solve. Many teachers intervene in a group by having members set aside their task, pointing out the problem, and asking the group to come up with an adequate solution. (The last thing teachers want to happen is for the students to learn to come running to the teacher with every problem.)

In one third grade class, the teacher noticed when passing out papers that one student was sitting back away from the other three. A moment later the teacher glanced over and only three students were sitting where four were a moment before. As she watched, the three students came marching over to her and complained that Johnny was under the table and wouldn't come out. "Make him come out!" they insisted (the teacher's role: police-officer, judge, and executioner). The teacher told them that Johnny was a member of their group and asked what they had tried to solve their problem. "Tried?" the puzzled reply. "Yes, have you asked him to come out?" the teacher suggested. The group marched back and the teacher continued passing out papers to groups. A moment later the teacher glanced over to their table and saw no heads above the table (which is one way to solve the problem). After a few more minutes, four heads came struggling out from under the table and the group (including Johnny) went back to work with great energy. We don't know what happened under that table, but whatever it was, it was effective. What makes this story even more interesting is that the group received a 100 percent on the paper and later, when the teacher was standing by Johnny's desk, she noticed he had the paper clutched in his hand. The group had given Johnny the paper and he was taking it home. He confided to the teacher that this was the first time he could ever remember earning a 100 percent on anything in school. (If that was your record, you might slip under a few tables yourself.)

The best time to teach cooperative skills is when the students need them. Intervening should leave a cooperative learning group with new skills that will be useful in the future. It is important that the cooperative skills be taught in the context of the class where they are going to be used, or are practiced in that setting, because transfer of skill learning from one situation to another cannot be assumed. **Students learn about cooperative skills when they are taught them, and learn cooperative skills when applying them in the midst of science, math, or English.** The good news about cooperative skills is that they are taught and learned like any other skill. At a minimum:

1. **Students need to recognize the need for the skill.**

2. **The skill must be defined clearly and specifically including what students should say when engaging in the skill.**

3. **The practice of the skill must be encouraged.** Sometimes just the teacher standing there with a clipboard and pencil will be enough to promote student enactment of the skill.

4. **Students should have the time and procedures for discussing how well they are using the skills.** Students should persevere in the practice until the skill is appropriately internalized. We never drop a skill, we only add on.

For older students (upper elementary school and above) the skills have been well described in **Joining Together** (Johnson & F. Johnson, 1991) and **Reaching Out** (Johnson, 1990). For younger students, teachers may need to revise and rename cooperative skills. Some primary teachers use symbols like traffic signs with a "green light" to represent encouraging participation, a "stop sign" to mean time to summarize, and "slippery when wet" to mean "say that over again, I didn't quite understand." Sometimes a more mechanistic structure is beneficial for young students. In one first grade class the teacher had a number of students who liked to take over the group and dominate. One day in frustration, she formed groups and handed out to each group member five poker chips with a different color for each group member. The students were instructed to place a chip in the box every time they spoke while they worked on the worksheet. When a student had "spent" all his or her chips, he or she could not speak. When all the chips were in the box, they could get their five colored chips back and start again. There were several surprised students when their five chips were the only chips in the box! Teachers only have to use this once or twice to get the message across (although first grade students can get addicted to chips, so watch out). This technique was later used in a monthly principals' meeting. As the principals came in, each was handed several colored strips of paper. When they spoke...

Teaching your students how to work together effectively is a necessary part of implementing cooperative learning into your classroom. We would recommend that only a few skills be taught in one semester. Most of the curriculum programs with cooperative learning groups written into them feature about five to eight cooperative skills for a year.

Providing Closure to the Lesson

At the end of the lesson students should be able to summarize what they have learned and to understand where they will use it in future lessons. Teachers may wish to summarize the major points in the lesson, ask students to recall ideas or give samples, and answer any final questions students have.

Evaluating the Quality and Quantity of Students' Learning

The product required from the lesson may be a report, a single set of answers that all members of the group agree to, the average of individual examination scores, or the number of group members reaching a specific criterion. Whatever the measure, the learning of group members needs to be evaluated by a criterion-referenced system. The procedures for setting up and using such an evaluation system are given in Johnson and Johnson (1991). Besides assessing students on how well they learn the assigned concepts and information, group members should also receive feedback on how effectively they collaborated. Some teachers give two grades, one for achievement and one for collaborative behavior.

Assessing How Well the Group Functioned

An old observational rule is, **if you observe, you must process your observations with the group.** Even if class time is limited, some time should be spent talking about how well the groups functioned today, what things were done well, and what things could be improved. Each learning group may have its own observer and spend time discussing how effectively members are working together. Teachers may also wish to spend some time in **whole-class processing** where they give the class feedback and have students share incidents that occurred in their groups and how they were solved. Names do not need to be used, but the feedback should be as specific as possible.

Discussing group functioning is essential. A common teaching error is to provide too brief a time for students to process the quality of their collaboration. Students do not learn from experiences that they do not reflect on. If the learning groups are to function better tomorrow than they did today, members must receive feedback, reflect on how their actions may be more effective, and plan how to be even more skillful during the next group session.

Every small group has two primary goals: (1) to accomplish the task successfully, and (2) to build and maintain constructive relationships in good working order for the next task. Learning groups are often exclusively task oriented and ignore the importance of maintaining effective working relationships among members. Group sessions should be enjoyable, lively, and pleasant experiences. If no one is having fun, something is wrong. Problems in collaborating should be brought up and solved and there should be a continuing emphasis on improving the effectiveness of the group members in collaborating with each other.

Often during the "working" part of the class period, students will be very task-oriented and the "maintenance" of the group may suffer. During the processing time, however, the emphasis is on maintenance of the group and the students leave the room ready for (a better?) tomorrow. If no processing is done, teachers may find the group's functioning decaying and important relationship issues left undiscussed. Processing may not need to occur each day in depth, but it should happen often. **Processing the functioning of the group needs to be taken as seriously as accomplishing the task.** The two are very much related. Teachers often have students turn in a "process sheet" along with the paper from the task assignment.

Group processing provides a structure for group members to hold each other accountable for being responsible and skillful group members. In order to contribute to each other's learning, group members need to attend class, be prepared (i.e., have done the necessary homework), and contribute to the group's work. A student's absenteeism and lack of preparation often demoralizes other members. Productive group work requires members to be present and prepared, and there should be some peer accountability to be so. When groups "process," they discuss any member actions that need to be improved in order for everyone's learning to be maximized.

Groups new to processing often need an agenda, including specific questions each group member must address. Inexperienced groups tend to say, "We did fine. Right? Right!" and not deal with any real issues. A simple agenda could be to have each group name two things they did well (and document them) and one thing they need to be even better at, or would like to work harder on.

Structuring Academic Controversies

For the past several years we have been training teachers and professors throughout North America in the use of structured academic controversies. The basic format for doing to consists of:

1. *Choose a topic that has content manageable by the students and on which at least two well-documented positions (pro and con) can be prepared. Topics on which we have developed curriculum units include:*

   - *Should the wolf be a protected species?*

- Should coal be used as an energy source?

- Should nuclear energy be used as an energy source?

- Should the regulation of hazardous wastes be increased?

- Should the Boundary Waters Canoe Area be a national park?

- How should acid precipitation be controlled?

and many others.

2. *Prepare the instructional materials so that group members know what position they have been assigned and where they can find supporting information.*

3. *Structure the controversy by:*

   a. *Assigning students to groups of four.*

   b. *Dividing each group into two pairs. Assign pro and con positions to the pairs.*

   c. *Highlighting the cooperative goal of reaching a consensus on the issue and writing a quality group report on which all members will be evaluated.*

4. *Conduct the controversy by (four class periods are recommended):*

   a. *Assigning each pair the cooperative task of learning their position and its supporting arguments and information.*

   b. *Having each pair present its position to the other. The group discusses the issue, critically evaluating the opposing position and its rationale, defending positions, and comparing the strengths and weaknesses of the two positions.*

   c. *Having the pairs reverse perspectives and positions by presenting the opposing position as sincerely and forcefully as they can.*

   d. *Having the group members drop their advocacy, reach a decision, and write a group report that includes their joint position and the supporting evidence and rationale. A test on the content covered in both positions may be given with the groups whose members all score above the preset criteria of excellence receiving bonus points.*

A more detailed description of conducting academic controversies may be found in Johnson, Johnson and Smith (1986) and Johnson and Johnson (1987). Peggy Tiffany, a 4th-grade teacher in Wilmington, Vermont, regularly conducts an academic controversy on whether or not the wolf should be a protected species. She gives students the cooperative assignment of writing a report on the wolf in which they summarize what they have learned about the wolf and recommend the procedures they think are best for regulating wolf populations and preserving wolves within the continental United States. Students are randomly assigned to groups of four, ensuring that both male and female and high-, medium-, and low-achieving students are all in the same group. The group is divided into two pairs and one pair is assigned the position of an environmental organization that believes wolves should be a protected species and the other pair is assigned the position of farmers and ranchers who believe that wolves should not be a protected species.

Each side is given a packet of articles, stories, and information that supports their position. During the first class period each pair develops their position and plans how to present the best case possible to the other pair. Near the end of the period pairs are encouraged to compare notes with pairs from other groups who represent the same position. During the second class period each pair makes their presentation. Each member of the pair has to participate in the presentation. Members of the opposing pair are encouraged to take notes and listen carefully. During the third class period the group discusses the issue following a set of rules to help them criticize ideas without criticizing people, differentiate the two positions, and assess the degree of evidence and logic supporting each position. During the first half of the fourth hour the pairs reverse perspectives and present each other's positions. Students drop their advocacy positions, clarify their understanding of each other's information and rationale and begin work on their group report. The first half of the fifth period is spent finalizing their report. The report is evaluated on the basis of the quality of the writing, the evaluation of opinion and evidence, and the oral presentation of the report to the class. The students then each take an individual test on the wolf and, if every member of the group achieves up to criterion, they all receive the bonus points. Finally, during the sixth class period each group makes a 10-minute presentation to the entire class summarizing their report. All four members of the group are required to participate orally in the presentation.

Within this lesson positive interdependence is structured by having each group arrive at a consensus and submit one written report and making one presentation, by jigsawing the materials to the pairs within the group, and by giving bonus points to members if all members learn the basic information contained in the two positions and score well on the test. Individual accountability is structured by having each member of the pair orally participate in the presentation of the position and in the perspective reversal, each member of the group orally participates in the group presentation, and each member takes an individual test on the material. The collaborative skills emphasized are those involved in systematically advocating an intellectual position and evaluating and criticizing the position advocated by others, as well as the skills involved in synthesis and consensual decision making. Numerous academic and social benefits are derived from participating in such structured controversies (Johnson & Johnson, 1987c; Johnson, Johnson & Smith, 1986).

Conclusions

These eighteen aspects of structuring learning situations cooperatively blend together to make effective, cooperative learning groups a reality in the classroom. They may be used in any subject area with any age student. One of the things we have been told many times by teachers who have mastered these strategies and integrated cooperative learning groups into their teaching is, "Don't say it is easy!" We know it's not. It can take years to become an expert. There is a lot of pressure to teach like everyone else, to have students learn alone, and not let students look at each other's papers. Students will not be accustomed to working together and are likely to have a competitive orientation. You may wish to start small by taking one subject area or one class and use cooperative learning until you feel comfortable, and then expand into other subject areas or other classes. In order to implement cooperative learning successfully, you will need to teach students the interpersonal and small group skills required to collaborate, structure and orchestrate intellectual inquiry within learning groups, and form collaborative relations with other others. **Implementing cooperative learning in your classroom is not easy, but it is worth the effort.**

Another statement of advice is, **start small and build**. Pick out a place in the school day where you are pretty sure it would work, plan carefully, and don't rush the process. We think cooperative learning groups should evolve into a teacher's program rather than become a part of every class on the first day. The good news is that many of your students will do well immediately. While one or two groups may struggle because of a lack of group skills, five will do well. Celebrate the five and problem-solve with the two. Keep in mind that the students who are most difficult to integrate into groups are very often the ones who need the peer support and positive peer pressure the most. Resist that advice you were given as a beginning teacher to isolate students who pester others or show that they lack interpersonal skills, and concentrate on integrating them into their peer group effectively. The other students can be the most powerful influence on isolated, alienated students, and we can't allow these students to make it through school alienated, disconnected, lonely, and bitter.

In addition, **cooperative, supportive relationships are just as productive for adults as they are for students** (see Chapter 7). Teachers are more effective when they have positive colleagial support and problem-solve together. Teachers need to give some thought to their "own" cooperative group as they implement cooperation in their classrooms.

It is also important to say again that **we would be disappointed if we ever visited a teacher's classroom and saw only cooperative learning groups.** The data is clear and will be discussed in detail in the next chapter. Cooperation should produce better results in school than having students work alone, individualistically or competitively. Yet there is an important place for competitive and individualistic goal structures within the classroom. The major problems with competition and individualistic efforts result from their being inappropriately used and overused. In addition to cooperative skills, students need to learn how to compete for fun and enjoyment (win or lose) and how to work independently, following through on a task until it is completed. The natural place for competitive and individualistic efforts is within the umbrella of cooperation. The predominant use of cooperation reduces the anxiety and evaluation apprehension associated with competition. It also allows for using individualistically structured learning activities as part of a division of labor within cooperative tasks. But, most of all, students should learn how to work together cooperatively, giving each other support in learning. Some teachers weave the three goal structures together, setting up individual responsibility (accountable to the group), peer teaching, competing as a light change of pace, and ending in a cooperative project. Thus, they do what schools should do--prepare students to interact effectively in cooperative, competitive, and individualistic structures.

Implementation Assignment

1. Read Chapter 3.

2. Plan at least one cooperative lesson to implement in your classroom. Use the lesson plan forms from this chapter. Keep track of the successes and problems encountered so they can be discussed next session. Bring to class the lesson plans and the written comments on successes and problems.

3. Choose the student who will be the subject of your case study.

⇥❲ Cooperative Learning Contract ❳⇤

Major Learnings	Implementation Plans

Date _____ Date of Progress Report Meeting _____

Participant's Signature _____

Signatures of Other Group Members _____ _____

_____ _____ _____

❋⟨ Cooperative Learning Progress Report ⟩❋

NAME _____   SCHOOL _____

AGE LEVEL _____   SUBJECT _____

DAY AND DATE	DESCRIPTION OF TASKS and ACTIVITIES PERFORMED	SUCCESSES EXPERIENCED	PROBLEMS ENCOUNTERED

Description of critical or interesting incidents:

EXERCISE

MATERIALS

The Jigsaw Strategy

For this session we are using a procedure for structuring cooperative learning groups called **jigsaw** (Aronson, 1978). Each group member will be given a different section of the material to be learned. Each member is dependent on the others for information to do well on the assignment. Each group member is accountable for teaching his or her information to the other group members and learning the information they are teaching. The **purposes** of the jigsaw strategy are to:

1. Provide an alternative method of introducing new materials besides reading and lecture.

2. Create information interdependence among participants to increase their sense of mutuality.

3. Ensure that participants orally rehearse and cognitively elaborate the information being learned.

4. Model a cooperatively structured lesson.

Cooperative Triads

Join a triad heterogeneous on the basis of subject area and grade level taught. Your **task** is to learn all the assigned material. Work **cooperatively** to ensure that all group members master all the assigned material.

Preparation To Teach By Pairs

Take one section of the material and find a member of another group who has the same section of the material as you do. Work cooperatively to complete these tasks:

1. **Learn and become an expert on your material.** Read the material together, discuss it, and master it. Use the **Search and Explain Procedure:**

   a. Both persons silently read a paragraph. Person A summarizes the content to Person B.

  b. Person B listens, checks for accuracy, and states how it relates to material previously learned.

  c. The two reverse roles and repeat the procedure.

2. **Plan how to teach your material to the other group members.** Share your ideas as to how best to teach the material. Make sure your partner is ready.

  a. As you read through the material, underline the important points, write questions or ideas in the margins, and add your own thoughts and suggestions.

  b. When finished, write down the major ideas and supporting details or examples.

  c. Prepare one or more visual aids to help you explain the material.

  d. Plan how to make the other members of your group intellectually active rather than passive while they listen to your presentation.

Practicing How To Teach In Pairs

Meet with another person who is from a different group but who prepared to teach the same section of the material as you did. Work cooperatively to complete these tasks:

1. Review what each person plans to teach his/her group and share ideas on how to teach the material. Incorporate the best ideas from both plans into each person's presentation.

2. Make sure the other person is ready to teach the material.

Cooperative Triads

Meet with your original triad and complete the cooperative task of ensuring that all triad members have mastered all the assigned material by:

1. Teaching your area of expertise to the other triad members.

2. Learning the material being taught by the other triad members.

The **presenter** should encourage:

1. Oral rehearsal.

2. Elaboration and integration.

3. Implementation ideas.

The role of the **listening members** is to:

1. Clarify the material by asking appropriate questions.

2. Help the presenter by coming up with clever ways of memorizing the important ideas or facts. Think creatively about the information being presented.

3. Relate (out loud) the information to previous learned knowledge. Elaborate the information being presented.

4. Plan (out loud) how the information can be applied in the immediate future.

Monitoring Of The Groups

The instructor monitors each group to make sure that what is being taught is accurate. Collect some data about the functioning of the triads to aid their later group processing.

Evaluating

The instructor assesses participants' mastery of all the material by giving every participant a written exam or randomly giving individual oral exams on the material being studied.

Processing

The instructor has the cooperative triads process briefly by identifying at least one action each member did to help the other members learn and at least three actions that could be added to improve members' learning next time.

The Teacher's Role in Cooperation

Make Decisions

Specify Academic and Collaborative Objectives. What academic and/or collaborative skills do you want students to learn or practice in their groups? Start with something easy.

Decide on Group Size. Students often lack collaborative skills, so start with groups of two or three students; later advance cautiously to fours.

Assign Students to Groups. Heterogeneous groups are the most powerful, so mix abilities, sexes, cultural backgrounds, and task orientations. Assign students to groups randomly or select groups yourself.

Arrange the Room. The closer the students are to each other, the better they can communicate. Group members should be "knee to knee and eye to eye."

Plan Materials. Materials can send a "sink or swim together" message to students if you give only one paper to the group or give each member part of the material to learn and then teach the group.

Assign Roles. Students are more likely to work together if each one has a job which contributes to the task. You can assign work roles such as Reader, Recorder, Calculator, Checker, Reporter, and Materials Handler or skill roles such as Encourager of Participation, Praiser, and Checker for Understanding.

Set the Lesson

Explain the Academic Task. Prepare students by teaching them any material they need to know, then make certain they clearly understand what they are to do in the groups. This might include explaining lesson objectives, defining concepts, explaining procedures, giving examples, and asking questions.

*Structure Positive Interdependence. Students must feel that they need each other to complete the group's task, that they "sink or swim together." Some ways to create this are by establishing mutual goals (students must learn the material and make certain group members learn the material), joint rewards (if all group members achieve above a certain percentage on the test, each will receive bonus points), shared materials and information, and assigned roles.

*Structure Individual Accountability. Each student must feel responsible for learning the material and helping the group. Some ways to ensure this feeling include frequent oral quizzing of group members picked at random, giving individual tests, having everyone in the group write (pick one paper at random to grade), or having students do work first to bring to the group.

Structure Intergroup Cooperation. Having groups check with and help other groups and giving rewards or praise when all class members do well can extend the benefits of cooperation to the whole class.

Explain the Criteria for Success. Student work should be evaluated on a criteria-referenced rather than a norm-referenced basis. Make clear your criteria for evaluating the groups' work.

Specify Expected Behaviors. The more specific you are about the behaviors you want to see in the groups, the more likely students will do them. Make it clear that you expect to see everyone contributing, helping, listening with care to others, encouraging others to participate, and asking for help or clarification. Younger students may need to be told to stay with their group, take turns, share, ask group members questions, and use quiet voices.

*Teach Collaborative Skills. After students are used to working in groups, pick one collaborative skill they need to learn, point out the need for it, define it carefully, have students give you phrases they can say when using the skill, post the phrases (praise, bonus points, stars), and observe for and encourage the use of the skill until students are doing it automatically. Then teach a second skill. Consider praising, summarizing, encouraging, checking for understanding, asking for help, or generating further answers.

Monitor and Intervene

*Arrange Face-to-Face Interaction. The beneficial educational outcomes of cooperative learning groups are due to the interaction patterns and verbal exchanges that take place among students. Make certain there is oral summarizing, giving and receiving explanations, and elaborating going on.

Monitor Students' Behavior. This is the fun part! While students are working, you circulate to see whether they understand the assignment and the material, give immediate feedback and reinforcement, and praise good use of group skills.

Provide Task Assistance. If students are having trouble with the task, you can clarify, reteach, or elaborate on what they need to know.

Intervene to Teach Collaborative Skills. If students are having trouble with group interactions, you can suggest more effective procedures for working together or more effective behaviors for them to engage in. You can ask students to figure out how to work more effectively together. If students are learning or practicing a skill, record on an observation sheet how often you hear that skill, then share your observations with the groups.

Evaluate and Process

Evaluate Student Learning. Assess how well students completed the task and give them feedback.

*Process Group Functioning. In order to improve, students need time and procedures for analyzing how well their group is functioning and how well they are using collaborative skills. Processing can be done by individuals, small groups, or the whole class. To start, have groups routinely list three things they did well in working together today and one thing they will do better tomorrow. Then summarize as a whole class.

Provide Closure. To reinforce student learning you may wish to have groups share answers or paper, summarize major points in the lesson, or review important facts.

COOPERATIVE LESSON WORKSHEET

Grade Level: _____   Subject Area: _____

Step 1.   Select a lesson: _____
_____

Step 2.   Make Decisions.

a. Group size: _____

b. Assignment to groups: _____
_____

c. Room arrangement: _____
_____

d. Materials needed for each group: _____
_____
_____

e. Assigning roles: _____
_____
_____

Step 3.   Set the Lesson. State, in language your students understand:

a. Task: _____
_____

b. Positive interdependence: _____
_____
_____

c. Individual accountability: _____
_____

d. Criteria for success: _____
_____

e. Specific behaviors expected: _____
_____

Step 4.   Monitor and Process

　　　a. Evidence of expected behaviors (appropriate actions):

_____

_____

　　　b. Observation form: _____

　　　　　Observer(s): _____

　　　c. Plans for processing (feedback): _____

_____

Step 5.   Evaluate Outcomes

　　　a. Task achievement: _____

_____

　　　b. Group functioning: _____

_____

　　　c. Notes on individuals: _____

_____

　　　d. Suggestions for next time: _____

_____

_____

_____

_____

_____

CURRICULUM ADAPTATION

*Changing lesson plans to include cooperative interaction can be time-consuming at first. H
is a quick lesson plan worksheet which can be used initially to ensure all the critical elem(
of cooperative learning are incorporated into your lessons. As you use groups more of
this form can be used as a quick self-check.*

SUBJECT AREA

I. **DECISIONS**

    LESSON: _____

    GROUP SIZE: _____

    ASSIGNMENT TO GROUPS : _____

    MATERIALS: _____

II. **SET THE LESSON**

    WHAT IS/ARE:

Academic Task:	Criteria for Success:

*Positive Interdependence:	*Individual Accountability:	*Expected Behavior:

III. ***MONITORING**

    WILL BE DONE BY: Teacher _____   Teacher/Student _____

    FOCUS WILL BE ON: Whole Class _____   Individual Groups _____   Individuals ___

    OBSERVATION SHEET INCLUDES THE BEHAVIORS OF: _____

    _____

    _____

    *PROCESSING/FEEDBACK: _____

    _____

    _____

----
*An essential element of cooperative groups

BEST ADVICE

. DECISIONS

LESSON: _Start with a short lesson, something you feel comfortable with._

GROUP SIZE: _Start small, a pair or a threesome (with larger groups more skills are necessary to be successful)._

ASSIGNMENT TO GROUPS: _You can randomly choose or assign students depending on the group's task. It is your choice._

MATERIALS: _Give each student materials or the group can have one set of papers. One group set helps create interdependence among members._

. SET THE LESSON

WHAT IS/ARE:

Academic Task:	Criteria for Success:
Clearly state what you want students to do: make a mural, complete the worksheet, answer the questions	_State how they will know they have been successful with the task:_ _90% Fantastic (A)_ _80% Very Good (B)_

*Positive Interdependence:	*Individual Accountability:	*Expected Behaviors:
The groups need to know they have to be concerned with each other's learning. They sink or swim together.	_Students should know they are each responsible for knowing the work--this can be done by testing each one._	_Specify how you want them to behave while they work. Name specific, observable, describable behaviors._

. *MONITORING _Start with the teacher as the observer to model how observing should be done._

WILL BE DONE BY: Teacher ___X___   Teacher/Student _____

FOCUS WILL BE ON: Whole Class ____   Individual Groups ____   Individuals ____

OBSERVATION SHEET INCLUDES THE BEHAVIORS OF: _Start small with just two or three behaviors. They should be positive behaviors not negative._

(Taking turns, sharing, praising, checking) (Refer to Expected Behaviors box above)

. *PROCESSING/FEEDBACK: _Take time to give feedback to your students._
Refer back to the behaviors you asked them to try, pointing out positive behaviors you noticed.

----

sential elements of cooperative groups   2:39

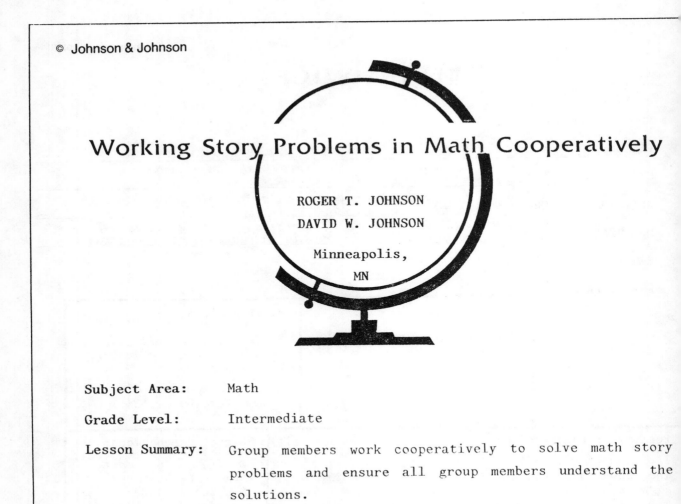

Working Story Problems in Math Cooperatively

ROGER T. JOHNSON

DAVID W. JOHNSON

Minneapolis,

MN

Subject Area: Math

Grade Level: Intermediate

Lesson Summary: Group members work cooperatively to solve math story problems and ensure all group members understand the solutions.

Instructional Objectives: Students will get practice and help in finding solutions to math story problems.

ITEM	NUMBER NEEDED
Story-Problem Worksheet (To be provided by teacher)	One per group
Observation Sheet	One per group
Role Cards	One set per group
Computation Sheet	One per student

Time Required: From twenty to sixty minutes

© Appears in Structuring Cooperative Learning: The 1987 Lesson-Plan Handbook by D. W. Johnson, R. T. Johnson, and Edythe Johnson Holubec. Edina, MN: Interaction Book Company, 1987.

≈ Decisions ≈

Group Size: Four

Assignment to Groups: Since there are twenty-eight students in your class, you have the class count off by seven. All the **Ones** make up one group, all the **Twos** make up another group, and so forth. By counting off you ensure heterogeneity in ability to do math. You want to have good and poor math students in every group.

Roles:

Reader: Reads the problem aloud to the group.

Checker: Checks to make sure all group members understand how to solve each problem.

Encourager: Watches to make sure everyone is participating and invites reluctant or silent members to join in.

Observer: Records the actions of each group member on an observation sheet while the group is solving the problems.

The students shuffle the role cards and deal them out so that each member is randomly assigned a role. The students are told to help each other fulfill the role, so, for example, a non-reader who ends up with the role of **Reader** will receive help from the other group members.

≈ The Lesson ≈

Instructional Task:

In this lesson you are to:

1. *Solve each of the problems on the worksheet correctly.*
2. *Understand the strategies required to do so.*
3. *Be able to show how you got your answer.*

Positive Interdependence

The tasks will be done cooperatively. This means:

1. One answer from the four of you.
2. Each member should understand how to solve the problem.
3. Each member should be able to explain the strategies required for solving the problem.

To help you work cooperatively, each member will be assigned a role. The **Reader** reads each problem clearly to the group. The **Checker** ensures that each member can explain at least one (and preferably two) ways to solve the problem. The **Encourager** acts as a cheerleader to ensure that everyone participates in the group discussion. The **Observer** records the actions of each group member on an observation sheet.

Individual Accountability

While discussing the problem, each member is expected to write out the computations required for the solution. The computation sheet from each member needs to be handed in with the group worksheet. Then I will call on individuals at random to explain how they worked a particular problem. On Friday, I will give you a test with similar problems to be taken individually and I will expect you to be able to solve these problems.

Criteria for Success

● If all group members can solve the problems correctly.

You will be able to earn bonus points for this activity. There may be more than one way to solve a problem in order to arrive at the correct answer. Your group will receive two bonus points for each additional strategy it finds.

Expected Behaviors:

I expect to see the following things as I observe the groups:

- *Make sure that all students get a chance to share their ideas.*
- *Say so when you don't understand an answer or question.*
- *Say so when you think someone's idea helps.*

Intergroup Cooperation:

When your group finishes, compare your answers with the answers of the surrounding groups. Identify at least two different strategies for solving the problem.

≈ Monitoring and Processing ≈

Monitoring: While the students are working, watch to see how easily they are solving the problems and how well they are working together. Occasionally, ask a student to explain one of the answers already agreed on and recorded to emphasize the fact that all group members need to be able to explain the answers. Often, turn students' questions back to the group to solve, or ask students to check with a neighboring group.

Intervening: When a group is obviously struggling, watch for a moment, then intervene. Point out the problem and ask the group what can be done about it. This establishes the teacher's role as one of consultant rather than answer giver. *What is the group going to do about this?* is a useful phrase for you in the cooperative goal structure. You can (and should) suggest possibilities along with the students, sometimes explain a skill, and help the group decide on an effective strategy. Then refocus the group on the task and move on.

Processing: At the end of the lesson, have the groups turn to their observation sheet. Ask them to discuss the findings of the

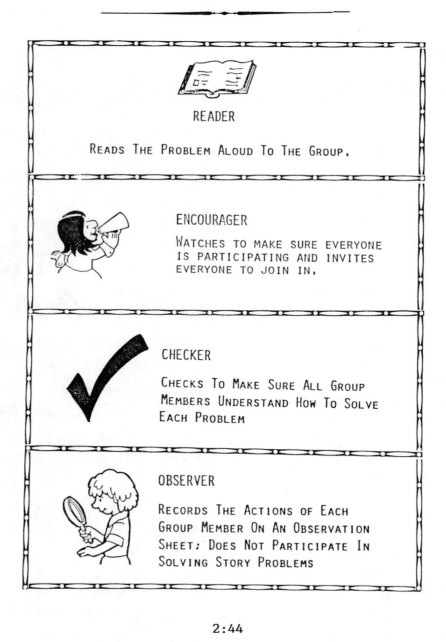

observer, and how they could work to improve their contributions to the group. Finally, lead a discussion on how well the groups worked together. Be careful to model good processing techniques by sticking close to actual observations and stressing positive behaviors. This processing is an important part of the lesson, so always leave time for it.

READER

READS THE PROBLEM ALOUD TO THE GROUP.

ENCOURAGER

WATCHES TO MAKE SURE EVERYONE IS PARTICIPATING AND INVITES EVERYONE TO JOIN IN.

CHECKER

CHECKS TO MAKE SURE ALL GROUP MEMBERS UNDERSTAND HOW TO SOLVE EACH PROBLEM

OBSERVER

RECORDS THE ACTIONS OF EACH GROUP MEMBER ON AN OBSERVATION SHEET; DOES NOT PARTICIPATE IN SOLVING STORY PROBLEMS

OBSERVATION SHEET

SKILL	GROUP MEMBERS		
Asks for Help			
Shares Ideas			
Gives Help			

COMMENTS:

Lesson Planning Project

Task: Plan a lesson to be taught cooperatively.

Cooperative: One lesson plan from the two of you. Members sign the to indicate that they have contributed their share of the work, that they agree with its content, and they can present/explain it.

Criteria For Success: A completed lesson plan that each group member can teach and is committed to teaching.

Individual Accountability:
1. Each group member may be given different color pens, markers, or pencils.
2. Each group member presents the lesson to a member of another group.

Expected Social Skills: Presenting ideas, eliciting ideas, and organizing work.

Ingroup Cooperation: Whenever it is helpful, check procedures, information, and progress with other groups.

Guided Practice In Structuring Cooperative Learning

An important aspect of mastering cooperative learning is actually using it. A teacher may need to structure and teach 20 to 30 lessons cooperatively before gaining a rudimentary competence in doing so. During this training you will practice structuring several lessons cooperatively.

Task: Take the lesson you have just planned. Practice presenting the task and the positive interdependence components of the lesson.

Cooperative: Working in a pair, role play teaching the task and positive interdependence components of the lesson. Present the lesson as if the other person were your class. Use the following procedure:

1. Present your lesson:

   a. *The **task** is . . .*

   b. *On this task I want you to work **cooperatively.** That means . . .*

2. Listen carefully while your partner presents his or her lesson.

3. Help each other make the task and positive interdependence statements even more effective. After a cooperative goal, what other methods of positive interdependence could be added? How could the statements be more precise and specific next time?

Expected Criteria For Success: Both persons able to present the task and positive interdependence components of a cooperative lesson.

Individual Accountability: One member from your group will be randomly chosen to present his or her task and positive interdependence statements.

Expected Behaviors: Presenting, listening, processing, and encouraging.

Intergroup Cooperation: Whenever it is helpful, check your task and positive interdependence statements with another group.

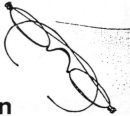

Reading Comprehension Lesson

Tasks:
1. Read the (poem, chapter, story, handout) and answer the questions.
2. Practice the skill of checking.

Cooperative:
1. One set of answers from the group, everyone has to agree, everyone has to be able to explain each answer.
2. If all members score 90 percent or better on the test, each member will receive 5 bonus points.
3. To facilitate the group's work, each member is assigned a role: Reader, recorder, checker.

Expected Criteria For Success: Everyone must be able to answer each question correctly.

Individual Accountability:
1. One member from your group will be randomly chosen to explain how to solve each problem.
2. A test will be given that each member takes individually.
3. Each group member will be required to explain the group's answers to a member of another group.

Expected Behaviors: Active participating, checking, encouraging, and elaborating by all members.

Intergroup Cooperation: Whenever it is helpful, check procedures, answers, and strategies with another group. When you are finished, compare your answers with those of another group and discuss.

Assignment

Rewrite the above assignment for a reading comprehension lesson in your classroom. If you are not a language arts teacher, modify the lesson into a reading comprehension lesson in your subject area. Script out exactly what you will say to your class. The lesson planning form on page 2:41 may be of help.

Joint Project

Task: Complete a project.

Cooperative: Each group completes one project. Members sign the project to indicate that they have contributed their share of the work, that they agree with its content, and they can present/explain it. When a variety of materials are used (such as scissors, paper, glue, markers), assign each team member a responsibility for one of the materials. If appropriate, assign each group member a specific role.

Criteria For Success: A completed project that each group member can explain/present.

Individual Accountability:
1. Each group member may be given different color pens, markers, or pencils.
2. Each group member presents the group project to a member of another group.
3. Each student takes a test individually on the content covered by the project.

Expected Social Skills: Presenting ideas, eliciting ideas, and organizing work.

Ingroup Cooperation: Whenever it is helpful, check procedures, information, and progress with other groups.

Examples:

1. Using compass readings, draw a treasure map for another group to follow.

2. Make a list of the reasons for not growing up (**Peter Pan** by J. M. Barrie).

Read And Explain Pairs

Task: Establish the meaning of each paragraph and then integrate the meaning of the paragraphs into the meaning of the assigned material as a whole.

Cooperative: Ensure that you and your partner become experts on the assigned material. Agree on the meaning of each paragraph. Formulate one summary from the two of you. Both of you must agree on and be able to explain the meaning of the assigned material. The following **procedure** is used:

1. Both persons silently read the first paragraph. Person A summarizes the content to Person B.
2. Identify the question being asked in the paragraph.
3. Agree on a summary of the paragraph that answers the question.
4. Relate the meaning of the paragraph to previous learning.
5. Move on to the next paragraph and repeat the procedure.

Expected Criteria For Success: Everyone must be able to explain the meaning of the assigned material correctly.

Individual Accountability: One member from your group will be randomly chosen to explain the meaning of the assigned material.

Expected Behaviors: Active participating, checking, encouraging, and elaborating by all members.

Intergroup Cooperation: Whenever it is helpful, check procedures, answers, and strategies with another group. When you are finished, compare your answers with those of another group and discuss.

Assignment

Think of a reading assignment you will give in the near future. Formulate a plan to use the <u>Read and Explain Pairs</u> for that assignment. Script out exactly what you will say to your class in assigning the procedure.

Jig-Saw Procedure

Task: Think of a reading assignment you will give in the near future. Divide the assignment in three parts. Plan how you will use the jig-saw procedure. Script out exactly what you will say to your class in using each part of the jig-saw procedure.

Procedure: One way to structure positive interdependence among group members is to use the jigsaw method of creating resource interdependence. The steps for structuring a "jigsaw" lesson are:

1. Cooperative Groups: Distribute a set of materials to each group. The set needs to be divisible into the number of members of the group (2, 3, or 4 parts). Give each member one part of the set of materials.

2. Preparation Pairs: Assign students the cooperative task of meeting with someone else in the class who is a member of another learning group and who has the same section of the material and complete two tasks:

   a. Learning and becoming an expert on their material.

   b. Planning how to teach the material to the other members of their groups.

3. Practice Pairs: Assign students the cooperative task of meeting with someone else in the class who is a member of another learning group and who has learned the same material and share ideas as to how the material may best be taught. These "practice pairs" review what each plans to teach their group and how. The best ideas of both are incorporated into each's presentation.

4. Cooperative Groups: Assign students the cooperative tasks of:

   a. Teaching their area of expertise to the other group members.

   b. Learning the material being taught by the other members.

5. Evaluation: Assess students' degree of mastery of all the material. Reward the groups whose members all reach the preset criterion of excellence.

2:51

Turn To Your Neighbor

When a teacher asks a class who knows the answer and one student is chosen to respond, that student has an opportunity to clarify and extend what he or she knows through explaining. In this situation only one student is involved and active. The rest of the class is passive. A teacher may ensure that all students are active by using a procedure that requires all students to explain their answers simultaneously. When each student has to explain his or her answer and reasoning to a classmate, all students are active and involved. No one is allow to be passive. There are two basic ways of structuring simultaneous explaining: (a) the individual student formulates an answer and then explains to a classmate or (b) a small group formulates an answer and each member explains their group's answer and reasoning to a member of another group.

Tasks: Explain answers and reasoning to a classmate and practice the skill of explaining.

Cooperative Procedure: Students create a joint answer within a pair through the following procedure:
1. **Formulate** an answer (either individually or in a group depending on the teacher's instructions).
2. **Share** their answers and reasoning with a newly assigned partner.
3. **Listen** carefully to their partner's explanation.
4. **Create** a new answer that is superior to their initial formulations through the processes of association, building on each other's thoughts, and synthesizing.

Expected Criteria For Success: Each student must be able to explain the answer.

Individual Accountability: Each member explains.

Expected Behaviors: Explaining and synthesizing.

Assignment

List upcoming instances in your teaching where students are required to formulate a series of answers. Plan how to use simultaneous responding procedures for each of these instances.

Teacher's Role In Cooperation

A	PI	IA	SS	MIP

Step 1: Specifying Objectives
1. Academic
2. Social Skills

Step 2: Making Preinstructional Decisions
1. Decide On Group Size.
2. Assign Students To Groups.
3. Arrange The Room.
4. Arrange Materials.
5. Decide On Roles.
6. Plan Monitoring Procedures And Forms.

Step 3: Setting The Lesson
1. Explain Academic Task And Procedure.
2. Explain Criteria For Success.
3. Structure Cooperation.
4. Structure Individual Accountability.
5. Specify (And Teach) Expected Social Skills.
6. Structure Intergroup Cooperation.

Step 4: Monitoring And Intervening
1. Arrange Face-To-Face Interaction Among Students.
2. Monitor Students' Behavior.
3. Provide Task Assistance.
4. Provide Social Skills Prompting And Encouragement.

Step 5: Evaluating And Processing
1. Evaluate And Celebrate Student Learning.
2. Process Group Functioning And Use Of Social Skills.
3. Provide Closure.

Chapter 3

Research On Cooperative Learning

Table Of Contents

Introduction

Linda Scott, in her Moundsview, Minnesota 5th-grade classroom, assigns her students a set of math story problems to solve. She assigns her students to groups of three, ensuring that a high-, medium-, and low-performing math students and both male and female students in each group. The instructional task is to solve each story problem correctly and to understand the correct process for doing so. Each group is given a set of story problems (one copy for each student) and a set of three "role" cards. Each group member is assigned one of the roles. The **reader** reads the problem aloud to the group. The **checker** makes sure that all members can explain how to solve each problem correctly. The **encourager** in a friendly way encourages all members of the group to participate in the discussion, sharing their ideas and feelings.

Within this lesson **positive interdependence** is structured by the group agreeing on (1) the answer and (2) the process for solving each problem. Since the group certifies that each member (1) has the correct answer written on their answer sheet and (2) can correctly explain how to solve each problem, **individual accountability** is structured by having the teacher pick one answer sheet at random to score for the group and to ask randomly one group member to explain how to solve one of the problems. The **cooperative skills** emphasized in the lesson are checking and encouraging. Finally, at the end of the period the groups **process** their functioning by answering two questions: (1) What is something each member did that was helpful for the group and (2) What is something each member could do to make the group even better tomorrow?

As a result of structuring this math lesson cooperatively, what instructional outcomes can the teacher expect?

Working together to get the job done can have profound effects on students and staff members. A great deal of research has been conducted on the relationship among cooperative, competitive, and individualistic efforts and instructional outcomes (Johnson & Johnson, 1974, 1978, 1983, 1989a; Johnson, Nelson, & Maruyama, 1983; Johnson, Maruyama, Johnson, Nelson, & Skon, 1981; Pepitone, 1980; Sharan, 1980; Slavin, 1983). These research studies began in the late 1890's when Triplett (1897) in the United States, Turner (1889) in England, and Mayer (1903) in Germany conducted a series of studies on the factors associated with competitive performance. The amount of research that has been conducted since is staggering. During the past 90 years over 600 studies have been conducted by a wide variety of researchers in different decades with different age subjects, in different subject areas, and in different settings. We know far more about the efficacy of cooperative learning than we know about lecturing, age grouping, beginning reading instruction at age six, departmentalization, or almost any other facet of education. While there is not space enough in this chapter to review all of the research, a comprehensive review of all studies may be found in Johnson and Johnson (1989a). In most cases, references to individual studies are not included in this chapter. Rather, the reader is referred to reviews that contain the references to the specific studies that corroborate the point being made.

Building on the theorizing of Kurt Lewin and Morton Deutsch, the premise may be made that the type of interdependence structured among students determines how they interact with each other which, in turn largely determines instructional outcomes. The quality of peer relationships, furthermore, has widespread and powerful impact on individuals' cognitive and social development. In this chapter, therefore, the importance of high quality peer relationships, student-student interaction patterns, and the instructional outcomes promoted by the three goal structures are discussed.

Part 1: Importance of Peer Relationships

Children and adolescents live in an expanding social world. From relating primarily to adult caretakers, young children begin interacting with other adults and with other children. As children become older, they have more interaction with other children and less interaction with adults. Yet, traditionally, adults in the United States have viewed the interaction between adults and children as the most important vehicle for ensuring the effective socialization and development of children and adolescents. Child-child relationships have been assumed to be, at best, relatively unimportant and, at worst, unhealthy influences.

This adult-centric view is reflected in the policies of our schools. In schools most legitimate peer interaction among students has been limited to extracurricular activities. These activities rarely deal directly with the basic issues of classroom life. The system of instruction emphasizes teacher lectures and seatwork done by students individualistically. Student attempts to interact with each other are seen as disruptive of this system. Furthermore, the rigid age segregation usually applied in school classrooms (and also fostered by the

subdividing of school programs for administrative purposes into elementary, junior, and senior high schools) often limits peer interaction within a narrowly confined age span. Finally, educators systematically fail to train students in the basic social skills necessary for interacting effectively with peers (in this chapter the word **peer** means a wide range of other children or adolescents). These skills are not considered pedagogically useful. Essentially, the typical adult-child dyadic view of teaching and learning has deemphasized student-student relationships in the classroom.

Despite these patterns of deemphasis, **peer relationships are a critical element in the development and socialization of children and adolescents** (Hartup, 1976; Johnson, 1980). In fact, the primary relationships in which development and socialization may take place may be with peers. Compared with interactions with adults, interactions with peers tend to be more frequent, intense, and varied throughout childhood and adolescence. Experiences with peers are not superficial luxuries to be enjoyed during lunch or on a Saturday afternoon. Constructive relationships with peers are a necessity.

There are numerous ways in which peer relationships contribute to (a) social and cognitive development and (b) socialization. Some of the more important consequences correlated with peer relationships are (the specific supporting evidence may be found in Johnson, 1980, and Johnson & Johnson, 1989a):

1. **In their interactions with peers, children and adolescents directly learn attitudes, values, skills, and information unobtainable from adults.** In their interactions with each other, children and adolescents imitate each other's behavior and identify with friends possessing admired competencies. Through providing models, reinforcement, and direct learning, peers shape a wide variety of social behaviors, attitudes, and perspectives.

2. **Interaction with peers provides support, opportunities, and models for prosocial behavior.** It is within interactions with other children and adolescents that one helps, comforts, shares with, takes care of, assists, and gives to others. Without peers with whom to engage in such behaviors, many forms of prosocial values and commitments could not be developed. Conversely, whether adolescents engage in problem or transition behavior, such as the use of illegal drugs and delinquency, is related to the perceptions of their friends' attitudes toward such behaviors. Being rejected by one's peers tends to result in antisocial behavioral patterns characterized by aggressiveness, disruptiveness, and other negatively perceived behavior.

3. Children and adolescents frequently lack the time perspective needed to tolerate delays in gratification. As they develop and are socialized, the focus on their own immediate impulses and needs is replaced with the ability to take longer perspectives. **Peers provide models of, expectations of, directions for, and reinforcements of learning to control impulses.** Aggressive impulses provide an example. Peer interaction involving such activities as rough-and-tumble play promotes the acquisition of a repertoire of effective aggressive behaviors and helps establish the necessary regulatory mechanisms for modulating aggressive effect.

4. **Children and adolescents learn to view situations and problems from perspectives other than their own through their interaction with peers.** Such perspective taking is one of the most critical competencies for cognitive and social development. All psychological development may be described as a progressive loss of egocentrism and an increase in ability to take wider and more complex perspectives. It is primarily in interaction with peers that egocentrism is lost and increased perspective taking is gained.

5. **Autonomy** is the ability to understand what others expect in any given situation and to be free to choose whether to meet their expectations. Autonomous people are independent of both extreme inner- or outer-directedness. When making decisions concerning appropriate social behavior, autonomous people tend to consider both their internal values and the situational requirements and then respond in flexible and appropriate ways. Autonomy is the result of (1) the internalization of values (including appropriate self-approval) derived from caring and supportive relationships, and (2) the acquisition of social skills and sensitivity. **Relationships with other children and adolescents are powerful influences on the development of the values and the social sensitivity required for autonomy.** Children with a history of isolation from or rejection by peers, furthermore, often are inappropriately other directed. They conform to group pressures even when they believe the recommended actions are wrong or inappropriate.

6. While adults can provide certain forms of companionship, **children need close and intimate relationships with peers with whom they can share their thoughts and**

feelings, aspirations and hopes, dreams and fantasies, and joys and pains. Children need constructive peer relationships to avoid the pain of loneliness.

7. Throughout infancy, childhood, adolescence, and early adulthood, a person moves through several successive and overlapping identities. The physical changes involved in growth, the increasing number of experiences with other people, increasing responsibilities, and general cognitive and social development all cause changes in self-definition. The final result should be a coherent and integrated identity. In peer relationships children and adolescents become aware of the similarities and differences between themselves and others. They experiment with a variety of social roles that help them integrate their own sense of self. In peer relationships values and attitudes are clarified and integrated into an individual's self-definition. **It is through peer relationships that a frame of reference for perceiving oneself is developed.** Gender typing and its impact on one's identity is an example.

8. **Coalitions formed during childhood and adolescence provide help and assistance throughout adulthood.**

9. The ability to maintain interdependent, cooperative relationships is a prime manifestation of psychological health. Poor peer relationships in elementary school predict psychological disturbance and delinquency in high school, and poor peer relationships in high school predict adult pathology. **The absence of any friendships during childhood and adolescence seems to increase the risk of mental disorder.**

10. **In both educational and work settings, peers have a strong influence on productivity.** Greater achievement is typically found in collaborative situations where peers work together than in situations where individuals work alone. Especially when a child or adolescent has poor study skills or is unmotivated, cooperative interaction with peers has powerful effects on productivity. Supportive relationships with peers are also related to using one's abilities in achievement situations.

11. **Student educational aspirations may be more influenced by peers than by any other social influence.** Similarly, ambition in career settings is greatly influenced by peers.

Within instructional situations, peer relationships can be structured to create meaningful interdependence through learning cooperatively with peers. Within cooperative learning situations students experience feelings of belonging, acceptance, support, and caring, and the social skills and social roles required for maintaining interdependent relationships can be taught and practiced.

Through repeated cooperative experiences students can develop the social sensitivity of what behavior is expected from others and the actual skills and autonomy to meet such expectations if they so desire. Through holding each other accountable for appropriate social behavior, students can greatly influence the values they internalize and the self-control they develop. It is through belonging to a series of interdependent relationships that values are learned and internalized. It is through prolonged cooperative interaction with other people that healthy social development with the overall balance of trust rather than distrust of other people, the ability to view situations and problems from a variety of perspectives, a meaningful sense of direction and purpose in life, an awareness of mutual interdependence with others, and an integrated and coherent sense of personal identity, takes place (Johnson, 1979; Johnson & Matross, 1977).

In order for peer relationships to be constructive influences, they must promote feelings of belonging, acceptance, support, and caring, rather than feelings of hostility and rejection (Johnson. 1980). Being accepted by peers is related to willingness to engage in social interaction, utilizing abilities in achievement situations, and providing positive social rewards for peers. Isolation from peers is associated with high anxiety, low self-esteem, poor interpersonal skills, emotional handicaps, and psychological pathology. Rejection by peers is related to disruptive classroom behavior, hostile behavior and negative affect, and negative attitudes toward other students and school. In order to promote constructive peer influences, therefore, teachers must first ensure that students interact with each other and, second, must ensure that the interaction takes place within a cooperative context.

Summary

Educators who wish to promote constructive relationships among students will wish to (Johnson & Johnson, 1980):

1. Structure cooperative situations in which children and adolescents work with peers to achieve a common goal.

2. Emphasize joint rather than individual products whenever possible.

3. Directly teach the interpersonal skills needed to build and maintain collaborative relationships with peers.

4. Give children and adolescents meaningful responsibility for the well-being and success of their peers.

5. Encourage the feelings of support, acceptance, concern, and commitment that are part of collaborative situations.

6. Hold children and adolescents accountable for fulfilling their obligations and responsibilities to their collaborators and give them mutual authority over each other.

7. Ensure that students experience success in working cooperatively with peers.

Part 2: Interaction Patterns

Simply placing students near each other and allowing interaction to take place does not mean that high quality peer relationships will result and that learning will be maximized. The nature of interaction is important. Some interaction leads to students rejecting each other and defensively avoiding being influenced by peers. When student-student interaction leads to relationships characterized by perceived support and acceptance, then the potential effects described in the previous section are likely to be found.

There have been several hundred studies comparing the effects of cooperative, competitive, and individualistic goal structures on aspects of interpersonal interaction important for learning (see Johnson & Johnson, 1989a). A cooperative goal structure leads to a promotive interaction pattern among students. **Promotive interaction** occurs as individuals encouraging and facilitating each other's efforts to achieve. It is characterized by personal and academic acceptance and support, exchange of information, mutual help and assistance, high intrinsic achievement motivation, and high emotional involvement in learning.

A competitive goal structure results in an oppositional pattern of student-student interaction. **Oppositional interaction** occurs as individuals discouraging and obstructing each other's efforts to achieve. It results in rejection of classmates, obstruction of each other's work, avoidance of information exchange or communication, low achievement motivation, and psychological withdrawal and avoidance. The negative interdependence created by a competitive goal structure results in students having a vested interest in obstructing one another's learning. There are two ways to win in a competition--to do better than anyone else or to prevent anyone else from doing better than you. This is known as a good offense and a good defense. In a classroom, however, preventing against classmates learning more than you can create destructive interaction patterns that decrease learning for everyone.

An individualistic goal structure results in no interaction among students. **No interdependence** exists when individuals work independently without any interchange with each other. Students work alone without bothering their classmates. Such a goal structure minimizes peer relationships and interaction in learning situations.

Acceptance, Support, Trust, Liking

If you want students to encourage and support each other's efforts to achieve, and if you wish students to accept and trust each other, cooperative learning should dominate your classroom. Cooperative learning experiences, compared with competitive and individualistic ones, have been found to result in stronger beliefs that other students (and teachers) care about how much one learns and want to help one learn (Johnson & Johnson, 1989a). Furthermore, cooperative attitudes are related to mutual acceptance, respect, liking, and trust among students.

From Table 3.1 it may be seen that cooperation resulted in greater social support than did competitive or individualistic efforts (effect sizes of 0.59 and 0.71 respectively). Social support tends to be related to (see Johnson & Johnson, 1989a):

1. Achievement, successful problem solving, persistence on challenging tasks under frustrating conditions, lack of cognitive interference during problem solving, lack of absenteeism, academic and career aspirations, more appropriate seeking of assistance, retention, job satisfaction, high morale, and greater compliance with regimens and behavioral patterns that increase health and productivity.

2. Living a longer life, recovering from illness and injury faster and more completely, and experiencing less severe illnesses.

3. Psychological health and adjustment, lack of neuroticism and psychopathology, reduction of psychological distress, coping effectively with stressful situations, self-reliance and autonomy, a coherent and integrated self-identity, greater psychological safety, higher self-esteem, increased general happiness, and increased interpersonal skills.

4. Effective management of stress by providing the caring, information, resources, and feedback individuals need to cope with stress, by reducing the number and severity of stressful events in an individual's life, by reducing anxiety, and by helping one appraise the nature of the stress and one's ability to deal with it constructively.

5. The emotional support and encouragement individuals need to cope with the risk that is inherently involved in challenging one's competence and striving to grow and develop.

The importance of social support has been ignored within education over the past 30 years. **A general principle to keep in mind is that the pressure to achieve should always be matched with an equal level of social support.** Challenge and support must be kept in balance. Whenever increased demands and pressure to be productive are placed on students (and teachers), a corresponding increase in social support should be structured.

Exchange of Information

The seeking of information, and utilizing it in one's learning, is essential for academic achievement. Students working within a cooperative goal structure (Johnson & Johnson, 1989a):

1. Seek significantly more information from each other than do students working within a competitive goal structure.

2. Are less biased and have fewer misperceptions in comprehending the viewpoints and positions of other individuals.

3. More accurately communicate information by verbalizing ideas and information more frequently , attending to others' statements more carefully, and accepting others' ideas and information more frequently.

4. Are more confident about the value of their ideas.

5. Make optimal use of the information provided by other students.

Motivation

Motivation is most commonly viewed as a combination of the perceived likelihood of success and the perceived incentive for success. The greater the likelihood of success and the more important it is to succeed, the higher the motivation. Success that is intrinsically rewarding is usually seen as being more desirable for learning than is having students believe that only extrinsic rewards are worthwhile. There is greater perceived likelihood of success and success is viewed as more important in cooperative than in competitive or individualistic learning situations (Johnson & Johnson, 1989a). In addition, cooperative learning tends to generate intrinsic motivation to learn while competitive and individualistic learning tend to be fueled by extrinsic motivation. Finally, students tend to be more emotionally involved in cooperative than in competitive or individualistic learning activities.

The more cooperative students' attitudes, the more they see themselves as being intrinsically motivated: They persevere in pursuit of clearly defined learning goals; believe that it is their own efforts that determine their school success; want to be good students and get good grades; and believe that ideas, feelings, and learning new ideas are important and enjoyable. These studies also indicate that the more competitive students' attitudes are, the more they see themselves as being extrinsically motivated in elementary and junior high schools. Competitive attitudes are, however, somewhat related to intrinsic motivation, to being a good student, and to getting good marks in senior high school. Individualistic attitudes tend to be unrelated to all measured aspects of the motivation to learn. Being part of a cooperative learning group has been found to be related to a high subjective probability of academic success and continuing motivation for further learning by taking more advanced courses in the subject area studied. There is also experimental evidence which indicated that cooperative learning experiences, compared with individualistic ones, will result in more intrinsic motivation, less extrinsic motivation, and less need for teachers to set clear goals for the students.

Cooperative Learning And Lecturing

"The best answer to the question, 'What is the most effective method of teaching?' is that it depends on the goal, the student, the content, and the teacher. But the next best answer is, 'Students teaching other students.' There is a wealth of evidence that peer teaching is extremely effective for a wide range of goals, content, and students of different levels and personalities."

Wilbert McKeachie, et al. (1986, p. 63).

There are many times when teachers will need to lecture. Direct teaching of new concepts is an example. In secondary and college classrooms the curriculums may assume that considerable lecturing will take place. The use of **informal cooperative learning groups** *can significantly increase the effectiveness of lecturing. The following procedure may help to plan a lecture that keeps students actively engaged intellectually. It entails having* **focused discussions** *before and after a lecture (i.e., bookends) and interspersing* **turn-to-your-partner discussions** *throughout the lecture.*

1. **Focused Discussion 1:** *Plan your lecture around a series of questions that the lecture answers. Prepare the questions on an overhead transparency or write them on the board so that students can see them. Students will discuss the questions in pairs. The discussion task is aimed at promoting advance organizing of what the students know about the topic to be presented and what the lecture will cover.*

2. **Turn-To-Your-Partner Discussions:** *Divide the lecture into 10 to 15 minute segments. This is about the length of time an adult can concentrate on a lecture. Plan a short discussion task to be given to pairs of students after each segment. The task needs to be short enough that students can complete it within three or four minutes. Its purpose is to ensure that students are actively thinking about the material being presented. The discussion task may be to:*

   a. *Summarize the answer to the question being discussed.*

b. *Give a reaction to the theory, concepts, or information being presented.*

c. *Elaborate (relate material to past learning so that it gets integrated into existing conceptual frameworks) the material being presented.*

d. *Predict what is going to be presented next.*

e. *Attempt to resolve the conceptual conflict the presentation has aroused.*

f. *Hypothesize answers to the question being posed.*

Each discussion task should have four components: **formulate** *an answer to the question being asked,* **share** *your answer with your partner,* **listen** *carefully to his or her answer, and to* **create** *a new answer that is superior to each member's initial formulation through the processes of association, building on each other's thoughts, and synthesizing. Students will need to gain some experience with this procedure to become skilled in doing it within a short period of time.*

3. **Focused Discussion 2:** *Prepare an ending discussion task to summarize what students have learned from the lecture.*

Once such preparation is completed the lecture may be given by:

1. *Having students choose partners. The person nearest them will do.*

2. *Giving the pairs the cooperative assignment of completing the initial (advance organizer) task. Give them only four or five minutes to do so.*

3. *Delivering the first segment of the lecture. Then give the pairs a discussion task. Give them only three or four minutes to complete it. Use the* **formulate/share/listen/create** *procedure. Randomly choose two or three students to give 30 second summaries of their discussions.*

4. *Delivering the second segment of the lecture and so forth until the lecture is completed.*

5. *Giving students the ending discussion task. Give them only five or six minutes to complete it. This task may point students toward what the homework will cover or what will be presented in the next class session.*

6. **It is important that students are randomly called on to share their answers after each discussion task.** *Such individual accountability ensures that the pairs take the tasks seriously and check each other to ensure that both are prepared to answer.*

7. *Until students become familiar and experienced with the procedure, process it regularly to help them increase their skill and speed in completing short discussion tasks.*

Part 3: Learning Outcomes

Different learning outcomes result from the student-student interaction patterns promoted by the use of cooperative, competitive, and individualistic goal structures (Johnson & Johnson 1989a). While space is too short here to review all of the research, some of the major findings are as follows.

Cooperative Efforts And Achievement / Productivity

"The highest and best form of efficiency is the spontaneous cooperation of a free people."

Woodrow Wilson

How successful competitive, individualistic, and cooperative efforts are in promoting productivity and achievement is the first question pragmatists ask about social interdependence. Over 375 studies have been conducted over the past 90 years to give an answer (Johnson & Johnson, 1989a). When all of the studies were included in the analysis, the average cooperator performed at about 2/3 a standard deviation above average student learning within a competitive (effect size = 0.66) or individualistic situation (effect size = 0.63). When only the high-quality studies were included in the analysis, the effect sizes are 0.86 and 0.59 respectively. Cooperative learning, furthermore, resulted in more higher-level reasoning, more frequent generation of new ideas and solutions (i.e., **process gain**), and greater transfer of what is learned within one situation to another (i.e., **group-to- individual transfer**) than did competitive or individualistic learning.

Some cooperative learning procedures contained a mixture of cooperative, competitive, and individualistic efforts while others are "pure." The original jigsaw procedure (Aronson,

Table 3:1 Social Interdependence: Weighted Findings

	Mean	s.d.	n
Achievement			
Cooperative vs. Competitive	0.66	0.94	128
Cooperative vs. Individualistic	0.63	0.81	182
Competitive vs. Individualistic	0.30	0.76	39
Interpersonal Attraction			
Cooperative vs. Competitive	0.65	0.47	88
Cooperative vs. Individualistic	0.62	0.59	59
Competitive vs. Individualistic	0.08	0.70	15
Social Support			
Cooperative vs. Competitive	0.59	0.39	75
Cooperative vs. Individualistic	0.71	0.45	70
Competitive vs. Individualistic	-0.12	0.37	18
Self-Esteem			
Cooperative vs. Competitive	0.60	0.56	55
Cooperative vs. Individualistic	0.44	0.40	37
Competitive vs. Individualistic	-0.19	0.40	18

et al., 1978), for example, is a combination of resource interdependence (cooperative) and individual reward structures (individualistic). Teams-Games- Tournaments (DeVries & Edwards, 1974) and Student-Teams- Achievement-Divisions (Slavin, 1980) are mixtures of cooperation and intergroup competition. Team- Assisted-Instruction (Slavin, Leavey, & Madden, 1983) is a mixture of individualistic and cooperative learning. When the results of "pure" and "mixed" operationalizations of cooperative learning were compared, the "pure" operationalizations produced higher achievement.

Since research participants have varied widely as to economic class, age, sex, and cultural background, since a wide variety of research tasks and measures of the dependent variables have been used, and since the research has been conducted by many different researchers with markedly different orientations working in different settings and in different decades, the overall body of research on social interdependence has considerable generalizability.

That working together to achieve a common goal produces higher achievement and greater productivity than does working alone is so well confirmed by so much research that

it stands as one of the strongest principles of social and organizational psychology. Cooperative learning is indicated whenever the learning goals are highly important, mastery and retention is important, the task is complex or conceptual, problem solving is desired, divergent thinking or creativity is desired, quality of performance is expected, and higher level reasoning strategies and critical thinking are needed.

What Mediates?

Why does cooperation result in higher achievement--what mediates? The critical issue in understanding the relationship between cooperation and achievement is specifying the variables that mediate the relationship. Simply placing students in groups and telling them to work together does not in and of itself promote higher achievement. It is only under certain conditions that group efforts may be expected to be more productive than individual efforts. Those conditions are:

1. **Clearly perceived positive interdependence.** From the research, it may be concluded that positive interdependence provides the context within which promotive interaction takes place, group membership and interpersonal interaction among students do not produce higher achievement unless positive interdependence is clearly structured, the combination of goal and reward interdependence increases achievement over goal interdependence alone, and resource interdependence does not increase achievement unless goal interdependence is present also (Johnson & Johnson, 1989a).

2. **Considerable promotive (face-to-face) interaction.** Within cooperative learning, compared with competitive and individualistic learning, students (a) provide others with efficient and effective help and assistance, (b) exchange needed resources such as information and materials and processing information more efficiently and effectively, (c) provide each other with feedback in order to improve their subsequent performance on assigned tasks and responsibilities, (d) challenge each other's conclusions and reasoning in order to promote higher quality decision making and greater insight into the problems being considered, (e) advocate exerting efforts to achieve mutual goals, (f) influence each other's efforts to achieve mutual goals, (g) act in trusting and trustworthy ways, (h) are motivated to strive for mutual benefit, and (i) feel less anxiety and stress (Johnson & Johnson, 1989a).

3. **Felt personal responsibility (individual accountability) to achieve the group's goals.** When groups work on tasks where it is difficult to identify members' contributions, when there is an increased likelihood of redundant efforts, and when there is lessened responsibility for the final outcome, the less some members will try to contribute to goal achievement. If, however, there is high individual accountability and it is clear how much effort each member is contributing, if redundant efforts are avoided, if every member is responsible for the final outcome, then the social loafing effect vanishes (Johnson & Johnson, 1989a). The smaller the size of the group the greater the individual accountability may be.

4. **Frequent use of relevant interpersonal and small group skills.** Social skills and competencies tend to increase more within cooperative than in competitive or individualistic situations (Johnson & Johnson, 1989a). Working together to get the job done requires students to provide leadership, build and maintain trust, communicate effectively, and manage conflicts constructively. The more socially skillful students are, and the more attention teachers pay to teaching and rewarding the use of social skills, the higher the achievement that can be expected within cooperative learning groups. In their studies on the long-term implementation of cooperative learning, Lew and Mesch (Lew, Mesch, Johnson, & Johnson, 1986a, 1986b; Mesch, Johnson, & Johnson, 1988; Mesch, Lew, Johnson, & Johnson, 1986) investigated the impact of a reward contingency for using social skills as well as positive interdependence and a contingency for academic achievement on performance within cooperative learning groups. In the cooperative skills conditions students were trained weekly in four social skills and each member of a cooperative group was given two bonus points toward the quiz grade if all group members were observed by the teacher to demonstrate three out of four cooperative skills. The results indicated that the combination of positive interdependence, an academic contingency for high performance by all group members, and a social skills contingency, promoted the highest achievement.

5. **Periodic and regular group processing.** Stuart Yager examined the impact on achievement of (a) cooperative learning in which members discussed how well their group was functioning and how they could improve its effectiveness, (b) cooperative learning without any group processing, and (c) individualistic learning (Yager, Johnson, & Johnson, 1985). The results indicate that the high-, medium-, and low-achieving students in the cooperation with group processing condition achieved higher on daily achievement, post-instructional achievement, and retention measures than did the students in the other two conditions. Students in the cooperation without group processing condition, furthermore, achieved higher on all three measures than did the students in the individualistic condition. Johnson, Johnson, Stanne, and Garibaldi (in press) conducted a

follow-up study comparing cooperative learning with no processing, cooperative learning with teacher processing (teacher specified cooperative skills to use, observed, and gave whole class feedback as to how well students were using the skills), cooperative learning with teacher and student processing (teacher specified cooperative skills to use, observed, gave whole class feedback as to how well students were using the skills, and had learning groups discuss how well they interacted as a group), and individualistic learning. Forty-nine high ability Black American high school seniors and entering college freshmen at Xavier University participated in the study. A complex computer- assisted problem-solving assignment was given to all students. All three cooperative conditions performed higher than did the individualistic condition. The combination of teacher and student processing resulted in greater problem-solving success than did the other cooperative conditions.

Critical Thinking Competencies

In many subject areas related to science and technology the teaching of facts and theories is considered to be secondary to the teaching of critical thinking and the use of higher level reasoning strategies. The aim of science education, for example, has been to develop individuals "who can sort sense from nonsense," or who have the critical thinking abilities of grasping information, examining it, evaluating it for soundness, and applying it appropriately. Cooperative learning promotes a greater use of higher reasoning strategies and critical thinking than do competitive and individualistic learning strategies (Johnson & Johnson, 1989a).

United States' students frequently believe that a learning task is completed when they have an answer in every blank in a worksheet. Sustained effort to comprehend material deeply seems to be rare. The Japanese, on the other hand, view academic success as a matter of disciplined, enduring effort aimed at achieving **satori**, or the sudden flash of enlightenment that comes after long, intensive, but successful effort. The achievement of satori is much more likely after a discussion in cooperative learning groups than after working alone, competitively, or individualistically to complete an assignment.

Attitudes Toward Subject Area

Cooperative learning experiences, compared with competitive and individualistic ones, promote more positive attitudes toward the subject area, more positive attitudes toward the instructional experience, and more continuing motivation to learn more about the subject area being studied (Johnson & Johnson, 1989a). These findings have important implications, for example, for influencing female and minority students to enter science and math oriented careers.

Interpersonal Relationships

Cooperative learning experiences, compared with competitive, individualistic, and "traditional instruction," promote considerably more liking among students (effect sizes = 0.65 and 0.62 respectively) (Johnson & Johnson, 1989a; Johnson, Johnson, & Maruyama, 1983). This is true regardless of differences in ability level, sex, handicapping conditions, ethnic membership, social class differences, or task orientation. Students who collaborate on their studies develop considerable commitment and caring for each other no matter what their initial impressions of and attitudes toward each other were. They also like the teacher better and perceive the teacher as being more supportive and accepting academically and personally.

In order to be productive, a class of students (or a school faculty) has to cohere and have a positive emotional climate. As relationships become more positive, absenteeism decreases, and increases may be expected in student commitment to learning, feelings of personal responsibility to do the assigned work, willingness to take on difficult tasks, motivation and persistence in working on learning tasks, satisfaction and morale, willingness to endure pain and frustration to succeed, willingness to defend the school against external criticism or attack, willingness to listen to and be influenced by peers, commitment to peer's success and growth, and productivity and achievement (Johnson & F. Johnson, 1987; Watson & Johnson, 1972). In addition, when students are heterogeneous with regard to ethnic, social class, language, and ability differences, cooperative learning experiences are a necessity for building positive peer relationships.

Psychological Health

When students leave school, we would hope that they would have the psychological health and stability required to build and maintain career, family, and community relationships, to establish a basic and meaningful interdependence with other people, and to participate effectively in our society. Our studies (Johnson & Johnson, 1989a) indicate that **cooperativeness** is positively related to a number of indices of psychological health, namely: emotional maturity, well-adjusted social relations, strong personal identity, and basic trust in and optimism about people. **Competitiveness** seems also to be related to a number of indices of psychological health, while **individualistic attitudes** tend to be related to a number of indices of psychological pathology, emotional immaturity, social maladjustment, delinquency, self-alienation, and self-rejection. To the degree that schools can contribute to a student's psychological well-being, they should be organized to reinforce those traits and tendencies that promote it.

Accuracy of Perspective Taking

Social perspective taking is the ability to understand how a situation appears to another person and how that person is reacting cognitively and emotionally to the situation. The opposite of perspective taking is egocentrism, the embeddedness in one's own viewpoint to the extent that one is unaware of other points of view and of the limitations of one's perspectives. Cooperative learning experiences tend to promote greater cognitive and affective perspective taking than do competitive or individualistic learning experiences (Johnson & Johnson, 1989a).

Self-Esteem

The data in Table 3.1 indicate that cooperation produced higher levels of self-esteem than did competitive and individualistic efforts (effect-sizes of 0.58 and 0.44 respectively). Individuals with low self-esteem tend to (Johnson & Johnson, 1989a):

1. Have low productivity due to setting low goals for themselves, lacking confidence in their ability, and assuming that they will fail no matter how hard they try.

2. Be critical of others as well as themselves by looking for flaws in others and trying to "tear them down."

3. Withdraw socially due to feeling awkward, self-conscious, and vulnerable to rejection.

4. Be conforming, agreeable, highly persuasible, and highly influenced by criticism.

5. Develop more psychological problems such as anxiety, nervousness, insomnia, depression, and psychosomatic symptoms.

Within **competitive** situations self-esteem tends to be based on the contingent view of one's competence that, "If I win, then I have worth as a person, but if I lose, then I have no worth." Winners attribute their success to superior ability and attribute the failure of others to lack of ability, both of which contribute to self-aggrandizement. Losers, who are the vast majority, defensively tend to be self-disparaging, apprehensive about evaluation, and tend to withdraw psychologically and physically. Within **individualistic** situations, students are isolated from one another, receive little direct comparison with or feedback from peers, and perceive evaluations as inaccurate and unrealistic. A defensive avoidance, evaluation apprehension, and distrust of peers results. Within **cooperative** situations, individuals tend to interact, promote each other's success, form multi-dimensional and realistic impressions of each other's competencies, and give accurate feedback. Such interaction tends to promote a basic self-acceptance of oneself as a competent person.

Understanding Interdependence

Cooperative learning simultaneously models interdependence and provides students with the experiences they need to understand the nature of cooperation (Johnson & Johnson, 1989a). The future of the world depends on the constructive and competent management of world interdependence as well as interdependence in family, work, community, and societal settings. Students who have had 12 to 20 years of cooperative learning will be better able to do so than will students who have had 12 to 20 years of competitive and individualistic learning.

Relationships Among Outcomes

There are bidirectional relationships among achievement, quality of interpersonal relationships, and psychological health (Johnson & Johnson, 1989a). Each influences the others. Caring and committed friendships come from a sense of mutual accomplishment, mutual pride in joint work, and the bonding that results from joint efforts. The more students care about each other, on the other hand, the harder they will work to

Figure 3.1

Outcomes
Of Cooperation

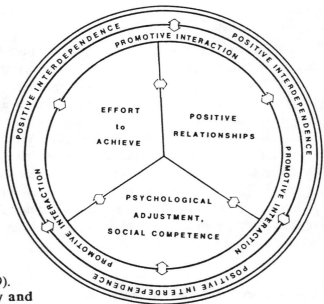

Taken from:

Johnson, D.W. & Johnson, R. T. (1989). **Cooperation and competition: Theory and research.** Edina, MN: Interaction Book Company.

achieve mutual learning goals. Long-term and persistent efforts to achieve do not come from the head, they come from the heart (Johnson & Johnson, 1989b). Individuals seek out opportunities to work with those they care about. As caring increases, so do feelings of personal responsibility to do one's share of the work, willingness to take on difficult tasks, motivation and persistence in working toward goal achievement, and willingness to endure pain and frustration on behalf of the group. All these contribute to group productivity.

In addition, the joint success experienced in working together to get the job done enhances social competencies, self-esteem, and general psychological health. The healthier psychologically individuals are, on the other hand, the better able they are to work with others to achieve mutual goals. Joint efforts require coordination, effective communication, leadership, and conflict management. States of depression, anxiety, guilt, shame, and anger decrease the energy available to contribute to a cooperative effort.

Finally, the more positive interpersonal relationships are, the greater the psychological health of the individuals involved. Through the internalization of positive relationships, direct social support, shared intimacy, and expressions of caring, psychological health and the ability to cope with stress are built. The absence of caring and committed relationships and destructive relationships tend to increase psychological pathology. On the other hand, states of depression, anxiety, guilt, shame, and anger decrease individuals' ability to build and maintain caring and committed relationships. The healthier psychologically individuals are, the more meaningful and caring the relationships they can build and maintain.

Reducing The Discrepancy

With the amount of research evidence available, it is surprising that classroom practice is so oriented toward individualistic and competitive learning and schools are so dominated by a competitive / individualistic structure. **It is time for the discrepancy to be reduced between what research indicates is effective in teaching and what teachers actually do.** In order to do so, educators must understand the role of the teacher in implementing cooperative learning experiences. That is the focus of the next chapter.

Summary

Achievement will be higher when learning situations are structured cooperatively rather than competitively or individualistically. Cooperative learning experiences, furthermore, promote greater competencies in critical thinking, more positive attitudes toward the subject areas studied, greater competencies in working collaboratively with others, and greater psychological health. The implications of these results for teachers are:

1. Cooperative learning procedures may be used successfully with any type of academic task, although the greater the conceptual learning required the greater will tend to be the efficacy of cooperation.

2. Whenever possible, cooperative groups should be structured so that controversy and academic disagreements among group members is possible and managed constructively.

3. Students should be encouraged to keep each other on task and discuss the assigned material in ways that ensure oral explanation and elaboration and the use of higher-level learning strategies.

4. Students should be encouraged to support each other's efforts to achieve, regulate each other's task-related efforts, provide each other with feedback, and ensure that all group members are verbally involved in the learning process.

5. As a rule, cooperative groups should contain low-, medium-, and high-ability students to help promote discussion, peer teaching, and justification of answers.

6. Positive relationships among group members should be encouraged.

Cooperative learning experiences, where students work together to maximize each other's achievement, tend also to promote positive relationships and a process of acceptance among students, thereby making an important contribution to the solution of the socialization crisis. More specifically, educators who wish to promote constructive relationships among students will wish to (Johnson & Johnson, 1982):

1. Structure cooperative situations in which children and adolescents work with peers to achieve a common goal.

2. Emphasize joint rather than individual products whenever possible.

3. Directly teach the interpersonal skills needed to build and maintain collaborative relationships with peers.

4. Give children and adolescents meaningful responsibility for the well-being and success of their peers.

5. Encourage the feelings of support, acceptance, concern, and commitment that are part of collaborative situations.

6. Hold children and adolescents accountable for fulfilling their obligations and responsibilities to their collaborators and give them mutual authority over each other.

7. Ensure that children and adolescents experience success in cooperative groups.

A Final Note

With the amount of research evidence available, it is surprising that classroom practice is so oriented toward individualistic and competitive learning and schools are so dominated by a competitive / individualistic structure. **It is time for the discrepancy to be reduced between what research indicates is effective in teaching and what teachers actually do.** In order to do so, educations must understand and be able to use the five essential components of cooperative learning. The most important of those components is positive interdependence. That is the focus of the next chapter.

Implementation Assignment 3

1. Read Chapter 3.

2. Fill out Lesson Plan Log on lessons taught.

3. Share informally with colleagues what you are doing with cooperative learning groups. Use these conversations as practice for the upcoming session with your principal. To promote interest in what you are doing, we suggest you leave your door open. Invite others in to see cooperative learning.

4. Conduct a formal conversation with your principal explaining why you are using cooperative learning groups and asking for his/her assistance. Prepare an outline and decide what written information you should copy from your book for your principal. Encourage questions and specify the kind of support you need.

5. Write down the highlights of your conversation to bring back and share with your base group.

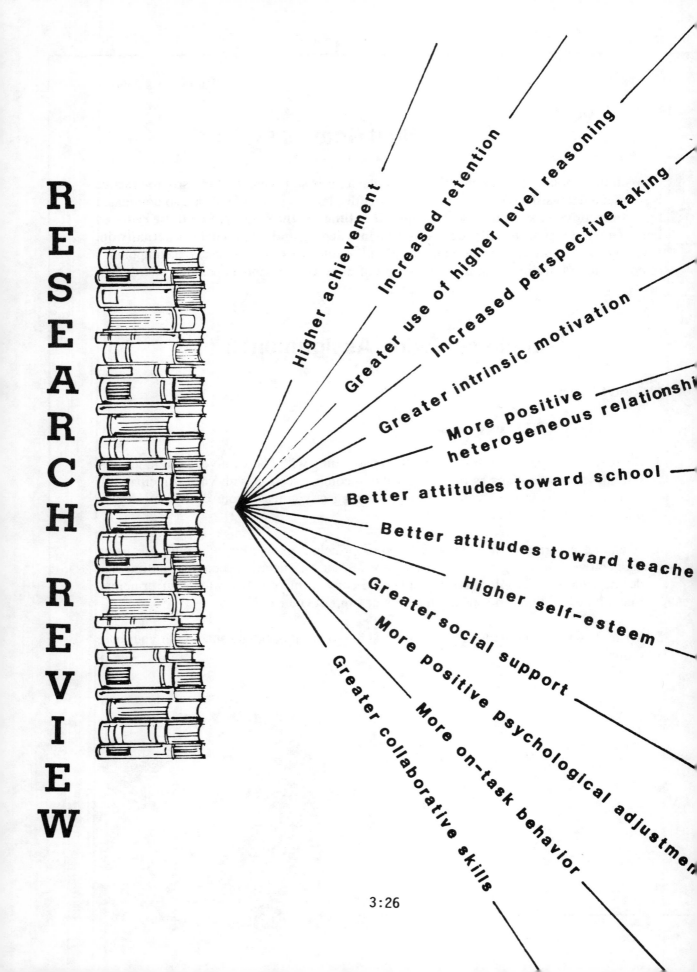

RESEARCH REVIEW

Higher achievement

Increased retention

Greater use of higher level reasoning

Increased perspective taking

Greater intrinsic motivation

More positive heterogeneous relationshi

Better attitudes toward school

Better attitudes toward teache

Higher self-esteem

Greater social support

More positive psychological adjustmen

More on-task behavior

Greater collaborative skills

3:26

⸙⸙⟦ Cooperative Learning Contract ⟧⸙⸙

Major Learnings	Implementation Plans

Date _____ Date of Progress Report Meeting _____

Participant's Signature _____

Signatures of Other Group Members· _____ _____

_____   _____   _____

⊰ Cooperative Learning Progress Report ⊱

NAME _____ SCHOOL _____

AGE LEVEL _____ SUBJECT _____

DAY AND DATE	DESCRIPTION OF TASKS and ACTIVITIES PERFORMED	SUCCESSES EXPERIENCED	PROBLEMS ENCOUNTERED

Description of critical or interesting incidents:

EXERCISE

MATERIALS

INK

Learning Outcomes Promoted By Cooperative Learning

1. Higher achievement and increased retention.

2. More frequent higher-level reasoning, deeper-level understanding, and critical thinking.

3. More ontask and less disruptive behavior.

4. Greater achievement motivation and intrinsic motivation to learn.

5. Greater ability to view situations from others' perspectives.

6. More positive, accepting, and supportive relationships with peers regardless of ethnic, sex, ability, social class, or handicapped differences.

7. Greater social support.

8. Greater psychological health, adjustment, and well-being.

9. More positive self-esteem based on basic self-acceptance.

10. Greater social competencies.

11. More positive attitudes toward subject areas, learning, and school.

12. More positive attitudes toward teachers, principals, and other school personnel.

Johnson, D. W., & Johnson, R. (1989). Cooperation and competition. Edina, MN: Interaction Book Company.

Research Rationale Statement

Task: Write an explanation why you are using cooperative learning. The written rationale statement should include:

1. An introduction that includes these two statements:
   a. *"Cooperative learning is not new, it is an American tradition."*
   b. *"In my classroom students learn in three ways: cooperatively, competitively, and individualistically."*
2. A definition of cooperative learning that includes an example.
3. A summary of the more important consequences of cooperative learning. State that, *"There is a great deal of research validating the use of cooperative learning."* Then include information about:
   a. The importance of peer relationships.
   b. The interaction process promoted by cooperation.
   c. The outcomes resulting from cooperative efforts.
   Also include the research outcomes most important to you and to the person asking, *"Why."*
4. At least one classroom incident that illustrates the power of cooperative learning.
5. A summary or conclusion.

Cooperative: All members must sign each other's rationale statements indicating that they agree with the statement and verify its quality. The signature also means that they have followed the peer editing procedure.

Criteria For Success: A well-written research rationale statement by each participant that they can deliver orally.

Individual Accountability:

1. Each participant understands the breadth and depth of the research on cooperative learning. This knowledge is reflected in his or her composition.
2. Each participant is able to explain why he or she is using cooperative learning to a member of another group.

Expected Behaviors: Explaining and listening.

Intergroup Cooperation: Whenever it is helpful to do so, check procedures and information with another group.

Peer Editing: Cooperative Learning In Composition

Task: Write a composition.

Cooperative: All group members must verify that each member's composition is perfect according to the criteria set by the teacher. One of their scores for the composition will be the total number of errors made by the pair (the number of errors in their composition plus the number of errors in their partner's composition). An individual score on the quality of the composition may also be given.

Procedure:

1. The teacher assigns students to pairs with at least one good reader in each pair. The task of writing individual compositions is given.

2. Student A describes to Student B what he or she is planning to write. Student B listens carefully, probes with a set of questions, and outlines Student A's composition. The written outline is given to Student A.

3. This procedure is reversed with Student B describing what he or she is going to write and Student A listening and completing an outline of Student B's composition, which is then given to Student B.

4. The students research individualistically the material they need to write their compositions, keeping an eye out for material useful to their partner.

5. The two students work together to write the first paragraph of each composition to ensure that they both have a clear start on their compositions.

6. The students write their compositions individualistically.

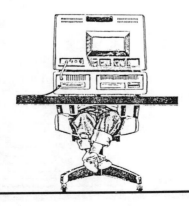

7. When completed, the students proofread each other's compositions, making corrections in capitalization, punctuation, spelling, language usage, topic sentence usage, and other aspects of writing specified by the teacher. Suggestions for revision are also encouraged.

8. The students revise their compositions, making all of the suggested revisions.

9. The two students then reread each other's compositions and sign their names (indicating that they guarantee that no errors exist in the composition).

While the students work, the teacher monitors the pairs, intervening where appropriate to help students master the needed writing and cooperative skills. When the composition is completed, the students discuss how effectively they worked together (listing the specific actions they engaged in to help each other), plan what behaviors they are goint to emphasize the next writing pair, and thank each other for the help and assistance received.

Criteria For Success: A well-written composition by each student. Depending on the instructional objectives, the compositions may be evaluated for grammar, punctuation, organization, content, or other criteria set by the teacher.

Individual Accountability: Each student writes his or her own composition.

Expected Behaviors: Explaining and listening.

Intergroup Cooperation: Whenever it is helpful to do so, check procedures with another group.

Chapter 4

Creating Positive Interdependence

Table Of Contents

o Johnson & Johnson

__Pretest__

After taking this pretest you should be able to define and give examples of positive interdependence and individual accountability. Find a partner. Take the following pretest while discussing each question arriving at one answer that both agree on. Fold a sheet of paper to cover the answers. With answers covered, read the first question. Move the folded paper down until the answer to Question 1 is uncovered. Check your answer to Question 1 before moving on to Question 2.

1. Not all groups are Cooperative Learning Groups.
   In order for a group to be a Cooperative Learning
   Group, there myst be, among other ingredients,
   both of the following essentials. One essential
   ingredient is positive interdependence. Thus,
   a Cooperative Learning Group must have _____   **POSITIVE**
   interdependence.

2. Positive interdependence ties the group members together
   in some way. A group in which the members are linked
   together has positive _____.   **INTERDEPENDENCE**

3. Dick and Jane have an assignment which they are
   to complete together. Having to work together
   is an example of positive
   i_____.   **INTERDEPENDENCE**

4. Jack and Jill will be graded on the total number of
   words they spell correctly. This is
   also an example of _____   **POSITIVE**
   i_____.   **INTERDEPENDENC**

5. For positive interdependence to be present,
   group members must be linked together in some
   way. Toad and mole are working at the same
   table on separate assignments. Is this positive
   interdependence?   _____

   NO

Written by Edythe Johnson Holubec, College of Education, University of Texas, Austin, Texas.

6. Tweedledum and Tweedledee are discussing their homework assignment. Is this positive interdependence? _____

    NO

7. Tolly and Toby are writing a paper together for their English assignment. Is this positive interdependence? _____

    YES

8. Lucy and Edmund are studying for a vocabulary test where their score will be the number they both get correct. Is this positive interdependence? _____

    YES

9. Tom and Huck will get bonus points only if they both turn in their homework on time. Is this an example of positive interdependence?

    _____

    YES

10. Thus, for positive interdependence to be present, group members must be _____ together in some way.

    LINKED

11. In addition to positive interdependence, a cooperative group must have individual account-ability. Making sure that each individual is accountable for the work of the group is individual _____.

    ACCOUNTABILITY

12. Even though students may have a group assignment, there is no guarantee that they will all help with it. Therefore, for Cooperative Learning Groups to work, there must be i_____ accountability.

    INDIVIDUAL

13. Individual accountability is making sure that each member of the group learns the material. Thus, testing all the group members over material learned in the group is an example of i_____ a_____.

    INDIVIDUAL ACCOUNTABILITY

14. Giving each group member a grade reflecting how well they contributed to the group is also an example of _____ _____.

    INDIVIDUAL ACCOUNTABILITY

15. After the group finishes writing its report, the teacher will pick one student at random to ex-plain the material. Is this an example of individual accountability? _____

    YES

16. Sherlock and Watson must give a report to the class on the material they researched. Both of them must participate in the report. Is this an example of individual accountability? _____

YES

17. A Cooperative Learning Group must include positive interdependence and individual accountability in order to be a Cooperative Learning Group. If both positive interdependence and individual accountability are present, then the group is a _____

_____ _____ .

COOPERATIVE LEARNING GROUP

18. Groucho, Harpo, and Zeppo are writing a movie script together. They will ggt a grade on the script and another grade reflecting how well they worked together in their group. Is this a Cooperative Learning Group?

_____

YES

19. Peter, Wendy, and Michael are to teach each other their vocabulary words. They will be tested individually and their grade will be their individual score plus a bonus based on how well the others do. Is this a Cooperative Learning Group? _____

YES

20. Bilbo, Frodo, and Sam are working on their geography maps at the same table. They will turn in their finished products. Is this a Cooperative Group? _____

NO

21. What essential ingredient is missing from the group above? _____ _____

POSITIVE INTERDEPENDENCE

22. Fern, Wilbur, and Charlotte have been told to read the chapter and answer the questions together. Is this a Cooperative Learning Group? _____

NO

23. What essential ingredient is missing from the group on the preceding question? _____

_____

INDIVIDUAL ACCOUNTABILITY

24. Flopsy, Mopsy, and Cottontail are each to investigate a different section of their report which they will then write together. Is this a Cooperative Learning Group? _____

YES

25. Thus, two elements essential to a Cooperative Learning Group are _____ _____ and _____ _____ .

POSITIVE
INTERDEPENDENCE
INDIVIDUAL
ACCOUNTABILITY

26. Which one of the following situations correctly describes a Cooperative Learning Group?

a. Athos, Porthos, and Aramis are sitting together while they write stories for a class assignment. Occasionally they ask each other how to spell certain words. Before turning in their writing, they read their stories to each other to get reactions and advice.

b. Mary, Jane, and Michael are working on a group report in their history class. Since Mary is the most motivated, she takes over and does most of the work while Jane and Michael chat. When it is finished, they all sign their names to the report and hand it in.

c. Christopher, Pooh, and Eeyore are working on a science lab experiment together. They argue over the procedure but finally get the experiment written up. The teacher picks one of them at random to explain how the experiment is done before their paper can be turned in.

ANSWER: _____

c

Key To Cooperation: We Instead Of Me

"United we stand, divided we fall."

Watchword of the American Revolution

Author William Manchester wrote several years ago in Life Magazine about revisiting Sugar Loaf Hill in Okinawa, where 34 years before he had fought as a Marine. He describes how he had been wounded, sent to a hospital and, in violation of orders, escaped from the hospital to rejoin his Army unit at the front. Doing so meant almost certain death. "Why did I do it?" he wondered. The answer lies in the power of positive interdependence.

Positive interdependence is the perception that (a) you are linked with others in a way so that you cannot succeed unless they do (and vice versa), and/or (b) their work benefits you and your work benefits them. It promotes a situation in which individuals work together in small groups to maximize the learning of all members. In such a situation individuals perceive:

1. Group members are striving for **mutual benefit** so that all members of the group will gain. There is recognition that what helps other group members benefits you and what promotes your productivity benefits the other group members. Each member invests time and energy into helping groupmates, which then pays dividends and capital gains when groupmates score high on tests and reciprocate the helping.

2. Group members share a **common fate** where they all gain or lose on the basis of their overall performance.

3. The performance of group members is **mutually caused**. Within a cooperative learning group, you are **responsible** for giving the help and assistance other members need to be productive and **obligated** to the other members for the support and assistance they gave to you. Each member is instrumental in the productivity of each other member. Your productivity, therefore, is perceived to be caused by (a) your own efforts and abilities and (b) the efforts and abilities of the other group members, and the performance of the other group members is perceived to be due partially to your encouragement and facilitation. The mutual responsibility and mutual obligation inherent in the mutual causation within cooperative learning groups results in a **mutual investment** by members in each other.

4. There is a **shared identity** based on group membership. Besides being a separate individual, you are a member of a team. The shared identity binds members together emotionally.

5. The **self-efficacy** of members is increased through the empowerment inherent in the joint efforts. Being part of a cooperative learning group increases students' confidence that if they exert effort, they will be successful. Cooperative groups empower their members to act by making them feel strong, capable, and committed. **Being part of a team effort changes feelings of "I can't do it" to "We can do it."** Success that is impossible for one person to achieve is attainable within a cooperative group. A student may believe, "I can't do algebra, it's too hard," until two other students say, "Stick with us; we'll get you through algebra with at least a 'B.'" The student then tends to believe, "We can do algebra."

6. There are **joint celebrations** based on (a) mutual respect and appreciation for the efforts of group members and (b) the group's success. Being part of a team effort results in feelings of (a) camaraderie, belonging, and pride and (b) success. Feelings of success are shared and pride is taken in others' accomplishments as well as one's own.

Barriers To Positive Interdependence: The Delusion Of Individualism

The feelings and commitment that drove William Manchester to risk his life to help protect his comrads do not automatically appear when students are placed in learning groups. There are barriers to positive interdependence. Among many current high school and college students, their own pleasures and pains, successes and failures, occupy center stage in their lives (Conger, 1988; Seligman, 1988). Each person tends to focus on gratifying his or her own ends without concern for others. Over the past 20 years, self-interest has become more important than commitment to community or country. Young adults have turned away from careers of public service to careers of self-service. Many young adults have a **delusion of individualism,**

believing that (a) they are separate and apart from all other individuals and, therefore, (b) others' frustration, unhappiness, hunger, despair, and misery have no significant bearing on their own well-being. With the increase in the past two decades in adolescents' and youth's concern for personal well-being, there has been a corresponding diminished concern for the welfare of others (particularly the less advantaged) and of society itself (Astin, Green, & Korn, 1987; Astin, Green, Korn, & Schalit, 1986).

The self is a very poor site for finding meaning. Hope does not spring from competition. Meaning does not surface in individualistic efforts aimed at benefiting no one but yourself. Empowerment does not come from isolation. Purpose does not grow from egocentric focus on own material gain. Without involvement in interdependent efforts and the resulting concern for others, it is not possible to realize oneself except in the most superficial sense. Contributing to the well-being of others within an interdependent effort provides meaning and purpose to life.

Power Of Positive Interdependence

For an individual, piloting a Boeing 747 is impossible. For the three-person crew, it is straightforward. The crew, furthermore, does not work in isolation. Large numbers of mechanics, service personnel, cabin attendants, air traffic controllers, pilot educators (who keep crew members abreast of the latest developments and sharp in their responses to problem situations), and many others are necessary to the flying of the plane. From the demands of repairing a flat tire on a dark highway ("You hold the light while I...") to the complex requirements of flying a modern passenger jet, teamwork is the most frequent human response to the challenges of coping with otherwise impossible tasks.

Within the real world, positive interdependence is pervasive on many levels. Individuals join together into a group that is structured around a mutual goal. The group fits into the larger mosaic of groups working toward a larger goal. Those groups also form a mosaic working toward even a larger superordinate goal. Thus, there are individuals who work within teams that work within departments that work within divisions that work within organizations that work within a societal economic system that works within the global economic system.

Life in the real world is characterized by layers of positive interdependence that stretch from the interpersonal to the international. Life in schools is dominated by competitive and individualistic activities that ignore the importance of positive interdependence. It is time for classrooms to become more realistic.

Positive Interdependence In The Classroom

The power of positive interdependence must be experienced to be believed. Teachers, when first discovering cooperative learning, often expect all their students to leap at the chance to work with classmates. Some students, however, may not want to work in learning groups and other students may refuse to work with anyone but their friends. Occasionally, a student may make statements such as: "Why should I help these dummies? What is in it for me?"

The primary reason why some students may **not** wish to participate in cooperative learning groups is that previous teachers (as well as society and parents) have taught them to work by themselves, hide their knowledge from others, hope that other students fail, and care only about themselves. The **bad news** is that students have successfully learned the "I, me, my" perspective. The **good news** is that they can be taught the "we, us, our" perspective. This reteaching involves more than wishing students would work together or crossing your fingers for cooperatively oriented students. Developing students' sense of mutuality and responsibility for others takes a careful and conscious effort to structure positive interdependence.

When positive interdependence is carefully structured, you tend to see students:

1. Putting their heads close together over their work.

2. Talking about the work.

3. Drilling each other on the material being learned.

4. Sharing answers and materials.

5. Encouraging each other to learn.

When positive interdependence has not been structured, teachers may see students:

1. Leaving their group impulsively.

2. Talking about topics other than the work.

3. Doing their own work while ignoring other students.

4. Not sharing answers or materials.

5. Not checking to see if others have learned the material.

To implement cooperative learning, you need to understand the types of positive interdependence and have specific strategies for implementing each one. In doing so you should follow the general procedure of:

1. **Structuring** positive goal interdependence within a lesson and supplementing it with a number of other types of positive interdependence.

2. **Informing** students of the types of positive interdependence present in the lesson and emphasize that they "sink or swim together."

3. **Monitoring** students' actions to ensure that they truly believe that they are responsible for each other's learning as well as their own.

4. Have groups **process** the extent to which they really believed that they were responsible for each other's learning and success.

With modifying a few words, this sequence may be called **STOP** (**S**tructure, **T**ell, **O**bserve, **P**rocess).

Types Of Positive Interdependence

Since at first most students (especially older ones) do not automatically care about their groupmates, positive interdependence must be consciously and clearly structured by the teacher. **Cooperative efforts begin with the establishment of mutual goals, around which the actions of each group member are organized.** To ensure that the group works productively and exerts considerable effort toward accomplishing the mutual goal, members with different resources are assigned roles and given a task that requires coordination of efforts. They are also given a team identity and a setting in which to work. To highlight the importance of the goal, the long-term implications of success are spelled out. Threats to team success are identified. Finally, the rewards of success are made salient to induce members to join in the joint effort.

The various ways of communicating to students that the learning situation is "sink or swim together" may be divided into outcome interdependence and means interdependence. **Outcome interdependence** exists when the goals and rewards directing individuals' actions are positively correlated, that is, if one person accomplishes his or her goal or receives a reward, all others with whom the person is cooperatively linked also achieve their goals or receive a reward. Outcome interdependence may be structured through assigning mutual goals and giving joint rewards. Learning goals may be actual, based on involvement in a fantasy situation, or based on overcoming an outside threat. **Means interdependence** specifies the actions required on the part of group members to achieve their mutual goals and rewards. There are three types of means interdependence: resource, task, and role. Finally, positive interdependence may be structured into a learning situation by requiring students to develop a shared identity or work within environmental boundaries. The types of positive interdependence are defined below and ways teachers may structure them are presented.

Positive Goal Interdependence 1: Learning Goals

The first step in structuring positive interdependence within a cooperative learning group is to set a mutual goal that establishes that members are responsible for each other's learning and success as well as their own. **Positive goal interdependence** exists when students perceive that they can achieve their learning goals if, and only if, all other members of their group also attain their goals. Members of a learning group have a mutual set of goals that they all are striving to accomplish. Success depends on all members reaching the goal. The goal might be that all group members understand how to do long division with remainders or that all group members be able to analyze the plot of **Hamlet.** All cooperative lessons need to include positive goal interdependence. Other types of positive interdependence support and supplement the effects of positive goal interdependence. Ways of structuring positive goal interdependence include the following:

1. **Teachers explain that the group goal is to ensure that all members achieve a prescribed mastery level on the assigned material.** This means each group member has

two responsibilities: (a) learn and (b) ensure that all other group members learn. Teachers may wish to say, "One answer from the three of you, everyone has to agree, and everyone has to be able to explain how to solve the problem or complete the assignment." Teachers may establish the prescribed mastery level as (a) individual levels of performance that each group member must achieve in order for the group as a whole to be successful (the group goal is for each member to demonstrate 90 percent mastery on a curriculum unit) or (b) improvement scores (the group goal is to ensure that all members do better this week than they did last week).

2. **Teachers "enlarge the shadow of the future" by:**

   a. Showing that the long-term benefits of cooperation outweigh the short-term benefits of taking advantage of the other group members or of not cooperating. Teachers may wish to demonstrate that sharing the work and helping each other learn is more productive and fun than competing or working alone. The long-term vision must be more compelling than the temptation of short-term personal advantage.

   b. Highlighting the facts that interactions among group members will be frequent and the relationships among team members will be durable. The shadow of the future looms largest when interactions among students are frequent and durable. **Durability** promotes cooperative efforts because it makes interpersonal relationships long lasting. It ensures that students will not easily forget how they have treated, and been treated by, each other. **Frequency** promotes stability by making the consequences of today's actions more salient for tomorrow's work. When students realize they will work with each other frequently and for a long period of time, they see the need to be cooperative and supportive in current dealings with each other.

3. **Teachers add the scores of all group members to determine an overall group score.** This score is compared with the preset criterion of excellence. Teachers may wish to say, "The goal of each triad is to reach a total group score of 135 out of 150 potential correct answers." Since there are 50 questions on the test, each member needs to get at least 45 correct on the test. To highlight the goal of maximizing the total group score teachers may wish to keep a group progress chart. Total group scores may be plotted each day or each week. Students are then responsible for raising their own and their groupmates' performances in order to show progress on the group chart.

4. **Teachers choose randomly the worksheet, report, or theme of one group member to be evaluated.** This means that members are responsible for reading and correcting each other's work to ensure that it is 100 percent correct before the teacher selects one representative paper on which to evaluate the group. Variations include randomly selecting one member to demonstrate mastery of a concept, translate a sentence in a foreign language class, or take the test for the group. Since this is a procedure to ensure each individual group member is accountable for learning the assigned material, it demonstrates that there is an intimate relationship between goal interdependence and individual accountability. **Individual accountability** is the measurement of whether or not each group member has achieved the group's goal. Individual accountability cannot exist unless goal interdependence has been previously established.

5. **Teachers request one product** (such as a report, theme, presentation, or answer sheet) from the group that is signed by all members. Signatures indicate that each member was active in creating the product, agrees with it, and can rationally defend its content. A variation on this procedure is to implement a rule that no group member receives credit for doing homework until all group members have handed in the homework assignment. Groups may be responsible for writing a newsletter or making a presentation, and each member does not receive credit unless all group members contribute an article to the newsletter or make part of the presentation. This may be extended into intergroup cooperation by having the class produce a newspaper in which each group has contributed a part (which in turn must contain work by each individual member), or by having the class give a Renaissance Day in which each group must make a presentation (which in turn must include all members).

Students will contribute more energy and effort to meaningful goals than to trivial ones. Being responsible for others' learning as well as for one's own gives cooperative efforts a meaning that is not found in competitive and individualistic learning situations. In cooperative learning situations, the efforts of each group member contribute not only to their own success, but also to the success of groupmates. When there is meaning to what they do, ordinary people exert extraordinary effort. It is positive goal interdependence that gives meaning to the efforts of group members.

Positive Goal Interdependence 2: Outside Enemy Interdependence

The goal of a learning group may be to learn more than other groups in order to win a competition. **Positive outside enemy interdependence** exists when groups are placed in competition with each other. Group members then feel interdependent as they strive to beat the other groups. A procedure we like is having students compete with the score made by last years' class or the total class score made last week. A teacher might say, "Last year's class made a total score of 647 on this test. Can you do better? Sure you can." Such competition reduces the negative behavior that often accompanies competing against other groups in the same class.

Positive Goal Interdependence 3: Fantasy Interdependence

The goals that learning groups strive to achieve do not have to be real. **Positive fantasy interdependence** exists when students imagine that they are in an emergency situation (such as surviving a ship wreak) or must deal with problems (such as ending air pollution in the world) that are compelling but unreal. A teacher may say, "You are the **world's leading scientists.** Your challenge is to save the world by finding the answers to these difficult and mystifying equations!" We like to tell students that they are **word detectives** who must look for a certain word in a reading assignment and describe how it is used by the author. Students may also be **character detectives** who analyze a character in a story or play.

Positive Reward / Celebration Interdependence

In order for students to look forward to working in cooperative groups, and enjoy doing so, they must feel that (a) their efforts are appreciated and (b) they are respected as an individual. Long-term commitment to achieve is largely based on feeling recognized and respected for what one is doing. Thus, students' efforts to learn and promote each other's learning need to be (a) observed, (b) recognized, and (c) celebrated. The celebration of individual efforts and group success involves structuring reward interdependence.

Positive reward interdependence exists when each group member receives the same reward for completing the assignment. A joint reward is given for successful group work. Everyone is rewarded or no one is rewarded. An example of reward interdependence is when every group member receives 5 bonus points (or 15 extra recess minutes) when all group members get 90 percent correct on a test. The rewards should be attractive to students, inexpensive, and consistent with your philosophy of teaching. It is important that groups that do not reach the criteria do not receive the reward. The rewards, furthermore, should probably be removed as soon as the intrinsic motivation inherent in cooperative learning groups becomes apparent. You will know when this happens when students pressure you to let them work in groups. Ways of structuring positive reward interdependence include the following:

1. Teachers give bonus points that are added to all members' academic scores when everyone in the group achieves up to criterion.

2. Teachers give nonacademic rewards (such as extra free time, extra recess time, stickers, stars, or food) when all group members reach criteria on an academic task.

3. Teachers give teacher praise (i.e., social rewards) for the group as a whole when all group members reach criteria.

4. Teachers give a single group grade for the combined efforts of group members. This should be cautiously done until all students (and parents) are very familiar with cooperative learning.

5. Group members swapping "good news" about each other's efforts to promote each other's learning and celebrating their joint success. Group members and teachers should:

   a. Seek out valuable, completed actions by group members in completing assignments and helping groupmates complete assignments.

   b. Honor the actions with all sorts of positive recognition. In doing so, interpersonal recognition rather than formal evaluation should be emphasized. Supportive, encouraging, and caring interaction among team members is the key. **There is nothing more motivating to students than having groupmates cheering them on and jointly celebrating their successes.**

Positive Resource Interdependence

Positive resource interdependence exists when each member has only a portion of the information, resources, or materials necessary for the task to be completed and members' resources have to be combined in order for the group to achieve its goal. Thus, the resources of each group member are needed if the task is to be completed. Ways of structuring positive resource interdependence include the following:

1. The teacher limiting the resources given to the group. Only one pencil, for example, may be given to a group of three students. Other resources that can be limited include textbooks, answer sheets, scissors, dictionaries, maps, typewriters, computers, and periodic charts of elements.

2. The teacher jigsawing materials so that each member has part of a set of materials. Materials that can be jigsawed include vocabulary words, lines of a poem, letters of a word, sentences of a paragraph to be sequenced, words for a sentence, pictures, definitions, puzzle pieces, problems, parts of directions, resource materials, lab equipment, parts of a map, art supplies, ingredients for cooking, and sections of a report. One social studies teacher gave each member of his cooperative learning groups a different social studies text and then gave assignments requiring students to share what each text had to say about the issue. Each member of a group may be given one sentence of a paragraph and the group is given the task of sequencing the sentences. A group could be given the assignment of writing a biography of Abe Lincoln and information on Lincoln's childhood given to one member, information on Lincoln's early political career given to another, information on Lincoln as president given to a third, and information on Lincoln's assassination given to the fourth member. A different type of jigsaw is created when the assignment is to make a collage and one member has the paste, another has the scissors, and a third has the magazines.

3. The teacher giving students a writing assignment with the stipulation that each member must offer a sentence in each paragraph, contribute an article to a newsletter, write a paragraph or an essay, or do a chapter in a "book."

Positive Task Interdependence

Positive task interdependence exists when a division of labor is created so that the actions of one group member have to be completed if the next team member is to complete his or her responsibilities. Dividing an overall task into subunits that must be performed **in a set order** is an example of task interdependence. This "factory-line" model exists when one student is responsible for obtaining swamp-water, another is responsible for making slides, another is responsible for viewing the slides through a microscope, and the fourth member is responsible for writing down the organisms found in the swamp- water. Another example is a "chain reaction" where a student named Bill learns a concept and then is responsible for teaching it to another student named Jane, and the test score received by Jane is given to

Bill. While task interdependence is closely related to resource interdependence, it is used much less frequently as not very many academic tasks lend themselves to such a "lock-step" division-of-labor.

Positive Role Interdependence

Positive role interdependence exists when each member is assigned complementary and interconnected roles that specify responsibilities that the group needs in order to complete a joint task. Any of the skills discussed in Chapter 5 may be used. Usually the roles are rotated daily so that each student obtains considerable experience in each role. Some roles to get you started are:

Reader: Reads the group's material out loud to the group, carefully and with expression, so that group members can understand and remember it.

Writer/Recorder: Carefully records the best answers of the group on the worksheet or paper, edits what the group has written, gets the group members to check and sign the paper, then turns it in to the teacher.

Materials Handler: Gets any materials or equipment needed by the group, keeps track of them, and puts them carefully away.

Encourager: Watches to make certain that everyone is participating, and invites reluctant or silent members to contribute. Sample statements: "Jane, what do you think?" "Robert, do you have anything to add?" "Nancy, help us out." "Juanita, what are your ideas on this?"

Checker: Checks on the comprehension or learning of group members by asking them to explain or summarize material learned or discussed. Sample statements: "Terry, why did we decide on this answer for number two?" "James, explain how we got this answer." "Anne, summarize for us what we've decided here."

Praiser: Helps members feel good about their contributions to the group by telling them how helpful they are. This is a good role to assign to help combat "put-downs." Sample statements: "That's a good idea, Al." "Sharon, you're very helpful." "Karen, I like the way you've helped us." "Good job, John."

Prober: In a pleasant way, keeps the group from superficial answering by not allowing the members to agree too quickly. Agrees when satisfied that the group has explored all the possibilities. Sample statements: "What other possibilities are there for this problem or question?" "What else could we put here?" "Let's double-check this answer."

Some other role possibilities include: **Noise Monitor** (uses a non-verbal signal to remind group members to quiet down), **Energizer** (energizes the group when it starts lagging), **Summarizer** (summarizes the material so that group members can check it again), **Observer** (keeps track of how well the team members are collaborating), **Time Keeper**, and **Paraphraser**. Come up with roles that fit the task and your students.

Identity Interdependence

Positive identity interdependence exists when the group establishes a mutual identity through a name, flag, motto, or song. English teachers may wish to give poet's names to groups (The Whitman's, Frost's, Cummings', and Hughes'). Science teachers can give famous scientists' names to groups. Teachers may let students think of their own group names, make a flag for their group, establish a group motto, or create some other symbol of their joint identity.

Environmental Interdependence

Environmental interdependence exists when group members are bound together by the physical environment in some way. Examples include giving each group a specific area to meet in, putting chairs or desks together, having group members hold hands or put their arms around each other, requiring group members to have their feet touching in a circle as they work, or placing a rope fence around the group. A first grade teacher we once worked with made circles on the floor with masking tape and required all group members to be within the circle while they worked together. Being stranded in the barn's haymow with your older brother because he carelessly knocked over the ladder is another example of environmental interdependence.

Conclusion

"Pull together. In the mountains you must depend on each other for survival."

Willi Unsoeld

Within Yosemite National Park lies the famous Half Dome Mountain. The Half Dome is famous for its 2000 feet of soaring, sheer cliff wall. Unusually beautiful to the observer, and considered unclimbable for years, the Half Dome's northwest face was first scaled in 1957 by Royal Robbins and two companions. This incredibly dangerous climb took five days, with Robbins and his companions spending four nights on the cliff, sleeping in ropes with nothing below their bodies but air. Even today, the northwest face is a death trap to all but the finest and most skilled rock climbers. And far above the ground, moving slowly up the rock face, are two climbers.

The two climbers are motivated by a shared vision of successfully climbing the northwest face. As they move up the cliff they are attached to each other by a rope (**"the life line"**). As one member climbs (**the lead climber**), the other (**the belayer**) ensures that the two have a safe anchor and that he or she can catch the climber if the climber falls. The lead climber does not begin climbing until the belayer says "go." Then the lead climber advances, puts in a piton, slips in the rope, and continues to advance. The pitons help the belayer catch the climber if the climber falls and they mark the path up the cliff. The life line (i.e., rope) goes from the belayer through the pitons up to the climber. When the lead climber has completed the first leg of the climb, he or she becomes the belayer and the other member of the team begins to climb. The pitons placed by the lead climber serve to guide and support the second member of the team up the rock face. The second member advances up the route marked out by the first member until the first leg is completed, and then leap- frogs and becomes the lead climber for the second leg of the climb. The roles of lead climber and belayer are alternated until the summit is reached.

All human life is like mountain climbing. The human species seems to have a **cooperation imperative**: We desire and seek out opportunities to operate jointly with others to achieve mutual goals. We are attached to others through a variety of "life lines" and we alternate supporting and leading others to ensure a better life for ourselves, our colleagues and neighbors, our children, and all generations to follow. Cooperation is an inescapable fact of life. From cradle to grave we cooperate with others. Each day, from our first waking moment until sleep overtakes us again, we cooperate within family, work, leisure, and community by working jointly to achieve mutual goals. Throughout history, people have come together to (a) accomplish feats that any one of them could not achieve alone and (b) share their joys and sorrows. From conceiving a child to sending a rocket to the moon, our successes require cooperation among individuals. The cooperation may be less clear than it is in climbing up a cliff, but it exists none the less.

Cooperative efforts begin when group members commit themselves to a mutual purpose and coordinate and integrate their efforts to do so. What is true of the real life needs to be true of classroom life. In the classroom, the mutual purpose and coordinated actions spring from the positive interdependence structured by you, the teacher. By structuring positive interdependence you remind your students, **None of us is as smart as all of us!**

The more ways you structure positive interdependence within learning groups, the better. **Never use one when two will do.** Many students are highly competitive and will initially not believe that they really do have to help others learn. Given that every cooperative lesson must include mutual goals, the more ways positive interdependence is structured within a lesson, the clearer the message will be to students that they must be concerned about and take responsibility for both their own and other's learning. The real test of whether or not positive interdependence has been successfully structured is whether group members really care about each other's learning. If they do not care whether or not groupmates learn, then they do not really believe that they sink or swim together.

Reducing Problem Behaviors

When students first start working in cooperative learning groups they sometimes engage in unhelpful behaviors. Whenever inappropriate student behavior occurs, the teacher's first move should be toward strengthening the perceived interdependence within the learning situation. Dishon and O'Leary (1984) state that four of the most common behavioral problems are passive uninvolvement, active uninvolvement, independence, and taking charge. They make the following recommendations.

Passive Uninvolvement

When you see students turning away from the group, not participating, not paying attention to the group's work, saying little or nothing, showing no enthusiasm, or not bringing their work or materials, you may wish to:

1. Jigsaw materials so that each member has information the others need. If the passive uninvolved member does not voluntarily contribute his or her information, the other group members will actively involve the student.

2. Divide up roles and assign the passive uninvolved student one that is essential to the group's success (such as reader).

3. Reward the group on the basis of their average performance. Since group members are penalized for the student's lack of effort, they will derive strategies for increasing his or her involvement.

Active Uninvolvement

When a student is talking about everything **but** the assignment, leaving the group without the group's permission, attempting to sabotage the group's work by giving wrong answers or destroying the group's product, refusing to do work, or refusing to work with another group member, you may wish to give a reward that this student or group finds especially attractive and structure the task so that all members must work steadily and contribute in order for the group to succeed and attain the reward.

Independence

When you see a student working alone and ignoring the group discussion, you can:

1. Limit the resources in the group. If there is only one answer sheet or pencil in the group, the member will be unable to work independently.

2. Jigsaw materials so that the student cannot do the work without the other members' information. To complete the task the independent student must interact and collaborate.

Taking Charge

When you see a student doing all the work, refusing to let other members participate, ordering other members around, bullying other members, or making decisions for the group without checking to see of the other members agree, you may wish to:

1. Jigsaw resources so that the task cannot be completed without the student encouraging others to participate and the student listening carefully to the other members' contributions.

2. Assign roles so that other group members have the most powerful roles such as reader, recorder, summarizer, and elaborator.

3. Reward the group on the basis of the lowest two scores by group members on a unit test. This will place pressure on the student taking charge to encourage and help other members learn the material and complete the task.

Positive Interdependence And Giving Grades

Ideally, each student in your classes will participate in a variety of cooperative, competitive, and individualistic instructional activities over the grading period. When summative grades are to be given, the number of points each student received in all three types of goal structures are added up to summarize achievement. A criterion-referenced evaluation procedure will have to be used if the student is to receive a specific single grade; a norm-referenced evaluation procedure will undermine all cooperative and individualistic learning activities in the future.

Giving Grades Exercise: Ms. Smith's Social Studies Class

In her social studies class over a six-week grading period, Ms. Smith has assigned six cooperative group projects (students worked in three different groups, each group completing two projects), three individualistic assignments, and two competitive drills. For each assignment, students received a grade of A, B, C, D, or F. On half of the cooperative assignments, all students within the same group received the same grade; on the other half students received their own score plus 10 bonus points if all group members reached the preset criterion. On the individualistic and competitive assignments, students received individual grades. At the end of the six-week period, Ms. Smith converted grades to points according to the following system: A = 4 points, B = 3 points, C = 2 points, D = 1 point, F = 0 points. In giving grades for the six-week period, Ms. Smith adopted the following criteria:

85 to 100 percent of the total possible points (37 to 44) = A
60 to 84 percent of the total possible points (31 to 36) = B
55 to 69 percent of the total possible points (24 to 30) = C
40 to 54 percent of the total possible points (18 to 23) = D
 0 to 39 percent of the total possible points (0 to 17) = F

Given below is a summary of the points earned by each student in Ms. Smith's math class. Find a partner. Your task is to give each student a grade using Ms. Smith's criteria. Working **cooperatively**, describe in writing the strengths and weaknesses of each student in performing in cooperative, competitive, and individualistic learning activities. Then give each student an overall grade. Next, give each student a grade using only the competitive and individualistic grades and compare with the overall grade. Join another pair and compare your grades and statements. Be prepared to share your evaluations with the entire class. One of you will be randomly selected by the instructor to do so.

| NAME | COOPERATIVE | | | | | | INDIVIDUALISTIC | | | COMPETITIVE | | TOTAL |
	1	2	3	4	5	6	1	2	3	1	2	
John A	4	3	3	4	4	3	4	4	4	4	3	40
Jean B	4	3	4	3	4	3	4	3	3	2	3	36
Jane C	4	3	2	2	4	3	3	2	3	2	2	30
Jack D	4	3	3	4	4	3	0	0	0	0	4	28
Julie F	2	2	4	3	4	4	2	2	3	3	1	30
Jon F	2	2	2	2	4	4	2	2	2	2	2	26
Judy G	2	2	3	4	4	3	2	3	3	2	2	30
Chris H	2	2	4	3	4	3	3	2	2	1	2	28
Char I	3	3	2	2	4	3	3	3	2	1	0	26
Cathy J	3	3	3	4	4	4	4	4	4	4	4	41
Ralph K	3	3	4	3	4	4	4	4	4	3	3	39
Ruth L	3	3	2	2	4	3	3	3	2	3	1	29

Communicating Grades

To communicate better with students, parents, school personnel, and other interested audiences, teachers may wish to use a multidimensional summary of each student's performances. A summary sheet for such a purpose is on the following page. This summary sheet can be used in two ways. An individual student may be evaluated by entering the student's points in the table and giving the student one of five ratings: excellent, good, satisfactory, unsatisfactory, and unacceptable. The instructional program may be evaluated by summarizing the scores of all the students in a group mean or average and entering the results in the table. Either may be done by:

1. Collect and store information on each student.

2. For cooperative and individualistic sessions, set criteria for making categorical judgments about student performance. You may wish to seek help from the curriculum coordinator, subject matter specialists, teacher committees, the school administration, and from parents and students in doing so.

3. For competitive sessions, rank the students from best to worse.

4. Standardize the scoring system. Each student will participate in a variety of cooperative, competitive, and individualistic learning situations over a period of time. Students will need to understand the scoring system and how points are totaled in the evaluation process.

5. When the points for each student are totaled and a grade given, a criterion-reference system needs to be used.

6. Personalize the evaluation by including notes on incidents and behaviors, conferences with parents and other teachers, and long-term growth information. This is the material students and parents may be most interested in.

7. Do not let students, parents, school personnel, or other audiences make competitive comparisons of the overall grade given to a student.

Summary Table

Student's Name _____ Date _____

Teacher's Name _____ Class _____

	OUTCOMES	POINTS	RATING
COGNITIVE	Mastery of assigned skills (Assignments, quizzes, reports, work units, homework)		
	Mastery of assigned skills (work units, use in problem-solving situations, homework)		
	Mastery of concepts and principles (group scores, reports, homework, observations)		
	Verbal ability 1. Communicates ideas and feelings effectively (observations, direct discuss.)		
	2. Participates actively in problem-solving groups		
	Writing ability (homework, reports)		
	Cooperative ability (observations, group products)		
	Competitive ability (observations, performances in competitions)		
	Ability to work independently (observations, performances in individualized activities)		
	Ability to apply knowledge and resources to the solution of problems (observations, group products)		
AFFECTIVE	Has appreciation of subject area		
	Appreciates learning (receives enjoyment and satisfaction from learning)		
	Aware of and appreciates own abilities, achievements, talents, and resources		
	When appropriate, helps others, shares resources, expresses warmth & caring, trusts		
	Accepts and appreciates cultural, ethnic, and individual differences		
	Willingness to meet the expectations of others when it is appropriate		
	Values free and open inquiry into all problems		

Giving Students Grades in Cooperative Learning Situations

Grades represent the most common reward given in most classrooms. Current grading systems, however, have created a tragedy within many schools in America. Almost every child comes to school optimistic about his or her chances for success. Most end up believing they are failures and losers. Ask first-grade students entering school how they are going to do academically. Most will respond, "I am going to do well." By the end of second grade, however, many are not so sure. By the end of elementary school, many students believe they are not intelligent and are poor students.

One cause is the evaluation and recognition systems used in our classrooms. Some students consistently receive recognition and others never do. If you compare the initial fall test scores in a classroom with final grades in June, there is a high correlation. All year long, the top students are given recognition for being successful. Other students receive little or none. There are winners and there are losers.

The situation is changed dramatically when high-, medium-, and low-achieving students are placed in a cooperative learning group. When the group succeeds, all members are recognized as having contributed to their joint success. Even low-ability students believe, **we** can succeed, **we** are successful. Being part of a cooperative learning group empowers each student by increasing his or her **self-efficacy**--the belief that if effort is exerted, success is possible. All students are recognized as contributing to the group's success.

The way grades are given depends on the type of interdependence the teacher wishes to create among students. Norm-referenced grading systems place students in competition with each other. Criterion-referenced grading systems require students to either work individualistically or cooperatively. How to give grades to communicate to students that they "sink or swim together" is one of the most difficult aspects of structuring learning situations cooperatively. Here are a number of suggestions.

1. **Individual score plus bonus points based on all members reaching criterion**: Group members study together and ensure that all have mastered the assigned material. Each then takes a test individually and is awarded that score. If all group members achieve over a preset criterion of excellence, each receives a bonus. An example is as follows:

Criteria for Bonus Points	Group	Scores	Total
100 15 points	Bill	100	110
90 - 99 10 points	Sally	90	100
80 - 89 5 points	Jane	95	105

2. **Individual score plus bonus points based on lowest score**: The group members prepare each other to take an exam. Members then receive bonus points on the basis of the lowest individual score in their group. An example is as follows:

Criteria for Bonus Points		Group	Scores	Total
71 - 75	1 point	Bill	100	103
76 - 80	2 points	Sally	98	101
81 - 85	3 points	Jane	84	87
86 - 90	4 points			
91 - 95	5 points			
96 - 100	6 points			

This procedure emphasizes encouraging, supporting, and assisting the low achievers in the group. The criterion for bonus points can be adjusted for each learning group, depending on the past performance of their lowest member.

3. **Individual score plus group average**: Group members prepare each other to take an exam. Each takes the examination and receives his or her individual score. The scores of the group members are then averaged. The average is added to each member's score. An example is given below.

Student	Individual Score	Average	Final Score
Bill	66	79	145
Sally	89	79	168
Jane	75	79	154
David	86	79	165

4. **Individual score plus bonus based on improvement scores**: Members of a cooperative group prepare each other to take an exam. Each takes the exam individually and receives his or her individual grade. In addition, bonus points are awarded on the basis of whether members percentage on the current test is higher than the average percentage on all past tests (i.e., their usual level of performance). Their percentage correct on past tests serves as their base score that they try to better. Every two tests or scores, the base score is updated. If a student scores within 4 points (above or below) his or her base score, all members of the group receive 1 bonus point. If they score 5 to 9 points above their base score, each group member receives 2 bonus points. Finally, if they score 10 points or above their base score, or score 100 percent correct, each member receives 3 bonus points.

5. **Totaling members' individual scores**: The individual scores of members are added together and all members receive the total. For example, if group members scored 90, 85, 95, and 90, each member would receive the score of 360.

6. **Averaging of members' individual scores**: The individual scores of members are added together and divided by the number of group members. Each member then receives the group average as their mark. For example, if the scores of members were 90, 95, 85, and 90, each group member would receive the score of 90.

7. **Group score on a single product**: The group works to produce a single report, essay, presentation, worksheet, or exam. The product is evaluated and all members receive the score awarded. When this method is used with worksheets, sets of problems, and examinations, group members are required to reach consensus on each question and be able to explain it to others. The discussion within the group enhances the learning considerably.

8. **Randomly selecting one member's paper to score**: Group members all complete the work individually and then check each other's papers and certify that they are perfectly correct. Since each paper is certified by the whole group to be correct, it makes little difference which paper is graded. The teacher picks one at random, grades it, and all group members receive the score.

9. **Randomly selecting one member's exam to score**: Group members prepare for an examination and certify that each member has mastered the assigned material. All members then take the examination individually. Since all members have certified that each has mastered the material being studied, it makes little difference which exam is scored. The teacher randomly picks one, scores it, and all group members receive that score.

10. **All members receive lowest member score**: Group members prepare each other to take the exam. Each takes the examination individually. All group members then receive the lowest score in the group. For example, if group members score 89, 88, 82, and 79, all members would receive 79 as their score. This procedure emphasizes encouraging, supporting and assisting the low-achieving members of the group and often produces dramatic increases in performance by low-achieving students.

11. **Average of academic scores plus collaborative skills performance score**: Group members work together to master the assigned material. They take an examination individually and their scores are averaged. Concurrently, their work is observed and the

frequency of performance of specified collaborative skills (such as leadership or trust-building actions) is recorded. The group is given a collaborative skills performance score, which is added to their academic average to determine their overall mark.

12. **Dual academic and nonacademic rewards**: Group members prepare each other for a test, take it individually, and receive an individual grade. On the basis of their group average they are awarded free-time, popcorn, extra recess time, or some other valued reward.

Myth: A Single Group Grade Shared by Group Members Is Not Fair

Having students work together on a joint product is viewed by many educators as being less fair to each student than is having each student work alone to produce an individual product for which he or she receives an individual grade. Most students would disagree. It is important that students perceive the distribution of grades and other rewards as being fair, otherwise they may become unmotivated and withdraw psychologically or physically. There have been a number of investigations of students' views of the fairness of various grading systems. There are five major findings:

1. Students who "lose" in a competitive learning situation commonly perceive the grading system as being unjust and, consequently, dislike the class and the teacher (Johnson & Johnson, 1983, 1989a).

2. Before a task is performed, students generally perceive a competitive grading system as being the most fair, but after a task is completed, having all members receive the same grade or reward is viewed as the fairest (Deutsch, 1979).

3. The more frequently students have experienced long-term cooperative learning experiences, and the more cooperative learning was used in their classes, then the more the students believed that everyone who tries has an equal chance to succeed in class, that students get the grades they deserve, and that the grading system is fair (Johnson & Johnson, 1983).

4. Students who have experienced cooperative learning prefer group grades over individual ones (Wheeler & Ryan, 1973).

5. Achievement is higher when group grades (compared with individual ones) are given (Johnson & Johnson, 1989a). The implications of this research for teachers is that

group grades may be perceived to be unfair by students before the students have participated in a cooperative learning activity. Once cooperation has been experienced for a while, however, a single group grade will probably be perceived as the fairest method of evaluation.

There are three general systems for distributing rewards within our society: **equity** (where the person who contributed the most or scored the highest receives the greatest reward), **equality** (where every participant receives the same reward), and **need** (where those who have the greatest need receive the greatest reward) (Deutsch, 1975). All three systems operate within our society and all three systems have their ethical rationale. Typically, the equality system assures members of a family, community, organization, or society that their basic needs will be met and that diverse contributions will be equally valued. The need system assures members that in moments of crisis others will provide support and assistance. And the equity system assures members that if they strive for excellence, their contributions will be valued and rewarded. Educators who wish to give rewards in the classroom only on the basis of equity may be viewing "fairness" from too limited a perspective.

In the ideal classroom, at the end of a grading period, each student will have a number of grades resulting from collaborative efforts, a number of grades resulting from individualistic efforts, and a number of grades resulting from competitive efforts. When these grades are added together, teachers we have worked with inevitably find that high-achievers get "A's." Because of the higher achievement found in cooperative learning situations, however, middle- and low-achievers may receive higher grades than they would if the classroom was dominated by competitive or individualistic learning situations. The number of students receiving "B's" and "C's" will tend to grow larger as the positive peer pressure and support raise achievement. The number of "D's" and "F's" will tend to disappear as collaborators refuse to allow unmotivated students to stay that way. In order not to undermine the overall class collaborativeness it is important to use a criterion-referenced evaluation system in determining final grades.

For teachers who want to give individual grades within cooperative learning situations there are a number of alternatives that have been successfully used:

1. Bonus point method: Students work together in cooperative learning groups, prepare each other for the test, take the test individually, and receive an individual grade. If all members of their group, however, achieve up to a preset criterion of excellence, then each member is rewarded bonus points.

2. Dual grading system: Students work together in cooperative learning groups, prepare each other for the test, take the test individually, and receive an individual grade. They then receive a second grade based on the total performance of all group members.

3. Alternative reward: Same as "2" except that the group grade is used to determine whether group members receive a nonacademic reward, such as free-time, extra recess time, or popcorn.

Wayne Schade, a science teacher in Austin, Texas, uses a grading system we like. Students work in cooperative learning groups during the week. The students take a weekly examination individually and their score becomes their base score. They then receive 5 bonus points if all group members score above 60 percent on the test. This encourages intergroup cooperation. His latest addition to the system is to give another 5 bonus points to every student if all students in the five science classes score above 60 percent on the test. This encourages cooperation across classes. We have a mental image of students going through the hall asking others, "Are you taking science? Take your book home and study!"

Positive Interdependence And Individual Accountability

In cooperative situations, participants share responsibility for the joint outcome. Each group member takes personal responsibility for (a) contributing his or her efforts to accomplish the group's goals and (b) helping other group members do likewise. The greater the positive interdependence structured within a cooperative learning group, the more students will feel **personally responsible** for contributing their efforts to accomplish the group's goals. The shared responsibility adds the concept of **ought** to members' motivation--one ought to do one's share, contribute, and pull one's weight. The shared responsibility also makes each group member personally accountable to the other group members. Students will realize that if they fail to do their fair share of the work, other members will be disappointed, hurt, and upset.

Positive Interdependence And Intellectual Conflict

The greater the positive interdependence within a learning group, the greater the likelihood of intellectual disagreement and conflict among group members. When members of a cooperative learning group become involved in a lesson, their different information, perceptions, opinions, reasoning processes, theories, and conclusions will result in intellectual disagreement and conflict. When such controversies arise, they may be dealt with constructively or destructively, depending on how they are managed and the level of interpersonal and small group skills of the participants. When managed constructively, controversy promotes uncertainty about the correctness of one's conclusions, an active search for more information, a reconceptualization of one's knowledge and conclusions and, consequently, greater mastery and retention of the material being discussed and the more frequent use of higher-level reasoning strategies (Johnson & Johnson, 1987, 1989a). Individuals working alone in competitive and individualistic situations do not have the opportunity for such intellectual challenge and, therefore, their achievement and quality of reasoning suffer.

Conclusions

In revisiting Sugar Loaf Hill in Okinawa William Manchester gained an important insight. "I understand at last, why I jumped hospital that long-ago Sunday and, in violation of orders, returned to the front and almost certain death. It was an act of love. Those men on the line were my family, my home. They were closer to me than I can say, closer than any friends had been or ever would be. They were comrades; three of them had saved my life. They had never let me down, and I couldn't do it to them. I had to be with them, rather than let them die and me live with the knowledge that I might have saved them. Men, I now knew, do not fight for flag or country, for the Marine Corps or glory or any other abstraction. They fight for their friends."

Positive interdependence results in individuals striving together to achieve mutual goals which, in turn, promotes caring and committed relationships. The more caring and committed the relationships, furthermore, the more interdependent individuals will perceive themselves to be and the more individuals will dedicate themselves to achieving the group's goals. Positive interdependence is the essence of cooperative learning. There are a number of ways of structuring positive interdependence. Teachers may structure positive goal interdependence, reward interdependence, resource interdependence, role interdependence, task interdependence, outside enemy interdependence, fantasy interdependence, identity interdependence, and environmental interdependence. The more types of positive interdependence teachers structure, the more effective cooperative learning will be. Many of the problems in student participation within learning groups may be prevented or resolved through the systematic use of positive interdependence. Grades are one of the ways in which students are given the message, "We sink or swim together."

After positive interdependence is carefully structured, teachers may wish to focus on teaching students the cooperative skills they need to function effectively within the learning groups. The next chapter focuses on this topic.

Implementation Assignment

1. Read Chapter 5.

2. Working individualistically, take a sheet of paper and divide it into two columns. Label the first column "Procedures for structuring positive interdependence I have used" and the second column "Procedures I would like to try." List at least five procedures in the second column.

3. Try out five new procedures for structuring positive interdependence with your class. Interview students about the differences among the ways (old and new) of structuring positive interdependence. Find out which methods they perceive as most effective. Bring back written notes on the class interview to share with your base group.

∼ **Positive Interdependence Posttest** ∼

Given below are a number of ways of structuring positive interdependence. Pick a partner from your group. Working as a pair, decide which type of positive interdependence is operationalized in each method listed. The types of positive interdependence are:

G = Goal   Rw = Reward

Rs = Resource   Ro = Role

T = Task   I = Identity

O = Outside enemy   F = Fantasy

E = Environmental   N = None

_____ 1. Asking each group to design a group flag based on a group motto.

_____ 2. Each group member having a section of homework to do to complete the assignment.

_____ 3. Giving free time to all group members when each scores above the 90 percent correct level on a test.

_____ 4. Asking members to imagine that they have just been stranded in the desert and have to derive a plan to survive.

_____ 5. Drawing a circle on the floor, designating it as the group's meeting place, and requiring all group members to stay within the circle.

_____ 6. Assigning the roles of summarizer, elaborator, questioner, and devil's advocate to different group members.

_____ 7. Asking students to sign their group's report to demonstrate their agreement with and mastery of the material.

_____ 8. Requiring every member to contribute a paragraph to a group theme.

_____ 9. Any student who achieves at the 90 percent correct level on a test receiving popcorn.

_____ 10. Calling randomly on one group member to explain the group's answer.

_____ 11. Requiring one student to write down the dictionary's definition of a word, a second student to learn how to pronounce the word, and a third student to use the word in a sentence.

_____ 12. Giving all members free time when each member has passed a test at the 90 percent correct level.

_____ 13. Giving only one textbook is given to each group.

_____ 14. Having five groups compete to see which attains the highest average score on a test.

_____ 15. Having groups imagine themselves as an animal and give themselves that name.

_____ 16. Each member receiving the grade he or she obtained on a unit test.

_____ 17. Having one student cut out circles, one write homonyms on the circles, and one staple the circles together to make a homonym worm.

_____ 18. Assigning each group member part of a famous person's life, an aspect of a war, or one of a series of events leading to a discovery, and then requiring them to combine their expertise in writing an overall report.

_____ 19. Requiring three kindergartners to draw a picture that includes six different colors, and then giving each two crayons of different colors, so that each has to draw part of the picture.

_____ 20. Adding the test scores of all members together and giving each member the total score for the group.

⊷[Cooperative Learning Contract]⊷

Major Learnings	Implementation Plans

Date _____ Date of Progress Report Meeting _____

Participant's Signature _____

Signatures of Other Group Members _____ _____

_____ _____ _____

❧ Cooperative Learning Progress Report ❧

NAME _____ SCHOOL _____

AGE LEVEL _____ SUBJECT _____

DAY AND DATE	DESCRIPTION OF TASKS and ACTIVITIES PERFORMED	SUCCESSES EXPERIENCED	PROBLEMS ENCOUNTERED

Description of critical or interesting incidents:

4:37

EXERCISE

MATERIALS

Types of
Positive Interdependence

Positive Goal Interdependence: Students perceive that they can achieve their learning goals if and only if all the members of their group also attain their goals. Members of a learning group have a mutual set of goals that they are all striving to accomplish.

Positive Reward Interdependence: Each group member receives the same reward for completing the assignment. A joint reward is given for successful group work. Everyone is rewarded or no one is rewarded.

Positive Resource Interdependence: Each member has only a portion of the information, resources, or materials necessary for the task to be completed and the members' resources have to be combined in order for the group to achieve its goal.

Positive Task Interdependence: A division of labor is created so that the actions of one group member have to be completed if the next team member is to complete his or her responsibility.

Positive Role Interdependence: Each member is assigned complementary and interconnected roles that specify responsibilities that the group needs in order to complete a joint task.

Positive Identity Interdependence: The group establishes a mutual identity through a name, flag, motto, or song.

Positive Outside Enemy Interdependence: Groups are placed in competition with each other. Group members then feel interdependent as they strive to beat the other groups and win the competition.

Positive Fantasy Interdependence: A task is given that requires members to imagine that they are in a life or death situation and must collaborate in order to survive.

Environmental Interdependence: Groups members are bound together by the physical environment in some way. An example is putting people in a specific area in which to work.

Positive Interdependence: Instructions

The **purposes of this chapter** are to have you:

1. Review the conceptual definition of positive interdependence.

2. Generate a list of specific procedures to structure positive interdependence among your students.

3. Try out several of the positive interdependence procedures in your classroom.

4. Understand a variety of different procedures for assigning grades within cooperative learning lessons.

To achieve these purposes you should **complete the following tasks**:

1. **Pretest:** Find someone who teaches the same grade level or subject area as you do. Form a pair. Complete the pretest, working cooperatively. There are two roles: reader and answerer. The reader reads the question, the answerer suggests an answer; if there is agreement the two check the answer. If there is disagreement the two discuss the question until they agree. Rotate the roles for each question.

2. **Types Of Positive Interdependence**: Working cooperatively as a pair, read the section of the chapter on the types of positive interdependence. Follow the **Reciprocal Learning Procedure**:

   a. Identify the question being asked in the paragraph or section.

   b. Read the section. Then agree on a summary that answers the question and gives examples of how the content may be implemented in your classrooms.

   c. Extend the section by adding additional information or examples or relate what is being learned to previously learned material.

   Work as quickly as you can. When you have finished, you and your partner should know what are the various types of positive interdependence and how each may be implemented within your classrooms.

3. **Lesson Plan Search**: There are a number of lesson plans included in this book. Your task is to analyze how positive interdependence is included in them. In doing so, work cooperatively as a pair. Agree on one set of answers and make sure that both of you are able to explain them. One member will randomly be selected to explain the group's answers.

   a. Review the lesson plans and select one.

   b. Identify the methods used to structure positive interdependence within the lesson.

   c. Add one that is missing.

   d. Pick a second lesson and repeat.

   e. Find another pair that has analyzed the same lesson plan you have. Share your analyses with each other.

4. **Application**: Plan how to operationalize the new procedures for structuring positive interdependence within the lessons you and your partner teach cooperatively. Be as specific as possible. Work cooperatively. Both members should understand how each member is planning to operationalize positive interdependence. Actively give each other suggestions for doing so.

5. **Posttest**: Take the posttest in your base group. This is a cooperative activity. Achieve consensus in your group on the answer to each question.

A Valediction: Encouraging Cooperation

TOM MORTON

Vancouver,
British Columbia

Subject Area: English

Grade Level: Secondary

Lesson Summary: Groups must match paraphrases with stanzas of John Donne's **A Valedication: Forbidding Mourning** and learn the target vocabulary. They then brainstorm comparisons with which they write a group poem containing metaphors.

Instructional Objectives: Students will gain practice in reading and interpreting poetry, will develop an awareness of metaphor, and will learn to write metaphors.

Materials:

ITEM	NUMBER NEEDED
A Valediction: Forbidding Mourning by John Donne	One per student
Set of role cards	One per group
Set of task cards	One per group
Instructions/Evaluation sheet	One per group

Time Required: One and one-half hours

© Appears in **Structuring Cooperative Learning: The 1987 Lesson-Plan Handbook** by D. W. Johnson, R. T. Johnson, and Edythe Johnson Holubec. Edina, MN: Interaction Book Company, 1987.

≋ Decisions ≋

Group Size: Three (four, if an observer is used)

Assignment To Groups: Either random or teacher assigned, with high, medium, and low achieving students in each group.

Roles: Reader of instructions/Checker of members to make certain they understand their roles, the instructions and the work

Recorder of answers/**Encourager** of participation

Reporter to the class/**Praiser** of contributions and efforts to practice the roles

Observer of group interactions (optional)

≋ The Lesson: Part One ≋

Instructional Task:

Discuss some of the background of John Donne and **A Valediction: Forbidding Mourning.** Born in 1572, Donne was a contemporary of Shakespeare. Passionate, charming, and intellectual, Donne sailed with Sir  Walter Raleigh on a raid against the Spanish Azores and wrote love poetry. He fell out of favor with the ruling class for secretly marrying his noble patron's sixteen-year-old niece. Although his marriage turned out to be a happy one, Donne was imprisoned for a time, lost his job, and lived in poverty for many years. In 1615 he became an Anglican minister and rose to prominence with his dramatic sermons and religious poetry as passionate as his earlier love poems. Donne wrote **A Valediction** to his wife before he visited the Continent in 1612. Donne had had a premonition of misfortune and on his return he found that his wife had given birth to a still-born child.

Distribute a copy of **A Valediction** and read it to the class. Explain that, in order to understand the poem fully, each group will be given a set of cards on each of which is a paraphrase of one of the stanzas of the poem. However, the cards are in a mixed order, so the group will have to sort them out, while following the instruction sheet carefully.

Positive Interdependence:

Students are all to agree on the answers of the group (consensus). Give the groups the role cards. Once each member has chosen and understood one of these roles, give the groups a set of task cards and an instruction sheet.

Individual Accountability:

Each member is to be ready to defend and explain the answers of the group. Their signatures at the end mean that they agree with the answer and can explain both it and the vocabulary.

∾ Monitoring and Processing ∾
Part One

Monitoring: First monitor the groups to check whether students can explain their group's decisions and the meaning of the vocabulary. Monitor the groups again to note the use of group skills.

Intervening: Comment on and praise those using the social skills. If there is a good opportunity to use a skill but a student does not do so -- for example, a worthwhile contribution that the praiser does not refer to -- encourage the use of that skill. Intervene as well to ask individuals to explain the group answers.

Processing: Once students have completed the task and signed their paper, ask them to discuss and write group answers to the processing questions at the bottom of the sheet.

Closing: Have students hand in their answers and processing, then discuss the poem as a class. At this stage you may wish to use a large compass to explain in detail Donne's extended metaphor in the last three stanzas or ask students for the explanation.

~ The Lesson: Part Two ~

Instructional Task:

For the following lesson, the ideas for teaching poetry from Kenneth Koch (**Rose, Where Did You Get That Red?**, Vintage, 1973, pp. 80–82) are combined with group brainstorming. Koch says that **A Valediction: Forbidding Mourning** offers [children] new things to write about [science and math], and shows them how they can use these things to talk about tender and passionate feelings. . .by means of mechanical, mathematical, and scientific analogies.

First, you need to be sure that students are familiar with **brainstorming:** The purpose is to generate as many ideas as possible; there is no criticism or discussion of ideas until afterwards; group members try to build on others' ideas if they can, and do not worry too much about the "right" response -- they just want to get the ideas flowing. Later, the group reviews the ideas and chooses the best. If the class is not familiar with brainstorming, teach and practice the process first.

The group's learning task is to use brainstorming to make a list of at least twelve comparisons of a serious feeling like love or loneliness to things in science or math. From this list the group will choose the most interesting or exciting ones to develop into a group poem of at least six lines. The poem may have a comparison in each line or the group may devote the whole poem to one or two comparisons as Donne did with the compass metaphor.

Koch gives a number of examples and questions to help a class start: What feeling do I have that is like magnetism? Electricity? Human feelings and relationships can be compared to ordinary mechanical things like turning on a light switch, a bulb burning out, or an electric eye. Brainstorming an example as a class creates the enthusiasm for groups to launch into their own idea generation.

Positive Interdependence:

The group is to complete one list from which it makes one poem.

Individual Accountability:

Individual responsibility is harder with brainstorming which depends on the free play of ideas back and forth, so the teacher should reiterate the group roles as one way to ensure that everyone contributes: The **recorder** writes down the brainstorming and the poem as well as encourages participation; the **checker** sees that everyone understands what to do and proofreads the final product; and the **praiser** gives verbal support and also reads the completed poem to the class.

Criteria for Success:

Evaluation will depend on the teacher's purpose and the level of the class. Completion of the minimum number of ideas and lines and the use of correct English would be part of the criteria. Originality and vividness of the metaphor could also be evaluated in a more advanced class.

Expected Behaviors:

Tell students that you expect everyone to participate in the brainstorming and to perform their roles.

≈ Monitoring and Processing ≈

Part Two

Monitoring and Intervening: The teacher monitors as before for the use of social skills but, depending on the class experience, there may need to be additional intervening to help students brainstorm.

Closing: Have each group's reporter read its poem to the class.

Processing: Because group members have so recently discussed their use of collaborative skills and given a suggestion on improving their group process, their processing could start there:

1. What was your suggestion for improvement from the last class? Did you improve on that skill?
2. What were two other things that your group did well that helped you to work together?
3. How effective was brainstorming for generating ideas?

Then, as a whole class, ask for responses from several groups for a discussion of group process, especially on the social skills with which students may have trouble and on the brainstorming. You could also refer to the written responses from the previous exercise.

Exercise on:
A VALEDICTION: FORBIDDING MOURNING

 Instructions

Deal out the cards equally to each group member. Do not show your cards to other group members. On each card is a number and one or two sentences that paraphrase one of the stanzas of **A Valediction: Forbidding Mourning**. However, they are not in the correct numbered order. Your group task is to understand the poem by putting the paraphrases in the order that reflects the sequence of stanzas in the poem and also by finding out the meaning of the vocabulary used.

You need to share what is written on your cards, but must do so orally and not show or give your cards to anyone. You are to reach group consensus on the order of the numbers with each member able to explain why the group chose that order and able to give the meaning of any word.

Following are some particular words that, either by referring to the dictionary or using the context, you should be ready to define: **valediction, profanation, laity, trepidation, sublunary, breach, hearkens, obliquely**.

After reaching consensus, you have agreed that the numbered order of the cards should be: _____, _____, _____, _____, _____, _____, _____, _____, _____.

Signatures: Your signature means you have participated in the assignment and understand the poem. You also agree with your answers and are able to explain them and the meaning of the poem's vocabulary.

_____   _____

_____   _____

Evaluation of Group Work

Discuss as a group and write down the answers to the following:
- Which of the cooperative skills did your group use successfully?
- What other things did your group do well?
- Which skills (if any) were harder to use?
- What one skill should your group try to improve next time?

A VALEDICTORY: FORBIDDING MOURNING
by John Donne

As virtuous men pass mildly away,
   And whisper to their souls to go,
Whilst some of their sad friends so say,
   "The breath goes now," and some say, "No,"

So let us melt, and make no noise,
   No tear-floods, nor sigh-tempests move;
'Twere profanation of our joys
   To tell the laity our love.

Moving of the earth brings harms and fears,
   Men reckon what it did and meant;
But trepidation of the spheres,
   Though greater far, is innocent.

Dull sublunary lovers' love
   (Whose soul is sense) cannot admit
Absence, because it doth remove
   Those things which elemented it.

But we, by a love so much refined
   That our selves know not what it is,
Inter-assured of the mind,
   Care less, eyes, lips, and hands to miss.

Our two souls therefore, which are one,
   Though I must go, endure not yet
A breach, but an expansion.
   Like gold to airy thinness beat.

If they be two, they are two so
   As stiff twin compasses are two:
Thy soul, the fixed foot, makes no show
   To move, but doth, if the other do;

And though it in the center sit,
   Yet when the other far doth roam,
It leans, and hearkens after it,
   And grows erect, as that comes home.

Such wilt thou be to me, who must,
   Like the other foot, obliquely run;
Thy firmness makes my circle just,
   And makes me end where I begun.

Task Cards

1

Yet our love, so special that we do not understand it, is strong in our minds and does not need us to be together physically.

2

People fear and puzzle over earthquakes, but they do not even notice the wobbling of the earth on its axis.

3

When good men die quietly and say their last words, their friends are not even sure that they are dead.

4

And so we will be the same: Like the outside foot of a compass, I must move away, but your steadiness will make me return home, just as the compass completes the circle.

5

Let us too be quiet and not cry aloud. To do so would be an insult to our great happiness.

6

Everyday physical love cannot last if the lovers are separated, because the source of their love is removed.

7

The two of us are united spiritually. Though I must leave, the separation will not break us apart, but only stretch our union.

8

Though your compass foot is fixed in the centre, when mine moves away, you lean towards my foot and then straighten up as mine returns to you.

9

We are like the two feet of a compass used for drawing a circle. You are the foot in the circle's centre that turns only if the outside foot does.

Math Drill-Review Pairs

Task: Correctly solve the problems.

Cooperative: The mutual goal is to ensure that both pair members understand the strategies and procedures required to solve the problems correctly. Two roles are assigned: **Explainer** (explains step-by-step how to solve the problem) and **accuracy checker** (verifies that the explanation is accurate, encourages, and provides coaching if needed). The two roles are rotated after each problem.

Procedure: Assign students to pairs. Assign each pair to a foursome. Implement the following procedure:

1. Person A reads the problem and explains step-by-step the procedures and strategies required to solve it. Person B checks the accuracy of the solution and provides encouragement and coaching if it is needed.

2. Person B solves the second problem, describing step-by-step the procedures and strategies required to solve it. Person A checks the accuracy of the solution and provides encouragement and coaching if it is needed.

3. When two problems are completed, the pair checks their answers with another pair. If they do not agree, they resolve the problem until there is consensus about the answer. If they do agree, they thank each other and continue work in their pairs.

4. The procedure continues until all problems are completed.

Individual Accountability: One member will be picked randomly to explain how to solve a randomly selected problem.

Assignment

Rewrite the above math procedure for a specific math assignment in your classroom. If you are not a math teacher, modify the lesson into a drill-review lesson in your subject area. Script out exactly what you will say to your class.

Preparing for a Test

Task: Understand how to answer correctly each study question. Give students (a) study questions on which the examination will be based and (b) class time to prepare for the examination.

Cooperative: Assign students to cooperative groups heterogeneous in terms of math and reading ability. The **cooperative goal** is to ensure that all group members know and understand the material on which they will be tested. Two roles are assigned: **Explainer** (explains step-by-step how to solve each study question) and **accuracy checker** (verifies that the explanation is accurate, encourages, and provides coaching if needed). The explainer reads a question and explains step-by-step how to answer it correctly. The other group members check for accuracy. The roles are rotated clockwise around the group after each problem. For any question for which there is disagreement among group members, the page number and paragraph on which the procedures required to attain the answer must be found.

Expected Criteria For Success: Each group member understands the material on which they are to be tested. If all group members score over 90 percent correct on the test, each will receive five bonus points.

Individual Accountability: Each student takes the examination individually.

Expected Behaviors: Helping and encouraging group members to do well on the test.

Intergroup Cooperation: Whenever it is unclear how to answer a question correctly, ask another group for help.

Assignment

Rewrite the procedure for the next test you plan to give. Script out exactly what you will say to your class.

Reviewing a Test

Two of the purposes of testing are to evaluate how much each student knows and assess what students need to review. Using the following procedure will result in achieving both purposes **and** students learning the material they did not understand before the test. It also prevents arguments with students over which answer is correct.

Task: Answer each test question correctly.

Cooperative Procedure:

1. Each student takes the test individually and hands their answers in to the teacher.

2. The next class period, students are randomly assigned to groups of four. Each group is divided into two pairs. Each pair retakes the test. The **cooperative goal** is to have one answer for each question that both agree upon and both can explain. They cannot proceed until they agree on the answer.

3. The groups of four meet. The **cooperative goal** is for all group members to understand the material covered by the test. Group members confer on each question. On any question to which the two pairs have different answers, they find the page number and paragraph in the textbook where the answer is explained. Each group is responsible for ensuring that all members understand the material they missed on the test. If necessary, group members assign review homework to each other.

Expected Criteria For Success: Each group member understands the material on which they were tested, especially the knowledge relevant to the questions they missed.

Individual Accountability: Students have to explain what they know to groupmates. Teacher randomly selects students to answer questions they missed on the test.

Assignment

Rewrite the above procedure for the next test you give. Formulate a plan to use the **Test Review Procedure**. Script out exactly what you will say to your class in assigning the procedure.

Checking Homework

Task: Bring completed homework to class and understand how to do it correctly.

Cooperative: Students enter the classroom and meet in their cooperative learning groups. The groups should be heterogeneous in terms of math and reading ability. One member (the **runner**) goes to the teacher's desk, picks up the group's folder, and hands out any materials in the folder to the appropriate members. The runner records how much of the assignment each member completed. At the end of the assigned review time, the members' homework is placed in the group's folder and the runner returns it to the teacher's desk.

Runn

The **cooperative goal** is to ensure that all group members bring their complete homework to class and understand how to do it correctly. Two roles ar assigned: **Explainer** (explains step-by-step how the homework is correctl completed) and **accuracy checker** (verifies that the explanation is accurat encourages, and provides coaching if needed). The explainer reads the first pa of the assignment and explains step-by-step how to complete it correctly. Th other group members check for accuracy. The roles are rotated clockwi around the group so that each member does an equal amount of explaining. Th group should concentrate on the parts of the assignments where members did n understand.

Expected Criteria For Success: All group members to have correctly complete the homework correctly and understand how to do it.

Individual Accountability: Regular examinations and daily random selection group members to explain how to solve randomly selected problems from t homework.

Alternative Of Directed Homework Review: Students are assigned to pairs. Teach randomly picks questions from the homework assignment. One student explai step-by-step the correct answer. The other student listens, checks f accuracy, and prompts the explainer if he or she does not know the answe Roles are switched for each question.

Assignment: Rewrite the above procedure for your next homework assignment. Script out exactly what you will say to your class.

Processing Starters

1. Name three things your group did well in working together. Name one thing your group could do even better.

2. Think of something each of your group members did that helped the group be effective. Tell them what it is.

3. Tell your group members how much you appreciate their help today.

4. Rate yourself from 1 (low) to 10 (high) on _____ (name a cooperative skill like **encouraging participation,** or **checking for understanding**). Share your rating with your group and explain why you rated yourself the way you did. Plan how to increase the frequency with which group members use this skill.

Chapter 5

Teaching Students Cooperative Skills

Table Of Contents

Part 1: The Importance of Cooperative Skills

"...instead of looking on discussion as a stumbling-block in the way of action, we think it an indispensable preliminary to any wise action at all."

Pericles

Children are not born instinctively knowing how to interact effectively with others. Interpersonal and group skills do not magically appear when they are needed. Students must be taught these skills and be motivated to use them. Many elementary and secondary students lack basic social skills such as correctly identifying the emotions of others and appropriately discussing an assignment. Their social ineptitude seems to persist into adulthood. Students who lack appropriate social skills find themselves isolated, alienated, and at a disadvantage in career training programs. It has often been estimated that over 10 percent of school children have no friends and perhaps a third of school children are not especially liked by any of their peers. Poor peer relationships have widespread immediate and long-term effects on children's cognitive and social development, well- being, happiness, success, and psychological health.

There is no way to overemphasize the importance of the skills required to work effectively with others. **Cooperative skills are the keystones to maintaining a stable family, a successful career, and a stable group of friends.** These skills have to be taught just as purposefully and precisely as reading and math skills. While many social skills are usually learned in family and community experiences, many contemporary children and adolescents lack basic social skills. One of the great advantages of cooperative learning is that important "life-survival" skills are required, used, reinforced, and mastered within a task situation. Participating in cooperative learning situations requires students to develop and use the social skills necessary for living productive and fulfilling lives as adults.

Since many students have never been taught how to work effectively with others, they cannot do so. Thus, the first experience of many teachers who try structuring lessons cooperatively is that their students cannot collaborate with each other. Teaching cooperative skills becomes an important prerequisite for academic learning since achievement will improve as students become more effective in learning from each other. It is within cooperative situations, where there is a task to complete, that social skills become most relevant and should ideally be taught. All students need to become skillful in communicating, building and maintaining trust, providing leadership, engaging in fruitful controversy, and managing conflicts (Johnson, 1990, 1991; Johnson & F. Johnson, 1990).

In this chapter we will review some of the assumptions that are vital to teaching cooperative skills, list and discuss some of the social skills, and describe a model for teaching them.

Teaching Cooperative Skills: Assumptions

There are four assumptions underlying teaching students cooperative skills. **The first is that prior to teaching the skills a cooperative context must be established.** The intent of cooperative learning is to create a perception that students "sink or swim together" and, therefore, must be actively involved in maximizing their own learning while at the same time maximizing the learning of groupmates. It is not to "win." When these overall cooperative goals are lacking, interaction among students becomes competitive, hostile, divisive, and destructive. Students who are competing want to "win," not learn the skills to cooperate. It makes little sense, furthermore, to teach students how to work more effectively with each other if they are expected to spend the school day working alone without interacting with classmates. Students' awareness of the need for collaborative skills is directly related to their being in cooperative situations. Implementing cooperative learning is vital to increasing students' collaborative competencies.

Second, cooperative skills have to be directly taught. Structuring lessons cooperatively is not enough. Students are not born with the interpersonal and group skills required to collaborate with each other, nor do the skills magically appear when the students need them. Learning how to interact effectively with others is no different from learning how to use a microscope, play a piano, write a complete sentence, or read. The same basic process is required for all skill learning.

Third, while it is the teacher who structures cooperation within the classroom and initially defines the skills required to collaborate, it is the other group members who largely determine whether the skills are learned and internalized. Teachers rely on the student's peers to cue and monitor the use of the skills, give feedback on how well the skills are being enacted, and reinforce their appropriate use. Peer accountability to learn cooperative skills must always be coupled with peer support for doing so. Group members need to communicate both, "We want you to practice this collaborative skill," and "How can we help you do so?" After the teacher instructs students as to what the cooperative skills are, and encourages students to practice the skills in their learning groups, peer support and feedback will determine whether the skills are used appropriately and frequently enough for the skills to be natural and automatic actions. Peer feedback will occur subtly while the groups are working and directly in formal feedback sessions structured by the teacher.

Fourth, the earlier students are taught cooperative skills, the better. There are procedures for kindergarten and even preschool teachers to use in teaching students collaborative skills. In elementary, secondary, and post-secondary settings teachers should be involved in improving students' competencies in working collaboratively with each other. To inform adults who are engineers, managers, supervisors, or secretaries that they need to learn how to cooperate more effectively with others is important, but a little late. Their education should have prepared them for the cooperation inherent in adult career and family life. There is a direct relation between schools demanding that students work alone without interacting with each other and the number of adults in our society who lack the competencies required to work effectively with others in career, family, and leisure settings.

Long-Term Outcomes Of Teaching Social Skills

In order to get the most out of cooperative learning groups, students must be taught interpersonal and small group skills. Doing so produces both short-term and long-term outcomes (Johnson & R. Johnson, 1989). The short-term outcomes include greater learning, retention, and critical thinking. The long-term outcomes include greater employability and career success.

Most people realize that a college education or vocational training improves their career opportunities. **Many people are less aware that interpersonal skills may be the most important set of skills to their employability, productivity, and career success.** Employers typically value verbal communication, responsibility, interpersonal, initiative, and decision-making skills. A question all employers have in mind when they interview a job applicant is, "Can this person get along with other people?" Having a high degree of technical competence is not enough to ensure a successful career. A person also has to have a high degree of interpersonal competence.

In 1982, for example, the Center for Public Resources published **Basic Skills in the U.S. Workforce**, a nationwide survey of businesses, labor unions, and educational institutions. The Center found that 90 percent of the people fired from their jobs were fired for poor job attitudes, poor interpersonal relationship, and inappropriate behavior. Being fired for lack of basic and technical skills was infrequent. Even in high-tech careers, the ability to work effectively with other high-tech personnel is essential, and so is the ability to communicate and work with people from other professions to solve interdisciplinary problems.

In the real world of work, the heart of most jobs, especially the higher-paying, more interesting jobs, is getting others to cooperate, leading others, coping with complex problems power and influence issues, and helping solve people's problems in working together. Millions of technical, professional, and managerial jobs today require much more than technical competence and professional expertise. They also require leadership. Employees are increasingly asked to get things done by influencing a large and diverse group of people (bosses, subordinates, peers, customers, and others), despite lacking much or any formal control over them, and despite their general disinterest in cooperating. They are expected to motivate others to achieve goals, negotiate and mediate, get decisions implemented, exercise authority, and develop credibility. The interpersonal and small group skills developed within cooperative efforts are important contributors to personal employability and career success.

In addition to career success, social skills are directly related to building and maintaining positive relationships and to psychological health. Maintaining a set of good friends your whole life long, being a caring parent, maintaining a loving relationship with your spouse, all directly relate to how interpersonally skilled you are. Quality of life as an adult largely depends on social skills. The more socially skilled a person is, furthermore, the healthier they tend to be psychologically. For these, and many other reasons, it is important that students learn the interpersonal and small group skills necessary to build and maintain cooperative relationships with others.

Coaching Social Skills

1. *Ensure that cooperative learning groups are being used.*

2. *Select the cooperative skill to be taught (such as "praising contributions") and make a "T-Chart" (Looks Like, Sounds Like) for the skill.*

3. *Take the target student from the regular classroom.*

4. *Explain the skill to the student.*

    a. *Ask the student to suggest a positive example of the skill and predict a possible consequence for engaging in the skill.*

    b. *Ask the student to suggest an opposite example of the skill and predict a possible consequence for his/her negative example.*

    c. *Acknowledge appropriate positive and negative examples and restate the skill.*

5. *Practice the skill with the student (**private guided practice**):*

    a. *Ask the student to role play the skill.*

    b. *Praise the student while discussing how well the skill was performed.*

    c. *Repeat until the student no longer awkwardly engages in the skill.*

6. *Explain how to use the skill in the student's cooperative group. Inform the student that you will be observing for the number of times he or she uses the skill in the group each day.*

7. *Observe the group session and record the frequency with which the student engages in the skill (**public guided practice**). Prompt the use of the skill if it is appropriate to do so. Record the frequency on a chart.*

8. *Just before the beginning of the next cooperative group meeting show the student his/her chart with the number of time he/she performed each skill the day (session) before. Discuss with the student the skills in which progress is good and the skills in which progress is slow. Ask the student why he/she is having difficulty with the skill. Set up criteria to reach in the cooperative session that is about to start, "Yesterday you praised a member's contributions four times. Let's see if you can praise contributions in today's session six times."*

9. *Repeat this procedure until the skill is firmly integrated into the student's behavior repertoire.*

Building a T-Chart

A very effective method of defining a social skill is to develop a T-Chart for it. Use the steps below to construct your chart.

1. Write the name of the skill to be learned and practiced at the top of the chart and draw a large T below it.

2. Label the left side of the T *"Looks Like"* and the right side *"Sounds Like."*

3. Think of an example for each of the columns and write that below the crossbar.

4. Ask for other behaviors that operationalize the skill and list those on the left side.

5. Ask for further phrases that operationalize the skill and list those on the right side.

6. Have group members practice both *Looks Like* and *Sounds Like* before the lesson is concluded.

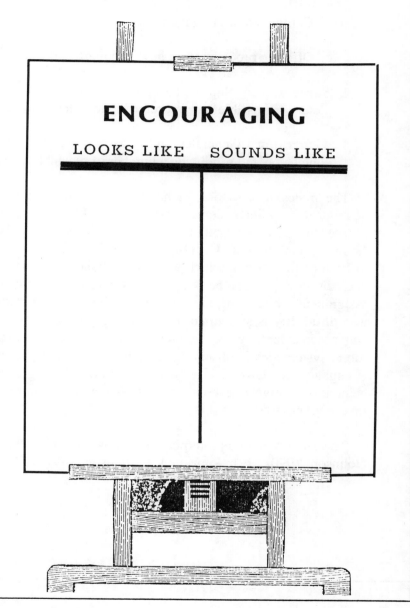

ENCOURAGING

LOOKS LIKE   SOUNDS LIKE

Part 2: What Skills Need To Be Taught?

John Dugan, in his 11th-grade English class in Suffern, New York, begins a unit on grammar with teaching students a set of leadership skills. He structures **positive interdependence** by giving students the assignment of (1) mastering the leadership skills and (2) ensuring that all members of their group master the leadership skills. The leadership skills he teaches are:

1. **Direction Giver**: Gives direction to the group's work by:

    a. Reviewing the instructions and restating the purpose of the assignment.

    b. Calling attention to the time limits.

    c. Offering procedures on how to complete the assignment most effectively.

2. **Summarizer**: Summarizes out loud what has just been read or discussed as completely as possible without referring to notes or to the original material.

3. **Generator**: Generates additional answers by going beyond the first answer or conclusion and producing a number of plausible answers to choose from.

The process he uses to teach the skills is as follows. **First**, he explains the skills. **Second**, he models the skills by demonstrating them. **Third**, he asks the class to generate a series of phrases that could be used to engage in the skills, such as "One way we could do this is...," "Another answer is..." **Fourth**, he next selects three students to role play a group session in front of the class in which the leadership skills are used. After the role play the whole class discusses each of the skills again. **Fifth**, students are told to complete the first grammar assignment while using the three leadership skills as frequently as possible. **Individual accountability** is structured by observing each group to verify that each group member engages in at least two of the three targeted leadership skills. John circulates throughout the room, systematically observing each group, recording how frequently each leadership role is engaged in. Groups in which each member engages in at least two of the leadership behaviors receive five bonus points on the first grammar assignment (**positive reward interdependence**).

There are numerous interpersonal skills that affect the success of collaborative efforts (Johnson, 1990, 1991; Johnson & F. Johnson, 1991; Johnson & R. Johnson, 1991). What cooperative skills teachers emphasize in their classes depends on what their students have and have not mastered. As teachers observe and monitor their students working in cooperative learning groups the teachers will notice where students lack important skills. Our list of required student behaviors may give teachers a starting point in examining how skillful their students are. There are four levels of cooperative skills:

1. **Forming**: The bottom-line skills needed to establish a functioning cooperative learning group.

2. **Functioning**: The skills needed to manage the group's activities in completing the task and in maintaining effective working relationships among members.

3. **Formulating**: The skills needed to build deeper-level understanding of the material being studied, to stimulate the use of higher quality reasoning strategies, and to maximize mastery and retention of the assigned material.

4. **Fermenting**: The skills needed to stimulate reconceptualization of the material being studied, cognitive conflict, the search for more information, and the communication of the rationale behind one's conclusions.

Forming

Forming skills are an initial set of management skills directed toward organizing the group and establishing minimum norms for appropriate behavior. Some of the more important behaviors in this category are:

1. **Move Into Groups Quietly:** Move into cooperative learning groups without undue noise and without bothering others. Work time is a valuable commodity and little time should be spent in rearranging furniture and moving into learning groups. Students may need to practice the procedure for getting into groups several times before they become efficient in doing so.

2. **Stay With The Group:** Moving around the room during group time is nonproductive for the student doing it as well as for the other group members. Let students know that leaving the group is not acceptable behavior.

3. **Use Quiet Voices**: Cooperative learning groups do not need to be noisy. Students can learn to work very quietly when that norm is set for them and positively reinforced.

Assigning one student in each group the job of reminding group members to speak quietly can help (noise monitor). Teaching students to use "12-inch" voices and measuring noice distance with a ruler is another possibility.

4. **Take Turns**. All group members need to share in the learning and be part of the group's efforts to achieve. Taking turns is one way to formalize this.

5. **Other forming skills** include keeping your hands (and feet) to yourself, looking at the paper, using names, looking at the speaker, and eliminate "put-downs."

Functioning

The second level of cooperative skills are the **functioning skills** involved in managing the group's efforts to complete their tasks and maintain effective working relationships among members. Some of these skills are:

1. **Share Ideas And Opinions**: All group members need to share their ideas (and materials).

2. **Ask For Facts And Reasoning** (ask questions; seek ideas and opinions from others): Members need to ask questions to get others to share their ideas and thinking processes. Group members can then understand, discuss, and correct each other's thinking.

3. **Give Direction To The Group's Work**: Helping the group move ahead rather than staying stalled for lack of direction can be done by:

   a. Stating and restating the purpose of the assignment ("We are supposed to...").

   b. Setting or calling attention to time limits ("Can we do it this way in the time we have left?").

   c. Offering procedures on how to most effectively complete the assignment ("Why don't we try this?").

4. **Encourage Everyone To Participate**: Asking other members to share what they are thinking or what their ideas are is important for getting everyone's ideas as well as making others feel that their ideas are valued ("Nancy, what do you think?").

5. **Ask For Help Or Clarification**: Asking groupmates for help and assistance when it is needed is essential for group success ("I don't understand. I'm not sure what you mean.").

6. **Express Support And Acceptance**: Support can be expressed both verbally and nonverbally. Nonverbal support can be expressed through eye contact, nodding, and a look of interest. Verbal support includes praising and seeking others' ideas and conclusions.

7. **Offer To Explain Or Clarify**: When group members think that others may not understand, they should offer to explain or clarify ("Would you like me to go over this again?").

8. **Paraphrase**: Restating what other members have said in order to make certain that a message is understood or clarified. The purpose of paraphrasing is to negotiate for accurate understanding ("So you think that...?" "Do I understand you correctly to say...?").

9. **Energize The Group**: Members can energize the group to work hard to achieve their goals when motivation is low by suggesting new ideas, through humor, or by being enthusiastic ("Come on, let's get moving!").

10. **Describe Feelings**: There are times when describing feelings will be helpful to the group ("I'm puzzled about why we didn't do better." "Everyone got an A! That makes me happy.").

The mixture of keeping members on task, finding effective and efficient work procedures, and fostering a pleasant and friendly work atmosphere is vital for effective leadership in cooperative learning groups.

Formulating

Formulating skills are needed to provide the mental processes needed to build deeper level understanding of the material being studied, to stimulate the use of higher quality reasoning strategies, and to maximize mastery and retention of the assigned material. Since the purpose of learning groups is to maximize the learning of all members, there are skills specifically aimed at providing formal methods for processing the material being studied. They include:

1. **Summarize Out Loud**: Summarizing out loud what has just been read or discussed as completely as possible without referring to notes or to the original material. All the important ideas and facts should be included in the summary. Every member of the group must summarize from memory often if their learning is to be maximized.

2. **Seek Accuracy (Correct)**: Seeking accuracy by correcting a member's summary, adding important information he or she did not include, and pointing out the ideas or facts that were summarized incorrectly is important ("I'm not sure that is right, I thought it was...").

3. **Seek Elaboration**: Elaborating occurs when students relate material being learned to earlier learned material and to other things they know. Asking other group members to elaborate is an important aspect of learning ("This is like what we studied last week..." How does this relate to...?").

4. **Help The Group Remember**: Members should seek clever ways of remembering the important ideas and facts by using drawings, mental pictures, and other memory aids ("Here is a way to remember this...").

5. **Check For Understanding (Demand Vocalization)**: Demanding vocalization to make the implicit reasoning process being used by other members overt and thus open to correction and discussion.

6. **Ask For Others To Plan Out Loud**: Members should ask groupmates to plan out loud how they would teach or tell others about the material being studied. Planning how best to communicate the material can have important effects on quality of reasoning strategies and retention ("Here is how I would teach this material...").

Fermenting

Fermenting includes the skills needed to engage in **academic controversies** to stimulate reconceptualization of the material being studied, cognitive conflict, the search for more information, and the communication of the rationale behind one's conclusions. Some of the most important aspects of learning take place when group members skillfully challenge each other's conclusions and reasoning (Johnson & R. Johnson, 1979, 1987). Academic controversies cause group members to "dig deeper" into the material, to assemble a rationale for their conclusions, to think more divergently about the issue, to find more information to support their positions, and to argue constructively about alternative solutions or decisions. Some of the skills involved in academic controversies are:

1. **Criticize Ideas Without Criticizing People**: An important skill is intellectually challenging groupmates by criticizing their ideas while communicating respect for other group members ("I respect you, but in this case I have to disagree with your thinking.").

2. **Differentiate Ideas And Reasoning Of Group Members**: First find out how members' thinking differs ("How do our information and conclusions differ?").

3. **Integrate Ideas Into Single Positions**: After differentiating members' ideas and reasoning, students should synthesize and integrate them ("Would this combine everyone's ideas into a single conclusion?") .

4. **Ask For Justification**: Members should ask other members to give the facts and reasoning that justify why the member's conclusion or answer is the correct or appropriate one ("Why do you think this answer is correct?").

5. **Extend Answers**: Members should extent other members' answers or conclusions by adding further information or implications ("Here is something else to consider..." I also know...").

6. **Probe By Asking Indepth Questions**: Members ask questions that lead to deeper understanding or analysis ("Would it work in this situation . . .?" "What else makes you believe . . .?").

7. **Generate Further Answers**: Students should go beyond the first answer or conclusion by going beyond the first answer or conclusion and producing a number of plausible answers to choose from ("Would this also work...? Would this be another possibility?").

8. **Test Reality By Checking The Group's Work**: Members should check out the group's work with the instructions, available time, and other examples of reality ("Do we have enough time to do the work this way?").

These skills are among those that keep group members motivated to go beyond the quick answer to the highest quality one. They are aimed at stimulating the thinking and intellectual curiosity of group members.

Summary

Typically, teachers begin with the forming skills to ensure that the group members are present and oriented toward working with each other. The functioning skills then assist the group in operating smoothly and building constructive relationships among members. The formulating skills ensure that high quality learning takes place within the group and that the members engage in the necessary cognitive processing. The fermenting skills are the most complex and the most difficult to master. They ensure that intellectual challenge and disagreement take place within the learning groups.

The above skills are discussed in terms of upper elementary, secondary, and post-secondary students. Primary and preschool students will need simplified versions of the skills. It is important that teachers translate cooperative skills into language and images that their students can understand and identify with. For example, the fermenting skills could be simplified to skills such as adding an idea, asking for proof, and seeing the idea from the other person's shoes.

Section 3: How Do You Teach Cooperative Skills?

Learning cooperative skills is first of all procedural learning, very similar to learning how to play tennis or golf, how to perform brain surgery, or how to fly an airplane. Being skilled in managing conflicts involves more than simply reading material for a recognition-level or even a total-recall-level of mastery. It requires learning a procedure that is made up of a series of actions. **Procedural learning** exists when individuals:

1. Learn conceptually what the skill is and when it should be appropriately used.

2. Translate their conceptual understanding into a set of operational procedures (phrases and actions) appropriate for the people they are interacting with.

3. Actually engage in the skill.

4. Eliminate errors by moving through the phases of skill mastery.

5. Attain a routine-use, automated level of mastery.

Procedural learning involves breaking a complex process into its component parts and then systematically learning the process until it becomes automatic. It differs from simply learning facts and acquiring knowledge by relying heavily on feedback about performance and modifying one's implementation until the errors of performance are eliminated. It is a gradual process--one's efforts to perform the skill will fail to match the ideal of what one wishes to accomplish for a considerable length of time until the new strategy is overlearned at a routine-use, automated level. Failure is part of the process of gaining expertise, and success is inevitable when failure is followed by persistent practice, obtaining feedback, and reflecting on how to perform the skill more competently. Any complex process is best learned if it is proceduralized. The ultimate goal of procedural learning is to have students automatically perform the skill without having to think about it.

Learning a cooperative skill results from a process of:

1. Engaging in the skill.

2. Obtaining feedback.

3. Reflecting on the feedback.

4. Modifying one's enactment and engaging in the skill again.

5. Repeating steps 2, 3, and 4 again and again and again until the skill is appropriately used in a more and more automated fashion.

Gaining expertise takes "learning partners" who are willing to trust each other, talk frankly, and observe each other's performance over a prolonged period of time and help each other identify the errors being made in implementing the skill. Unless students are willing to reveal lack of expertise to obtain accurate feedback, expertise cannot be gained. In other words, procedural learning, and the mastery of all skills, requires cooperation among students.

One of the most important aspects of conducting cooperative learning lessons is identifying the students who are having difficulty in arguing effectively because of missing or underdeveloped cooperative skills. The part of the teacher's role dealing with monitoring highlights the importance of gathering data on students as they work and intervening to encourage more appropriate behavior. Teachers often assume that students have the social skills necessary for working cooperatively with others. This is often not the case, even when students are in high school or college. Family background, role models and the nature of the students' peer group all influence the development of such skills. The exciting part of teaching students to be more effective working with others is that the students not only gain a valuable set of skills for life, but have an excellent chance of raising their achievement as well.

There are five major steps in teaching cooperative skills:

1. Ensuring students **see the need** for the skill.

2. Ensuring students **understand** what the skill is and when it should be used.

3. Setting up **practice** situations and encouraging mastery of the skill.

4. Ensuring that students have the time and the needed **procedures for processing** (and receiving feedback on) how well they are using the skill.

5. Ensuring that students **persevere** in practicing the skill until the skill seems a natural action.

Step 1: Helping Students See the Need for the Skill

To be motivated to learn cooperative skills, students must believe that they are better off knowing, than not knowing, the skills. Teachers can promote students' awareness of the need for cooperative skills by:

1. **Displaying** in the room posters, bulletin boards, and other evidence that the teacher considers the skills to be important. It is often easy to see what is important in a classroom by looking at the walls, boards, and seating arrangements of the room.

2. **Communicating** to students why mastering the skills is important. With many students, sharing information about the need for cooperative skills in career and family settings is enough. Other students may benefit from experiencing how the skills help them do better work.

3. **Validating** the importance of the skills by assigning a grade or giving a reward to groups whose members demonstrate competence in the skills. Many teachers give learning groups two grades: one for achievement and one for the appropriate use of targeted cooperative skills.

There are other ways to communicate the importance of cooperative skills--covering the walls with postures, telling students how important the skills are, and rewarding students who use the skill, get teachers off to a good start.

Step 2: Ensuring Students Understand What the Skill Is

To learn a skill, students must have a clear idea of what the skill is and how to perform it. There is little chance of being too concrete in defining cooperative skills. Every student needs to know what to say or do to perform the skill. A number of strategies teachers can use in ensuring students understand what a skill is and when it is to be appropriately used are:

1. **Helping students generate specific phrases and behaviors that express the skill.** "Do you agree?" asks for a "yes" or "no" answer and is, therefore, a much less effective encouraging question than is "How would you explain the answer?" The class may

wish to list phrases the teacher should hear in each group as the teacher monitors the group's effectiveness. The list can then be prominently displayed for reference.

2. **Demonstrating, modeling, and having students role play the skill** are all effective procedures for clearly defining the skill. Setting up a short counter-example where the skill is obviously missing is one way to emphasize the skill and illustrate the need for it at the same time.

Teachers should not try to teach too many skills at the same time. Start with one or two. One first-grade curriculum unit we have helped with teaches eight skills over a year's time, starting with "Everyone does a job" and including "Sharing ideas and materials," "Giving directions without being bossy," and "Caring about others' feelings."

Step 3: Setting Up Repetitive Practice Situations

To master a skill, students need to practice it again and again. Students should be asked to role play the skill several times with the person sitting next to them immediately after the skill is defined. An initial practice session should be long enough for the skill to be fairly well learned by each student, and then short practice sessions should be distributed across several days or weeks. As students practice, teachers should continue to give verbal instructions and encourage students to perform the skills with proper sequence and timing. Some of the strategies found effective for encouraging practice are:

1. **Assigning specific roles to group members to ensure practice of the skills.** A teacher, for example, could assign the roles of reader, encourager, summarizer, and elaboration-seeker to the members of a cooperative learning group. The roles could be rotated daily until every student has been responsible for each role several times.

2. **Announcing that the occurrence of the skills will be observed.** It is surprising how much practice of a skill occurs when the teacher announces that he or she will be looking for a specific skill and stands next to a group with an observation sheet. The teacher's presence and the knowledge that the frequency of the skills is being counted and valued by the teacher (or a student observer) is a potent motivater of practice.

3. **Using nonacademic skill-building exercises to provide students with a chance to practice cooperative skills.** There may be times when an exercise that is fun and not part of the ongoing work of the class can be used to encourage students to practice specific skills. There are many such exercises available (Johnson, 1990, 1991; Johnson & F. Johnson, 1991; Johnson & R. Johnson, 1991).

New skills need to be cued consistently and reinforced for some time. Teachers should be relentless in encouraging prolonged use of cooperative skills.

Step 4: Ensuring That Students Process Their Use of the Skills

Practicing cooperative skills is not enough. **Students must process how frequently and how well they are using the skill.** Students need to discuss, describe, and reflect on their use of the skills in order to improve their performance. To ensure that students discuss and give each other feedback about their use of the skills, teachers need to provide a regular time for group processing and give students group processing procedures to follow. The following strategies may help:

1. **Provide regular time for processing.** Ten minutes at the end of each period, or 20 minutes once a week are typical.

2. **Provide a set of procedures for students to follow**. A processing sheet that the group fills out together, signs, and then hands in may be useful. Questions might include, "How many members felt they had a chance to share their ideas in their group?" and "How many members felt listened to?" The most effective procedure, however, is to have one member of the group observe the frequency with which each member engages in one of the targeted conflict management skills and, in the discussion at the end of the period, give each member feedback about his or her performance.

3. **Provide opportunities for positive feedback among group members.** One procedure is to have each member told by every other member one action that reflected effective use of a conflict management skill.

A standard processing task is, "Name three things your group did well and name one thing your group could do even better next time." Such group processing will not only increase students' interpersonal and small group skills, it will also increase achievement (Johnson, Johnson, Stanne, & Garibaldi, in press; Yager, Johnson, & Johnson, 1985) and the quality of the relationships developed among students (Putnam, Johnson, Rynders, & Johnson, 1989). Teachers may have to model the processing initially and periodically so that students will take the processing seriously and become adept at doing it.

Step 5: Ensuring That Students Persevere in Practicing the Skills

With most skills there is a period of slow learning, then a period of rapid improvement, then a period where performance remains about the same, then another period of rapid improvement, then another plateau, and so forth. **Students have to practice cooperative skills long enough to make it through the first few plateaus and integrate the skills into their behavioral repertoires.** There are a set of stages that most skill development goes through:

1. **Awareness** that the skill is needed.

2. **Understanding** of what the skill is.

3. Self-conscious, **awkward engaging** in the skill. Practicing any new skill feels awkward. The first few times someone throws a football, plays a piano, or paraphrases, it feels strange.

4. Feelings of **phoniness** while **engaging** in the skill. After a while the awkwardness passes and enacting the skill becomes more smooth. Many students, however, feel unauthentic or phony while using the skill. Teacher and peer encouragement are needed to move the students through this stage.

5. Skilled but **mechanical use** of the skill.

6. **Automatic, routine use** where the skill is fully integrated into students' behavior repertoire and seems like a natural action to engage in.

In order for students to move from awareness to the automatic use of the skills teachers have to encourage sustained practice of the skills over a long period of time. **Persistence in practicing the cooperative skills is essential.** Whenever students feel awkward in engaging in the skill, when they feel phony, or when it feels mechanical, the immediate response by the teacher should be that more practice is needed. Make sure that lots of practice occurs. The goal for all cooperative skill learning is to reach the stage where teachers can structure a lesson cooperatively and have students automatically and naturally engage in a high level of cooperative skills while achieving their learning goals. Ways to ensure that students persevere are to continue to assign the skill as a group role, continue to give students feedback as to how frequently and how well they are performing the skill, and reinforcing the groups when members use the skill. We have found that students (even socially isolated and withdrawn students) learned more social skills and engaged in them more frequently when the group was given bonus points for members doing so (Lew, Mesch, Johnson, & Johnson, 1986a, 1986b).

Using Bonus Points To Teach Social Skills

Many teachers may want to use a structured program to teach students the interpersonal and small group skills they need to cooperative effectively with classmates. Such a program will provide students with the opportunity to help earn bonus points for their groups as a result of their using targeted cooperative skills. These points can be accumulated for academic credit or for special rewards such as free time or minutes listening to one's own choice of music. The procedure for doing so is as follows:

1. **Identify, define, and teach a social skill** you want students to use in working cooperatively with each other. This skill becomes a target for mastery. The skills may be **forming** skills of staying with your group and using quiet voices, **functioning** skills of giving direction to the group's work and encouraging participation, **formulating** skills of explaining answers, relating present learning to past learning, and **fermenting** skills of criticizing ideas without criticizing people, asking probing questions, and requesting further rationale (Johnson, Johnson, & Holubec, 1988).

2. **Use group points** and group rewards to increase the use of the cooperative skill:

   a. Each time a student engages in the targeted skill, the student's group receives a point.

   b. Points may only be awarded for positive behavior.

   c. Points are added and never taken away. All points are permanently earned.

3. **Summarize total points daily.** Emphasize daily progress toward the goal. Use a visual display such as a graph or chart.

4. **Develop an observational system** that samples each group an equal amount of time. In addition, utilize student observers to record the frequency of students using the targeted skills.

5. **Set a reasonable number of points for earning the reward.** Rewards are both social and tangible. The **social rewards** are having the teacher say, "That shows thought," "I like the way you explained it," "That's a good way of putting it," "Remarkably well done." The **tangible reward** is the points earned, which may be traded in for free time, computer time, library time, time to a play a game, extra recess time, and any other activity that students value.

6. In addition to group points, **class points** may be awarded. The teacher, for example, might say, "Eighteen people are ready to begin and helped the class earn a reward," or "I noticed 12 people worked the last 25 minutes." Class points may be recorded with a number line, beans in a jar, or checks on the chalk board.

7. In addition to social skills, **potential target behaviors** include following directions, completing assigned tasks, handing in homework, behaving appropriately in out-of-class settings such as lunch or assemblies, or helping substitute teachers.

Group Size And Social Skills

The larger the group the more the social skills required for members to interact effectively. The number of response bonds in a group is determined by $n(n-1)$, that is, the number of group members multiplied by one less than that number. In a dyad, there are two response bonds to manage. In a triad, there are six response bonds to manage. In a group of four, there are twelve response bonds to mange. In a group of five, there are 20 response bonds to manage. Considerable more skill is required to interact within a group of four than a group of three.

Conclusion

If the potential of cooperative learning is to be realized, students must have the prerequisite interpersonal and small group skills and be motivated to use them. These skills need to be taught just as systematically as math and social studies. Doing so involves communicating to students the need for the social skills, defining and modeling the skills, having students practice the skills over and over again, processing how effectively the students are performing the skills, and ensuring that students persevere until the skills are fully integrated into their behavioral repertoires. Doing so will not only increase student achievement, it will also increase students' future employability, career success, quality of relationships, and psychological health.

Nothing we learn is more important than the skills required to work cooperatively with other people. Most human interaction is cooperative. Without some skill in cooperating effectively, it is difficult (if not impossible) to maintain a marriage, hold a job, or be part of a community, society, and world. In this chapter we have only discussed a few of the interpersonal and small group skills needed for effective cooperation. For a more thorough and extensive coverage of these skills see **Reaching Out** (Johnson, 1990), **Joining Together** (Johnson & F. Johnson, 1991), **Human Relations and Your Career** (Johnson, 1991), and **Learning Together And Alone** (Johnson & R. Johnson, 1991).

Implementation Assignment 5

1. Read Chapter 6.

2. Review the behaviors you have been encouraging when you structure cooperative lessons. Ask your class what behaviors are needed to make cooperative learning groups effective and list them. Have the class star the three behaviors they think are the most important.

3. For each of the three skills identified above have your students construct a T-Chart. Bring the charts to class to share with your base group.

4. Teach one cooperative skill to the whole class.

5. Note in your journal the cooperative skills you wish to improve on.

⚔️ Cooperative Learning Contract ⚔️

Major Learnings	Implementation Plans

Date _____ Date of Progress Report Meeting _____

Participant's Signature _____

Signatures of Other Group Members _____ _____

_____ _____ _____

⚔ Cooperative Learning Progress Report ⚔

NAME _____   SCHOOL _____

AGE LEVEL _____   SUBJECT _____

DAY AND DATE	DESCRIPTION OF TASKS and ACTIVITIES PERFORMED	SUCCESSES EXPERIENCED	PROBLEMS ENCOUNTERED

Description of critical or interesting incidents:

EXERCISE

MATERIALS

Social Skills Planning Unit

David W. Johnson and Roger T. Johnson

What Are the Social Skills You Are Going to Teach?

1. _____
2. _____
3. _____
4. _____

STEP 1: How Are You Going to Communicate the Need for the Social Skills?

_____ 1. Room displays, posters, bulletin boards, and so forth.

_____ 2. Telling students why the skills are needed.

_____ 3. Jigsawing materials on the need for the skills.

_____ 4. Having groups work on a cooperative lesson and then asking students to brainstorm what skills are needed to help the group function effectively.

_____ 5. Giving bonus points or a separate grade for the competent use of the skills.

_____ 6. Other(s): _____

_____

_____

STEP 2: How Are You Going to Define the Skill?

1. Phrases (list 3):

_____

_____

_____

2. Behaviors (list 3):

_____

_____

_____

Social Skills Planning Unit

3. How will you explain and model each social skill?

_____ a. Demonstrating the skill, explaining each step of engaging in
           the skill, and then redemonstrating the skill.

_____ b. Using a videotape or film to demonstrate and explain the skill.

_____ c. Asking each group to plan role-play demonstrations of the
           skill to present to the entire class.

_____ d. Other(s): _____

           _____

           _____

STEP 3: How Will You Ensure that
Students Practice the Skill?

_____ 1. Assigning specific roles to group members ensuring practice of the
           skills.

_____ 2. Announcing that you will observe for the skills.

_____ 3. Having specific practice sessions involving nonacademic tasks.

_____ 4. Other(s): _____

           _____

           _____

STEP 4: How Will You Ensure Students Receive
Feedback and Process Their Use of the Skills?

Teacher Monitoring

_____ 1. Structured observation with the Social Skills Observation
           sheet, focusing on each learning group an equal amount of time
           (30 minutes, 6 groups, each group is observed for 5 minutes).

_____ 2. Structured observation with the Social Skills Observation
           sheet, focusing only on the learning groups in which target stu-
           dents (emotional/behavior problem students, handicapped students,
           low achieving students, and so forth) are members.

_____ 3. Anecdotal observation (eavesdropping) to record the significant,
           specific events involving students engaging in interaction with
           each other.

_____ 4. Other(s): _____

           _____

           _____

Teacher Intervening

1. If the social skills are not being used in a cooperative group, I will:

    _____ a. Ask the group what it has done so far and what it plans to try next to increase the use of the controversy skills.

    _____ b. Other: _____

    _____

2. If the social skills are being used in a cooperative group, I will:

    _____ a. Note it on the observation sheet or anecdotal record and come back to the group during the processing time, call attention to the use of the skills, and compliment the group.

    _____ b. Interrupt the group, call attention to the use of the skills, and compliment the group.

    _____ c. Call attention to it during the whole-class processing.

    _____ d. Other: _____

    _____

Student Observing

1. Student observers will be selected by: _____

2. Student observers will be trained by: _____

3. Time for the student observers to give group members feedback will be provided by:

    _____

During the group processing time, students will:

_____ 1. Receive feedback from the teacher.

_____ 2. Receive feedback from the student observer.

_____ 3. Complete a skills checklist or say/write: *Things I did today that helped my group are . . .*

_____ 4. Say/write: *Things I plan to do differently next time to help my group work better are . . .*

_____ 5. Say/write: *What I learned about being a good group member is . . .*

_____ 6. Other: _____

    _____

Social Skills Planning Unit

STEP 5: Ensure that Students Persevere
in Practicing the Skills

I will provide continued opportunity for students to practice and repractice the collaborative skills by:

_____ 1. Assigning the collaborative skills to group members for _____ sessions.

_____ 2. Assigning the collaborative skills to the groups as a whole with all members being responsible for their use _____ sessions.

_____ 3. Asking another teacher, an aide, or a parent volunteer to tutor and coach target students in the use of the skill.

_____ 4. Asking the groups to process how well each member is using the skill for _____ sessions.

_____ 5. Intermittently spending a class session on training students to use and reuse the skill.

_____ 6. Intermittently giving any group whose members use the skill above a certain criterion a reward of _____

_____ 7. Other(s):

_____

_____

_____

ADD-ON OBSERVATION SHEET

Start by teaching one skill and observing for it. Show students how well they do in practicing that skill; praise and otherwise reward their efforts. When they have mastered one skill, add and teach a second skill, etc.

DATE _____   PERIOD _____   OBSERVER _____

Skills	Group Members			

er Observation Notes: 5:31

© Johnson & Johnson

START

PROBE BY ASKING IN-DEPTH QUESTIONS

GENERATE FURTHER ANSWERS

TEST REALITY BY CHECKING THE GROUP'S WORK

EXTEND OTHER MEMBERS' ANSWERS

ASK FOR JUSTIFICATION

INTEGRATE IDEAS INTO SINGLE POSITIONS

DIFFERENTIATE WHEN THERE IS DISAGREEMENT

CRITICIZE IDEAS, NOT PEOPLE

FORMING

MOVE WITHOUT NOISE

STAY WITH THE GROUP

USE QUIET VOICES

FERMENT

ASK OTHER MEMBERS TO PLAN OUT LOUD

ENCOURAGE PARTICIPATION BY ALL

DEMAND VOCALIZATION

C O O P E R A T I V E

S K I L L S

FUNCTIONING

USE NAMES, LOOK AT THE SPEAKER AND USE NO PUT-DOWNS

SEEK CLEVER WAYS OF REMEMBERING IDEAS AND FACTS

DIRECT GROUP'S WORK

SEEK ELABORATION

EXPRESS SUPPORT

SEEK ACCURACY BY CORRECTING &/OR ADDING TO SUMMARIES

ASK FOR HELP OR CLARIFICATION

OFFER TO EXPLAIN OR CLARIFY

PARAPHRASE OTHERS' WORK

SUMMARIZE OUT LOUD

5:32

ENERGIZE THE GROUP

DESCRIBE FEELINGS WHEN APPROPRIATE

FORMULATING

𝔖𝔬𝔠𝔦𝔞𝔩 𝔖𝔨𝔦𝔩𝔩𝔰 𝔗𝔯𝔞𝔫𝔰𝔩𝔞𝔱𝔦𝔬𝔫 𝔖𝔥𝔢𝔢𝔱

What is the targeted social skill ? _____

_____

How will the skill be introduced so that each student sees a need to develop it?

_____

_____

_____

_____

How is the skill defined?

Specific phrases _____

_____

_____

Specific behaviors _____

_____

_____

How will the skill be practiced?

Teacher encouragement strategies _____

_____

_____

_____

Peer encouragement strategies _____

_____

_____

Parent encouragement strategies _____

_____

_____

_____

How will use of the skill be processed?

Teacher _____

_____

How will use of the skill be processed?

Peer _____

_____

How is perseverance going to be built in for this skill?

_____

_____

_____

_____

_____

What would you like your students to be like when this skill is mastered?

_____

_____

_____

Where can you get support for teaching and encouraging practice of this skill? _____

_____

_____

■ Guided Practice: Teaching A Social Skill ■

Task: Practice teaching social skills to your students.

Cooperative: Working in a pair, role play teaching a social skill to your classes. Teach the social skill as if the other person were your class. Use the following procedure:

1. Say to your class, *"Stop working, close your books, look at me."*

2. With the assistance of your students in a whole class discussion, construct a T-Chart for the skill.

3. State:
   a. *"Your task is to learn the skill of summarizing."*
   b. *"Work cooperatively. Make sure you can summarize, everyone in your group can summarize, and every group member can explain what the skill of summarizing is."*

4. Have the students practice the skill twice, using two different phrases.

5. Instruct students to resume work. Observe each group and note whether the skill of summarizing is being used by group members.

6. Repeat the above sequence with the following skills (each person teaches two social skills):
   a. Giving direction to the group's work.
   b. Asking for help or clarification.
   c. Criticizing ideas without criticizing people.

Expected Criteria For Success: Both persons able to teach a social skill using a T-Chart.

Individual Accountability: Each person teaches two social skills to the other.

Expected Behaviors: Presenting, listening, processing, and encouraging.

Intergroup Cooperation: Whenever it is helpful, check your task and positive interdependence statements with another group.

Chapter 6

Processing For Effective Cooperation

Table Of Contents

What Is Group Processing?

Introduction

Groups need specific time to discuss how well they are (1) achieving their goals and (2) maintaining effective working relationships among members. Groups need to describe what member actions were helpful and unhelpful and make decisions about what member actions to continue or change. Such processing enables task groups to focus on group maintenance, facilitates the learning of collaborative skills, ensures members receive feedback on their participation, and reminds members to practice collaborative skills consistently. Having students reflect on how well they are collaborating need not always follow the same format or require the same degree of time and energy. Sometimes processing will be quite thorough and take some time. At other times processing will be quite brief and short. **Whether thorough or brief, having groups reflect on their effectiveness is an integral part of cooperative learning.**

After reading this chapter and implementing the recommended activities, you will:

1. Understand conceptually and operationally what group processing is.

2. Be prepared to monitor cooperative learning groups and structure group processing so that students:

   a. Receive feedback on how effectively they are collaborating with their peers.

   b. Make decisions on how to increase both members' learning and the quality of members' relationships.

3. Be skilled in:

   a. Observing and intervening within cooperative learning groups.

   b. Structuring cooperative learning groups so that a member of each group observes the group's functioning.

c. Promoting effective processing within each learning group.

d. Promoting effective whole class processing.

Nature Of Group Processing

A junior-high math teacher was puzzled because his students continued to use put-downs and would not help each other despite the emphasis the he was placing on support and assistance. When asked what his students said about why such behavior was taking place the teacher said, "We rarely have time to discuss how well the groups are functioning." The teacher immediately realized that it was the lack of self-examination by the groups that was creating the situation in which the destructive behavior could continue. The students needed to become more aware of the negative impact of put-downs and of the positive impact of supportive statements on the productivity of their learning groups.

There are two views of group processing, one differentiating outcome from process goals and one differentiating content from process. All teams have outcome goals, such as high productivity. In addition, cooperative learning groups have process goals, such as optimizing the utilization of all members' resources. A **process** is an identifiable sequence of events taking place over time, and **process goals** refer to the sequence of events instrumental in achieving outcome goals. Members engage in group processing when they discuss (1) how well their group is functioning and (2) how they may improve the group's effectiveness. More specifically, **group processing** may be defined as reflecting on a group session to (1) describe what member actions were helpful and unhelpful and (2) make decisions about what actions to continue or change. For example, members of a cooperative group may decide that they are all contributing well in getting the task done but that more praising would increase their productivity. They then would resolve to praise each other's contributions more frequently in the future. The purposes of group processing are to clarify and improve the effectiveness of the members in contributing to the collaborative efforts to learn.

A second view of group processing contrasts it with the content of the learning assignment. A distinction may be made between the **content** the group is discussing and the **process** by which the discussion is being conducted. Content is **what** is being discussed and process is **how** the group members are interacting and whether effective leadership, communication, decision-making, trust-building, and conflict-management skills are being employed.

One of the current disagreements among proponents of cooperative learning is whether or not cooperative learning groups need to process how well they are functioning. Aronson, Blaney, Stephan, Sikes, and Snapp (1978), DeVries, Slavin, Fennessey, Edwards, and Lombardo (1980), Sharan and Sharan (1976), and Slavin (1983) emphasize the achievement of outcome goals only. The authors of this book (Johnson & Johnson, 1987; Johnson, Johnson, & Holubec, 1986), and Dishon and O'Leary (1984) however, emphasize that cooperative learning groups need to process how well they are functioning in order to maximize their effectiveness. This latter view follows the group dynamics literature which has emphasized the importance of group processing (Cartwright & Zander, 1968; Johnson & F. Johnson, 1987; Napier & Gerschenfeld, 1981; Schmuck & Schmuck, 1982).

Research On Processing

Few attempts have been made to investigate the impact of group processing on group productivity. Recently, a study was completed on the impact of (a) cooperative learning in which members discussed how well their group was functioning and how they could improve its effectiveness, (b) cooperative learning without any group processing, and (c) individualistic learning on daily achievement, post-instructional achievement, and retention (Yager, Johnson, & Johnson, 1986). Eighty-four third-grade American students were randomly assigned to the three conditions stratifying for sex and ability level. Students worked for 35 minutes a day for 25 instructional days on a transportation unit.

The results indicate that the high-, medium-, and low-achieving students in the cooperation-with-group-processing condition achieved higher than did the students in the other two conditions. Students in the cooperation-without-group-processing condition achieved higher on all three measures than did the students in the individualistic condition. Having members of cooperative learning groups discuss how well their group is functioning and how they may improve its effectiveness had a sizable and positive effect on student achievement. Through gaining insight into how to behave more effectively and/or generating feedback that (a) informed group members how to improve their effectiveness and (b) reinforced them for engaging in collaborative skills, members increased their productivity. Up to three weeks after the end of the instructional unit, their achievement gains stayed considerably higher than those of members of cooperative learning groups that did not process their functioning and students working individualistically.

There are a few studies on the impact of self-monitoring on individual performance in group and organizational settings. Sarason and Potter (1983), for example, examined the impact of individual self-monitoring of thoughts on self-efficacy and successful performance and found that having individuals focus their attention on self-efficacious thoughts is related to greater task persistence and less cognitive interference. They conclude that the more people are aware of what they are experiencing, the more aware they will be of their own role in determining their success.

Models Of Group Processing

There are at least two models of group processing (Johnson, 1979; Johnson & F. Johnson, 1987). The first is a **"counseling" model**. It assumes that self-examination leads to insight, which leads to increased effectiveness. From the counseling model, group processing consists of members analyzing the group's functioning (self-examination), having insights into the strengths and problems in functioning, and planning for more effective actions to be taken in the future. The components of the counseling model include self-monitoring by observing the group's functioning, discussing the results of the observation, a heightened self-awareness of the effective and ineffective actions taken during the group meetings, public commitment to increase the frequency of effective actions and decrease the frequency of ineffective actions, and an increased sense of having the ability to be more effective if appropriate effort is exerted (i.e., **self-efficacy**).

The second is the **feedback model** (Johnson, 1979). From this model group processing is aimed at providing accurate and nonthreatening feedback concerning the procedures the group is using to achieve its outcome goals. The feedback gives group members information that helps them improve performance. And it reinforces students for engaging in collaborative skills. Both the information and reinforcement aspects of feedback are viewed as important aspects of group processing.

In both models, **group processing depends on**:

1. Observing student-student interaction.

2. Using the observations to provide feedback to individual students and the group as a whole.

3. Reflecting on the feedback to identify problems they have in functioning effectively.

4. Planning how to be more effective next time they work together.

Importance Of Group Processing

To be productive groups have to "process" how well they are working and take action to resolve any difficulties members have in collaborating together productively. **Every learning experience is also a lesson in learning how to collaborate when the**  **group members process how well their group functioned.** Group processing, however, has been relatively ignored in most models of cooperative learning. While a great deal of attention has been paid to structuring materials and organizing instruction to promote cooperative learning, little attention has been focused on training teachers (and students) to promote the processing by group members of their collaborative efforts to achieve. Theoretically, empirically, and practically, group processing has been ignored.

Just placing students in cooperative learning groups and telling them to collaborate does not mean that they can or will do so. Students must learn **what** social skills are needed for a cooperative learning group to function effectively and **when** the social skills should be used. To do this, students must discuss what collaborative skills are and are not being used in the group and plan how they may improve their performance. Following each learning session, or periodically during the life of the group, teachers will wish to schedule time for students to reflect on and process the effectiveness of their learning groups. This processing need not always follow the same format or require the same degree of time and energy. Sometimes processing will be quite brief and short. At other times processing will be quite thorough and take some time. Whether thorough or brief, an integral part of cooperative learning is having groups reflect on their effectiveness.

Group processing is important for the group as a whole and for individual students. **Some of the most important reasons for having cooperative groups process include the following:**

1. If students are to learn from their experience in working together, they must reflect on that experience. Unexamined experience rarely benefits anyone. Both self-efficacy and group-efficacy are built through examining the interaction among group members to determine how it may be modified to improve the group's productivity.

2. Problems in collaborating effectively may be prevented from reoccurring by group processing. By reflecting on problems in collaborating in September, groups will be managing those problems effectively in November.

3. Systematic processing of group functioning promotes the development and use of cooperative skills. Knowing that they are being observed to see how frequently they engage in targeted skills increases students' awareness of those skills and motivates them to use the skills. Conscious practice of collaborative skills in ensured by systematic group processing.

4. When groups first begin to work together, they tend to be very task oriented. Processing gives the groups the time they need to maintain effective working relationships.

Processing will especially help students who have difficulty in appropriately relating to classmates. Students who poke or push others, ridicule their classmates, are too shy to interact, do not do their homework or contribute to the group's success,

or otherwise indulge in behavior that keeps them from being accepted and liked by their classmates, will receive considerable benefit from the group processing. They will learn and practice acceptable behavior and start down the difficult path toward being more socially skilled.

Effective Vs. Ineffective Processing

Effective processing (a) promotes a sense of self-efficacy rather than helplessness, (b) focuses group members on positive rather than negative behaviors, and (c) creates meta-cognitive examination of individual and group functioning.

Processing And Self-Efficacy. One of the aims of group processing is to increase members' feelings of efficacy by empowering group members to feel that they can increase their productivity. **Self-efficacy** is the expectation of successfully obtaining valued outcomes through personal effort. Some of the consequences of an increased sense of self-efficacy are increased task orientation, increased persistence in completing learning tasks, greater confidence that they can successfully learn, and decreased self-doubt and self-preoccupation which may interfere with learning. **Group efficacy** is the expectation of successfully obtaining valued outcomes through the joint efforts of the group members. In cooperative learning situations the effort available includes one's own and the effort of one's collaborators. The knowledge that there is to be a team effort in achieving the group's goal provides added confidence that the group will be successful. The greater the sense of self- and joint-efficacy promoted by group processing, the more productive and effective group members and the group as a whole become.

Positive Versus Negative Categories. Monitoring of one's own and one's collaborators' actions begins with deciding which behaviors to direct one's attention towards. Knowing that certain behaviors are possible and reasonable can change a person's train of thought and cognitive focus. Individuals can focus either on positive and effective behaviors, or on negative and ineffective behaviors. A positive focus may result in feelings of satisfaction and efficacy. **Positive monitoring** is linked to the emission of thoughts and statements that reflect positively on oneself and one's collaborators. Someone whose attention is drawn to recent personal successes may come to attend to positive personal qualities. The more group members are aware of their competent, effective, successful actions, the more aware they will be of their own role in determining individual and group success, and the more confident they will be in their ability to be productive and effective. Positive attributions (e.g., "I'm an intelligent person who can do well on this task"; "We are a hard-working and committed group") are particularly effective in (a) countering the worrying and self-preoccupation that often cause poor performance and (b) fostering a sense of efficacy.

Negative monitoring is linked to negative statements about oneself and others. A negative focus may result in feelings of dissatisfaction and incompetence and can exacerbate the group's difficulties. Negative monitoring (that is, monitoring unpleasant, unrewarding, frustrating, destructive, counterproductive behaviors) may focus attention unduly on the stressful and unpleasant events in the group. Hypersensitivity to negative behaviors and attitudes and seeking to blame someone for any problems the group has in functioning may lead to destructive conflict, chronic complaining, and feelings of helplessness and dissatisfaction.

Meta-Cognitions. Meta-cognition is the "thinking about how one thinks" or the reflection on how one functions within a learning situation. When members of cooperative learning groups are discussing how they are interacting and functioning they are engaging in meta-cognitive activity. The more able students are to reflect on their functioning with academic learning situations, the better. Group processing is a structured way of requiring meta-cognitive thought.

Procedures For Processing

Scheduling processing involves two main elements:

1. Teachers must set aside time for students to reflect on their experiences in working with each other in their cooperative learning groups.

2. Teachers must give students a structure and a set of procedures for discussing how well the group is functioning and how well the members are using collaborative skills.

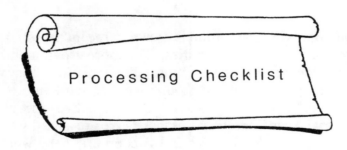

Processing Checklist

☐ 1. I have decided what two or three skills and behaviors I am going to concentrate on and observe for and have taught the students those skills.

☐ 2. I have appointed the observers (either teacher, students or visitor), prepared the appropriate observation form (one for each observer), and explained the form to the observers.

☐ 3. I have observed and intervened when necessary.

☐ 4. I have had the group members assess how often and well they performed the collaborative skills.

☐ 5. I have had the observer report to the group the information gathered and have had the group members report their impressions as to how they behaved.

☐ 6. I have had group members reflect on and analyze the effectiveness of their behavior by comparing the observed behavior with their own impressions of and expectations for their performance of the targeted collaborative skills. I have reinforced with compliments and praise those group members who used the skills frequently and appropriately.

☐ 7. I have had the group members set goals to strengthen their collaborative skills in the next group session.

Teachers have two basic options for providing students time to process how well they are collaborating. The first is to provide ten minutes or so at the end of each group session for immediate processing. The second is to take a longer period of time, such as thirty minutes, once every week or so. When cooperative learning groups first meet, it is best to use the first option and leave ten or fifteen minutes each day for the students to process. This helps emphasize the self-examination and reflection that is necessary for the groups to be effective. It also gives students an opportunity to discuss the group process while it is fresh in their memory, and helps immediately reinforce the use of group skills. After students become used to processing and become proficient in using collaborative skills, processing sessions can then become intermittent, perhaps once a week or so, just to remind students to stay focused on improving their collaborative skills.

The procedures for processing are:

1. **Decide** what skills and behaviors you are going to emphasize and observe for and **teach (or precue)** students the skills.

2. **Appoint** observers (teacher, students, visitor), **prepare** observation forms (one for each observer), **explain** observation form to observers.

3. **Observe** and **intervene** when necessary while groups complete the task.

4. Group members may **assess** how often and how well they individually performed the collaborative skills.

5. Observer **reports** to the group the information gathered and group members report their impressions as to how they behaved.

6. Group members **reflect on** and **analyze** the effectiveness of their behavior by comparing their observed behavior with their own impressions of and expectations for their performance of the targeted collaborative skills. Group members who used the skills frequently and appropriately are complimented **(reinforced)**.

7. Group members publicly **set goals** for performing collaborative skills in the next group session.

Deciding/Precuing

When setting the objectives for the lesson, both academic and collaborative skill objectives are usually set. At first the forming collaborative skills might need to be emphasized, with students practicing "twelve-inch" voices and staying with their group. Then functioning skills may be taught with the formulating and fermenting skills being emphasized once students have become skillful in cooperating. More specifically, teachers may wish to:

1. Prepare lists of collaborative skills that will be encouraged over an extended period of time. The goal is for **all** students to use the skills effectively.

2. Choose the collaborative skills that will be observed in the lesson.

3. Plan the daily observation sheet (or select one of the available ones). Observation Sheet 3 may save time when different collaborative skills are observed daily or weekly.

One procedure for precuing students as to the skills to be emphasized is through the use of **task cards**. Each day the groups can be given a card summarizing their tasks. The card lists the components of the task and includes a box to be marked when that component has been completed. An example of such a task card might be:

_____ Write down five causes of World War II.

_____ Each group member shares his or her ideas.

_____ Members encouraged each other to participate.

Appointing/Preparing/Explaining

There are three alternative sources of observers: the teacher, students, and visitors. The teacher may decide to be an observer or to use students or a visitor as observers, or to use some combination of the three. Often both the teacher and a student from each group are used as observers. After observers are appointed, an appropriate observation form is prepared (suitable to the age of the student and the behaviors to be observed), and it is explained both to the observers and to the class as a whole.

Observing

To process how productively cooperative groups are functioning there must first
be observation. **Observation** is aimed at
recording and describing members' behavior as it occurs in the group, that is, to
provide objective data about the interaction among group members. The behavior
of group members is observed so that students may be given feedback about their
participation in the group and so that inferences can be made about the ways in
which the group is functioning. Observation procedures may be structured or un-
structured. **There are five steps usually involved in structured observation:**

1. Decide which cooperative skills you wish to observe.

2. Construct or find an observation sheet that specifies the cooperative skills you wish to observe.

3. Observe the group and, on the observation sheet, record how often each student performs the specified behaviors.

4. Summarize your observations in a clear and useful manner and present them to the group as feedback.

5. Help group members make inferences from your observations about how well the group functioned, how frequently and well each member engaged in the targeted skills, and how the group process should be revised to make it more effective.

The purpose of the observation is to provide for the group an objective assessment of how well they used the targeted collaborative skills so they can discuss and

OBSERVATION

Directions for Use: (a) Put names of group members above each column. (b) Put a mark in the appropriate box each time a group member contributes. (c) Make notes o back when interesting things happen which are not captured by the categories. (d) It good idea to collect one (or more) good things that each group member does.

		Student A	Student B	Student C	Student D	Student E
1	CONTRIBUTES IDEAS					
2	DESCRIBES FEELINGS					
3	PARAPHRASES					
4	EXPRESSES SUPPORT, ACCEPTANCE, AND LIKING					
5	ENCOURAGES OTHERS TO CONTRIBUTE					
6	SUMMARIZES					
7	RELIEVES TENSION BY JOKING					
8	GIVES DIRECTION TO GROUP'S WORK					
	TOTALS					

Trusting: 1, 2; Trustworthy-Acceptance: 3, 4; Trustworthy-Reciprocation: 1, 2; **Lead** Task: 1, 2, 6, 7; Leadership-Maintenance: 3, 4, 5, 8; Communication: 1, 2, 3 (and, technica all the rest); Conflict-Resolution: 1, 2, 3.

modify group procedures and members' behavior. The untrained observer confuses two tasks:

1. Recording what the students do while they work in cooperative learning groups.

2. Making inferences and interpretations about how well the students are collaborating.

Observation should be descriptive, not interpretative. Providing groups with descriptive information about their functioning involves counting the frequency with which certain collaborative skills are used. Overall judgments about the skillfulness of the group members or interpretations about why the skills are not being used should be avoided. The observer collects descriptive information about group functioning. Group members make the inferences and interpretations about what the information means.

When structured observation sheets are used, the following general rules may be helpful:

1. Make a mark in the appropriate box on the observation sheet every time you see or hear a student using a collaborative skill.

2. Be alert for nonverbal messages, such as smiles, nods, pointing, eye contact, and so forth.

3. Do not worry about recording everything, but observe as accurately and as rapidly as possible.

4. Make notes on the back of the observation sheet if something that should be shared with the group takes place but does not fit into the categories being observed.

5. Collect one (or more) effective actions each member takes during the session.

6. Write down specific words or phrases to help you recall examples when you report your observations to the group.

The observation sheets should be kept to assess the growth of the students and the groups. The daily information may be transferred to long-term record sheets. When the group is observed more than once during a session, different colored ink may be used. This allows individuals to assess skill development at a glance.

Unstructured observations may be made by recording significant, specific events involving students collaborating with each other. The characteristics of such "eavesdropping" are that the observations are specific, they are brief enough to be written down quickly, they capture an important aspect of the behavior of one or more students, and they provide help in answering questions about the successful implementation of cooperative learning.

Gathering Impressions From Group Members

Besides the information gathered by observers, **information about how well the group functioned may be gathered from the group members.** The easiest way to do so is through a checklist or questionnaire about how the individual member or other group members behaved. Group members complete the checklist or questionnaire, giving their impressions as to how well they or the group functioned. **The focus of the questions could be what the member did (I, me), what other members did (you, they), or what all members did (we).** The "I" statements help students individually consider how they performed in the group. The "you" statements give students an opportunity to give other group members feedback about which behaviors were perceived as helpful or unhelpful. The "we" statements provide an opportunity for group members to reach consensus about which actions helped or hurt the group's work. The students then summarize their perceptions. At the very least this means that for each question the frequencies are summed and divided by the number of members in order to derive an average.

Another procedure is as follows. The teacher supplies questions. Each group member publicly shares his or her answers through a procedure called the whip. Each

◑ STUDENT CHECKLIST: Cooperation ◑

I contributed my ideas and information.

Always	Sometimes	Never

I asked others for their ideas and information.

Always	Sometimes	Never

I summarized all our ideas and information.

Always	Sometimes	Never

I asked for help when I needed it.

Always	Sometimes	Never

I helped the other members of my group learn.

Always	Sometimes	Never

I made sure everyone in my group understood how to do
the school work we were studying.

Always	Sometimes	Never

I helped keep the group studying.

Always	Sometimes	Never

I included everyone in our work.

Always	Sometimes	Never

group member is given 30 seconds to share his or her answer to each question about how well the group worked, with no comment allowed from other group members. The group hears the answers of each member by "whipping" through the group.

Each student names behaviors he or she performed that day that helped the group function more effectively, and then names one behavior that the member to his/her right (or left) performed that day that also helped the group.

Providing Feedback

When observers inform students how often they engaged in collaborative skills, they are giving feedback. **Feedback** is giving information to students so they can compare their actual performance with criteria for ideal performance. Feedback gives students information that helps them improve their performance and reinforces them for doing so. It is, therefore, probably the most important factor affecting students' learning of collaborative skills. **The purposes of feedback are to:**

1. **Fine-tune students' use of cooperative skills** by giving students information about whether they are engaging in the skills and whether they are using the skills accurately, appropriately, and effectively.

2. **Teach** students to use collaborative skills by helping students correct errors, identify problems in learning the skill, and compare their actual performance with the desired standard of performance (i.e., what they said and did with the actions that make up the skills).

3. **Reinforce** students for using the collaborative skills well and to identify progress in mastering the skills.

4. Promote students' positive **attitudes** and increased **commitment** toward using collaborative skills by giving them personal attention and support.

When feedback is given skillfully, it generates energy, directs the energy toward constructive action, and transforms the energy into action toward improved performance of the collaborative skills. Increased self-efficacy should result. Students should feel empowered to be even more effective next time. The following **checklist** may help in assessing the effectiveness of feedback:

1. Is feedback given?

2. Is energy generated in students?

3. What is the direction of the energy?

   a. Denial and/or flight (resistance, anxiety, no change).

   b. Using feedback to identify and solve problems so that performance is improved.

4. Do opportunities exist to turn the energy into action? If not, students will experience frustration and failure.

Feedback will be more helpful when students have clearly conceptualized the collaborative skills, when it is personal to each student, and when it is immediate. Feedback should encourage students to persevere in practicing the collaborative skills, since repetition is necessary for students to learn to use the skills easily and efficiently.

Remember to avoid negative feedback. **Some of the pitfalls of giving individuals, groups, or the entire class, negative feedback are:**

1. It confirms their apprehension about being evaluated and they will resist being observed in the future.

2. Criticism carries more weight than does praise. One critical remark often outweighs dozens of positive comments.

3. People bring more to criticism than to praise because of their past history. Feelings from criticism in the past are tapped when criticism is given in the present.

4. Weaknesses take more words to explain than do strengths.

5. Trust is easy to destroy but hard to build. Criticism often destroys trust.

The procedure for giving cooperative learning groups feedback is as follows:

1. Sum the frequencies for columns and rows on the observation sheet. This summarizes the data for each person's overall participation and for the overall frequency of each targeted collaborative skill.

2. Have group members summarize their impressions as to how well they utilized the targeted collaborative skills.

3. Give the group members the results of the observations by holding the observation sheet so that all group members can see it.

4. Ask the group members to summarize and draw conclusions about the data on the observation sheet. Remember that it is the person who talks the most who learns the most about student-student interaction within the group and who changes the most.

5. Using each student's name and making eye contact, give each student personal and positive feedback about his/her actions that helped the group function effectively.

The rules for giving personal feedback in a helpful, nonthreatening way are (Johnson, 1986):

1. **Focus feedback on the person's behavior, not on his or her personality.** Refer to what the person did, not to what you imagine his or her personality traits to be.

2. **Be descriptive.** Do not make judgments or give advice. Avoid all judgmental words and statements, such as "good," "excellent," "poor," and so forth.

3. **Be specific and concrete rather than general or abstract.** Refer to specific situations to help group members recall what you are describing.

4. **Make feedback as immediate as possible.**

5. **Be brief and concise.** Do not overload receivers with more feedback than they can understand at the time.

6. **Phrase feedback so it will review the definitions of the collaborative skills and help students better conceptualize what the skills are and how the skills are**

Giving Feedback: An Example

Suppose the observer has tallied the following observation sheet. In relating the data the observer might say:

"*Helen contributed ten times, Roger seven times, Edythe five times, and David twice. David encouraged others to participate ten times, Edythe five times, and Roger and Helen twice. Roger praised good ideas five times, David twice, and Helen and Edythe once.*"

Or, the observer might just show the observation sheet to the other group members and say:

"*What conclusions do you make for yourself and for the group?*"

In summarizing, the observer might say:

"*Each of you will wish to set a personal goal for how you can be an even more effective group member tomorrow than you were today. Ask yourself, who needs more encouragement? Who should we praise more? What other skills would help the group function better?*"

SKILL	ROGER	DAVID	HELEN	EDYTHE
Contributes Ideas	~~IIII~~ II	II	IIII IIII	IIII
Encourages Others to Contribute	II	IIII IIII	II	IIII
Praises Good Ideas	IIII	II	I	I

performed. Say, "I heard people who were encouraging say things like ...," "I noticed group members helping each other by ...," "I saw people who were checking do ..."

7. **Avoid negative comments and relate at least one positive incident for each group member that reinforces the use of cooperative skills** such as, "Did you notice how hard Edythe was working?" "Did you see how happy Roger was when he was praised for his contributions?" Affirm how well each student did, but do not give false complements or be unrealistically positive.

8. **Take ownership of the feedback.** Use personal descriptive statements like, "I observed ...," "I heard ...," "I saw ...," and "I noticed ..."

Frequently teachers will wish to give whole-class feedback. This may be done by making a large chart on which the frequency with which each targeted skill was performed is recorded. Either the results from the teacher's observations are recorded or student observations of each group are added together for a class total. If this chart is regularly updated, students can see how well they improved their behavior over a period of time. Teachers may wish to give a class reward when the class total exceeds a preset criteria of excellence. Not only does such a chart serve as a visual reminder of the skills students should practice while working in their groups, but it becomes a challenge that promotes class cooperation and encouragement. Expand this basic procedure by asking students to name skills they saw performed by anyone that day that helped their groups work well together.

Reflecting/Analyzing/Identifying Problems/Reinforcing

The group members need to reflect on and analyze the group session they just completed in order to discover what helped and what hindered them in completing the day's work and whether specific behaviors had a positive or negative effect. Such reflection and analysis is generally structured by the teacher. Some possible ways for doing so are:

1. Each group member is given 30 seconds to make a statement about his or her conclusions derived from the information shared by the observer and by the impressions of the group members. This procedure allows the group to hear from every member quickly, thus "whipping" through the group.

2. The group can be given a series of questions to discuss concerning their effective use of collaborative skills. Each group member gives his or her response and then consensus is achieved through discussion.

3. The last question on an assignment sheet can be a group-processing question. This signals that the group processing is an integral part of one's learning.

Teachers may conduct a whole-class processing discussion by:

1. Asking a group process question such as, "What actions did group members do that were helpful?"

2. Having each cooperative group discuss the question for a minute or two and arrive at a consensus on an answer.

3. Asking each group to announce its answer.

4. Repeating the process by asking another group-process question. Three questions may be as many as most teachers will wish to ask.

As the result of analyzing how well their group functioned, students can identify problems in individual and group functioning by comparing their desired level of collaborative skills with their actual behavior. To do this effectively, students need to receive enough information and feedback during processing so that they can accurately determine what behaviors are needed by the group and what collaborative skills they personally need to work on more. Identifying problems in group functioning leads directly into goal setting, which is discussed in the next session.

Students' engagement in the skills may be reinforced through the following sorts of procedures:

1. Focus on one member of the group. Every other member tells that person one thing he/she did that helped the group that day. The focus is rotated until all members have received positive feedback.

2. Each member writes a positive comment about each other member's effective use of collaborative skills on an index card. The students then give their written comments to each other so that every member will have, in writing, positive feedback from all the other group members.

Observation Sheet 1:
Teacher Observing Groups

GROUPS	EXPLAINING CONCEPTS	ENCOURAGING PARTICIPATION	CHECKING UNDERSTANDING	ORGANIZING THE WORK
1				
2				
3				
4				
5				

3. Each member comments on how well each other member used the collaborative skills by writing an answer to one of the following statements. The students then give their written statements to each other.

   a. I appreciated it when you . . .

   b. I liked it when you . . .

   c. I admire you . . .

   d. I enjoy it when you . . .

   e. You really helped out the group when you . . .

This procedure may also be done orally. In this case students look at the member they are complementing, use his or her name, and read their comments. The person receiving the compliment makes eye contact and says nothing or "thank you." Positive feedback should be directly and clearly expressed and should **not** be brushed off or denied.

Having each group summarize its processing and place its summary in a folder with its completed academic work is a good way for teachers to stay in touch with the functioning of each learning group.

Processing can and should be done in a variety of ways. Varying the procedures for processing keeps the activity vital and interesting to the students. Processing is a vital element of cooperative learning procedures and helps students develop collaborative skills as well as increasing group productivity.

Setting Goals For Improved Functioning

As the result of analyzing how well their group functioned, students can set goals for improving the functioning of their group. **Goal setting is the link between how students did today and how they will do tomorrow.** A vital aspect of group processing is, therefore, having students set goals about how they will function more effectively and skillfully in the next group work session. At the end of each processing session, students should publicly announce the behavior they plan to increase. Or they should write the behavior down and review it at the beginning of the next group session. Goal setting can have powerful impact on students' behavior in future cooperative learning situations. There is a powerful sense of ownership of and commitment to behaviors that a student has decided to engage in (as opposed to assigned behaviors). If students decide on how they will behave in the next group work session they will be more likely to engage in the behaviors. **Some procedures for goal setting are:**

1. Have students set specific behavioral goals for the next group session. Have each student pick a specific collaborative skill to use more effectively (an "I" focus) and/or have the group reach consensus about which collaborative skill all group members will practice in the next session (a "we" focus). The group can be required to hand in a written statement specifying which collaborative skill each member is going to emphasize during the next work session.

2. In a whole-class processing session, ask each group to agree on one conclusion to the statement, **"Our group could do better on collaborative skills by . . .",** and tell their answer to the entire class. You write the answers on the board under the title "goals." At the beginning of the next cooperative learning lesson, you publicly read over the goal statements and remind students what they agreed to work on during this session.

3. Have each student write an answer to one of the following questions before the next cooperative learning lesson:

   a. "Something I plan to do differently next time to help my group is . . ."

   b. "The collaborative skill I want to use next time is . . ."

   c. "How I can help my group next time is . . ."

   d. "Two things I will do to help my group next time are . . ."

   e. "One collaborative skill I will practice more consistently next time is . . . I will do this by (list specific behaviors)."

4. As an optional activity, have students plan where, outside of class, they can apply the collaborative skills they are learning in class. Ask them to make connections between the cooperative learning groups and the rest of their lives. Have them specify times in the hallway, playground, home, church, or

Date _____

Next Time We Will Be Better At _____

(Behavior)

Signed: _____ _____

_____ _____

Date _____

We Will _____
(Behavior)

_____ **Times Today**
(Number)

Signed _____ _____

_____ _____

community where they can use the same collaborative skills they are learning in class. Both "I" and "we" focuses are useful.

Observers

Teacher As Observer

After the lesson is planned, and students have been given their instructions, they begin work in their learning groups. At this point the teacher's job begins in earnest. **A major part of the teacher's role in conducting cooperative learning activities is to observe each group and intervene to improve their effectiveness when it is necessary.** Besides checking the groups to determine what, if any, problems they are having in completing the assignment, the teacher must monitor the learning groups to ensure that students are in fact collaborating effectively with each other. While the cooperative groups are working, the teacher circulates through the room and gathers information about the functioning of several or all of the learning groups. When first using cooperative learning groups, the teacher will probably be the only observer. It is only after learning groups become somewhat experienced that student observers are usually used.

Before the lesson begins teachers will need to plan how much time will be spent observing each learning group. Teachers will need to develop a **sampling plan** for obtaining information about the functioning of groups and students. The teacher may observe one learning group for the entire class period, collecting information on every member. Or, if the class period lasts for 50 minutes and there are ten groups in the class, the teacher may decide to observe each group for five minutes. Another alternative is to observe each group for two minutes and rotate through all the groups twice during the class period. Finally, only certain target students may be observed.

The teacher may use a structured or an unstructured observation procedure. When first using cooperative learning procedures, teachers should use a structured observation sheet to count the number of times appropriate behaviors are being used by students. The more concrete the information the teacher gathers, the more useful it is to both the teacher and the students. Look for positive behaviors in order to praise students when they are using the skills.

Unstructured observations may be added about skillful student interchanges to supplement the frequencies obtained through the structured observations.

Teacher Intervention

While monitoring a learning group the teacher may need to intervene occasionally to increase the group's effectiveness. **There are at least three reasons to intervene within a cooperative learning group:**

1. To correct misunderstandings or misconceptions about task instructions and the academic assignments they are completing.

2. To correct the absence, incorrect use, or inappropriate use of collaborative skills.

3. To reinforce the appropriate or competent use of collaborative skills.

There are a number of decisions teachers will have to make while observing students working collaboratively:

1. **Should I intervene now or wait for the processing time?** You may wish to stop the group's work and intervene immediately, or you may wish to wait until the processing time and then intervene.

2. **Should I intervene within this single group or should I intervene within the entire class?** Sometimes the problem is specific to a group and sometimes it is a generic problem that all groups may be experiencing.

3. **Should I tell students how to be more effective or structure a problem-solving process for them to discover the same point?** In a skillful intervention, you do not solve the problem for the group. You highlight a problem for the group to solve. Show the group the data collected by your observing and ask them to identify the problem and plan how to correct it. Often just the awareness of the recorded information (for example, showing the data indicating that group members are not sharing or helping) will get group members back on the right track. Students may lack skills or they may be inexperienced in using the skills. Avoid rescuing floundering groups. Guide them to a solution that they themselves discover and implement. It is only in the most ex-

⸻⟦ Long-Term Group Progress ⟧⸻

Curriculum Unit _____

Group Members _____

DATE	ADDED IDEAS	ENCOURAGED OTHERS	SUMMARIZED/ CLARIFIED	FINISHED WORK	ASKED FOR HELP

Comments:

treme cases that you may wish to tell students how to behave more appropriately and skillfully. You want students to learn how to diagnose and solve their problems in group functioning and, if you are too active in solving problems students are having in collaborating, they will not get the chance to do so.

4. **Should I have students talk about the issue or should I have them role play the situation and practice new behaviors?**

5. **Does the problem identified have a clear procedure to correct it?** If not, highlighting the problem may only create helplessness, demoralization, and frustration. For every problem in group functioning identified, students should always believe that there is something they can do to correct it.

In identifying problems groups members are having collaborating, it is always possible that it is you, the teacher, who needs to modify your actions. For example, you may have failed to make clear to students that they are to collaborate or what your expectations are for student-student interaction. The positive interdependence may not be strong enough.

Students As Observers

When students become experienced in working in cooperative learning groups, they should be trained to be observers. There are at least two reasons for doing so. **First,** student observers can collect considerably more information about interaction among group members than can a teacher circulating among all the groups in the class. **Second.** one of the most effective ways of teaching students collaborative skills is to assign them the role of observer and have them record how frequently their groupmates engage in the targeted skills. When students observe collaborative skills, the nature and execution of the skills becomes clarified. As the responsibility for observing rotates to each group member, all students understand more clearly the nature of the collaborative skills required for the group to function effectively.

The meta-goal of observing is for the students to become **participant/observers**, so that they can actively participate in the cooperative learning groups and simultaneously notice how well group members are interacting with each other. It is the mature, skilled group member that says, "Something is not working here; we need an observer."

Students may be used in two ways as observers. First, a student observer can circulate throughout the classroom as a roving observer. The procedures for doing so are the same as those for the teacher. During the processing of the lesson the teacher asks the roving student observer to report on the information he or she collected. The roving observer can be useful if the teacher finds only one student present for the group. If, for example, the speech therapist arrives to test Jenny, do not panic. Hand Jenny's partner a class list. He becomes a roving student observer! The **second** way to use student observers is to have one member of each cooperative learning group be an observer. Many teachers have success with doing so, even in kindergarten.

The procedure for using a student from each group as observers is as follows. First, an observer is chosen from each group. Students may volunteer or the teacher may randomly select an observer. The role of observer, however, should rotate so that every group member is an observer at some time. **Second**, the teacher explains the role of observer to the class. This explanation may include the teacher modeling the observer role and explaining to the class what is expected of the observer before commencing the group's work. Also, the teacher should discuss the contents of the observation sheet with the entire class, so that there are no surprises when the group receives feedback. **Third**, students observe by:

1. Recording the interaction among group members. Observers do not comment or intervene, but simply record on the observation sheet what they see and hear. Student observers use the structured observation sheets in the same way as modeled by the teacher.

2. Removing themselves slightly from the group so that they are not tempted to participate in the academic task but are close enough to see and hear the interaction among group members.

3. Learning as much about collaborative skills and group functioning as possible. Observers are to become acutely aware of effective member actions and then engage in the actions the next group session.

Fourth, to ensure that observers do not have a gap in their academic learning, a time near the end of the class period can be set aside for the learning groups to review the content of the lesson with the observer. While observers often know quite a bit about the lesson by this time, the group members often further their understanding of the academic material by conducting this review.

Observation Sheet 2: Intensive Observation

ACTIONS	ROGER	EDYTHE	HELEN	FRANK
ENCOURAGES OTHERS TO PARTICIPATE				
EXPLAINS CONCEPTS AND PRINCIPLES				
EXPRESSES SUPPORT				
GIVES DIRECTION				
ASKS FOR INFORMATION, RATIONALE				
PARAPHRASES				

Fifth, observers report the results of their observations to the group. This provides the group and individual members with constructive feedback. Observers should total the frequencies for rows and columns on the observation sheet, hold the sheet so that the members of the group can see it, and ask group members to summarize and make conclusions about the interaction among members.

It is not necessary to use student observers all the time. Until students have participated in cooperative learning groups a few times, the use of observers may not be productive. In the beginning it is enough for teachers simply to structure cooperative learning groups without worrying about using student observers too. And teachers do not have to use observers with every lesson.

While students are learning collaborative skills, however, observation and feedback are important. After students become skillful, observing can become something that is done less often, perhaps when new skills are added or when a group problem occurs.

Either the teacher or the groups should keep a folder with all of their observation sheets in it. These records can be used to decide how well the group is functioning or whether the group qualifies for rewards being given for using the collaborative skills effectively.

Visiting Observers

At times your colleagues may wish to observe you teach a cooperative lesson or you may invite a colleague to do so to help you diagnose the difficulties a group or student is having in collaborating effectively. A structured observation sheet may help the classroom visitor focus on critical aspects of cooperative learning. A visiting colleague may observe the overall structure of a cooperative lesson, the interaction among students in all the cooperative learning groups, one specific group, or one or more targeted students.

Classroom Observations

Teacher Observed _____

My focus as an observer for this lesson is: _____

_____

		COMMENTS
Subject Matter Obj.		
Social Skills Objec.		
Positive Interdependence	Group goal ☐ Group grade ☐ Division of Labor ☐ Materials Shared ☐ Bonus Points ☐ Roles Assigned ☐ Materials Jigsawed ☐ Other: ☐	
Group Composition	Homogeneous ☐ Heterogeneous ☐	
Seating Arrangement	Clear View of Others ☐ Clear View of Materials ☐	
Individual Accountability	Each Student Evaluated ☐ Students Check Each Other ☐ Random Student Evaluated ☐ Other: ☐	
Observation	Teacher ☐ Student ☐ Observation Form Used ☐ Informal ☐	
Teacher Feedback: Social Skills	Class as a Whole ☐ Group by Group ☐ Individual ☐	
Group Processing	Observation Data ☐ Social Skills ☐ Academic Skills ☐ Positive ☐ Goal Setting ☐	
General Climate	Group Products Displayed ☐ Group Progress Displayed ☐ Aids to Group Work Displayed ☐	

Observer _____ Date _____

Obstacles To Group Processing

Some of the common obstacles to group processing are given below (Dishon & O'Leary, 1984). For each obstacle a number of solutions are suggested.

1. **There is not enough time for group processing.** For many reasons (fire drills, announcements, assemblies, discipline problems) teachers often believe that they cannot take the time for group processing that day, week, or month. When such an attitude dominates, some suggestions are:

   a. Do quick processing by rapidly asking the class to tell how well their groups are functioning. Do this by making a statement and then having students indicate agreement or disagreement by: **agree** (hand in air), **do not know** (arms folded), **disagree** (hands down). Two or three statements can be made and responded to in a minute or so.

   b. Do processing now and either have students finish the work at home or else do it tomorrow in class.

2. **Processing stays vague.** When students conclude, "We did OK," "We did a good job," or "Everyone was involved," the teacher knows that the processing is not specific enough. Some suggested remedies are:

   a. Use specific statements students have to give detailed responses to.

   b. Use student observers so that specific frequencies of behaviors are recorded.

   c. Give groups specific questions to be answered about their functioning.

3. **Students stay uninvolved in processing.** Occasionally there will be groups where members consistently stay uninvolved in analyzing the group's functioning. In such a case, try:

   a. Asking for a written report from the group reporting the strengths and weaknesses of their functioning.

   b. Using processing sheets that require participation from everyone.

c. Assigning to the student most uninvolved in the processing the job of recorder or spokesperson for the group.

d. Having all members sign the processing statement to indicate they participated in the group processing and agree with the group's conclusions.

e. Giving bonus points for group processing reports.

4. **Written process reports are incomplete or messy.** There may be groups who hand in incomplete or messy reports of their group processing. You may wish to try:

a. Having group members sign each other's processing sheets to show that each has been checked for completeness and neatness.

b. Giving bonus points for neatness and completeness.

5. **Students use poor cooperative skills during processing.** When group members do not listen carefully to each other, when they are afraid to contribute to the processing, when the discussion becomes divisive, the teacher may wish to intervene by:

a. Assigning specific roles for the processing.

b. Having one group member observe the processing and have the group discuss the results.

Implementation Assignment 6

1. Read Chapter 7.

2. Review the processing forms in this chapter one by one. Select those you will use with your class. Plan for using a combination of individual, small group, and whole class processing methods.

3. Implement the group processing procedures in your classroom. Train your students to be observers. Record the results to share with your base group.

4. Make a journal entry concerning the use of processing procedures.

Processing Posttest

Working cooperatively with a partner, answer each question on the posttest. For each answer, both of you must agree, and each must be able to explain. Then combine with another pair and repeat the procedure, making sure that all four individuals agree on the answer to each question.

1. Processing is not very important.   *True   False*

2. During processing, the group discusses how well it is functioning.   *True   False*

3. Processing teaches students both what social skills are needed in a cooperative learning group and when to use the social skills.   *True   False*

4. In processing, students discuss:

    a. What skills are not being used in the group.
    b. How well the skills are being implemented.
    c. Whether their efforts are successful or unsuccessful.
    d. Plans for improving their group skills next time.
    e. All of the above.

5. Which of the following is <u>not</u> an important reason for processing?

    a. Processing helps the group members maintain effective working relationships.
    b. Processing helps students become aware of and develop collaborative skills.
    c. Processing gives the teacher a chance to give students positive feedback on how well they use collaborative skills.
    d. Processing reminds students that they should practice collaborative skills consistently.
    e. Processing gives the teacher time to regain sanity between lessons or classes.

6. When groups are just starting, it is best to plan a 30 minute process period once a week rather than 10 minutes a day.   *True   False*

7. It is best not to tell students what skills are being observed in order to surprise them.   *True   False*

8. Observation, either by the teacher or a student, is a good way for groups to get information about how well they are using collaborative skills.   *True   False*

9. Teachers should use informal methods of observation rather than formal ones.   *True   False*

10. Teachers can observe how well individuals are using the skills, or how well the class is using the skills.   *True   False*

11. All students should take a turn at being a group observer.   *True   False*

12. Observers learn about cooperative skills by looking for them.   *True   False*

13. A roving student observer usually is either the principal or custodian.   *True   False*

14. Student observers sit outside the group with an observation sheet and make a record of who uses what collaborative skills while the group is working.   *True   False*

15. Teachers should throw away the used observation sheets at the end of the day so they don't pile up.   *True   False*

16. Which of the following is <u>not</u> a rule for giving feedback?

    a. Focus on behavior, not on personality.
    b. Describe behaviors rather than judge them.
    c. Be specific rather than general.
    d. Wait several days before giving feedback.
    e. Don't give more feedback than a person can understand.

17. Teachers should wait until the processing session to point out inappropriate group behavior or to praise good use of skills.   *True   False*

⇥❰ Cooperative Learning Contract ❱⇤

Major Learnings	Implementation Plans

Date _____ Date of Progress Report Meeting _____

Participant's Signature _____

Signatures of Other Group Members _____ _____

_____ _____ _____

ᛞᚲ Cooperative Learning Progress Report ᚲᛞ

NAME _____   SCHOOL _____

AGE LEVEL _____   SUBJECT _____

DAY AND DATE	DESCRIPTION OF TASKS and ACTIVITIES PERFORMED	SUCCESSES EXPERIENCED	PROBLEMS ENCOUNTERED

Description of critical or interesting incidents:

6:41

EXERCISE

MATERIALS

Group Processing: Purposeful Reading

1. Read the first question. Find the answer in the text and discuss it with your partner.

2. Agree on the answer and summarize it. Both members should be able to explain the answer.

3. Relate the answer to previous learning (elaborate).

4. Move on to the next question and repeat the procedure.

Questions

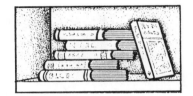

1. What is group processing?

2. What are the two views of group processing?

3. What are the two models of group processing?

4. Why is group processing important?

5. How do you tell effective processing from ineffective processing?

6. What two elements of processing does the teacher have to schedule?

7. What are the procedures for processing?

8. What are two procedures for deciding/precuing?

9. How may observing be defined?

10. What are the five steps of structured observation?

11. What is the purpose of observing?

12. What is the difference between descriptive and interpretative observations?

13. What are the general rules for observation?

14. What are unstructured observations?

15. What are "I," "you," and "we" statements?

16. What is feedback?

17. What are the purposes of feedback?

18. What does skillful feedback do?

19. What are the pitfalls of negative feedback?

20. What is the procedure for giving learning groups feedback?

21. What are the rules for giving nonthreatening feedback?

22. What is whole-class feedback?

23. What are possible ways for reflecting on and analyzing group sessions?

24. How may students' engagement in cooperative skills be reinforced?

25. What are procedures for goal setting?

26. Why would teachers intervene in cooperative groups?

27. Why should students be trained as observers?

28. What is the procedure for using student observers?

29. What is the procedure for utilizing visiting observers?

30. What are the obstacles to group processing and how may they be overcome?

They Will Never Take Us Alive Exercise

1. Form groups of five. One member volunteers to be an observer.

2. Each group member individually completes the **They Will Never Take Us Alive Ranking Task**.

3. The group decides by consensus on the best ranking possible on the **They Will Never Take Use Alive** items. There should be one ranking for the group, every member should agree with the ranking, and every member should be able to explain the rationale behind the ranking of each item.

4. Score the accuracy of the group's ranking by comparing it with the expert's ranking. Find the absolute difference between the group's ranking and the expert's ranking for each item and add them together. The lower the score the more accurate the group's ranking.

5. Using the observer's information, the members' impressions, and the group's accuracy score for the ranking, discuss how effectively the group functioned. Write down your group's conclusions.

6. Share your group's conclusions with the entire class.

© Johnson & Johnson

They Will Never Take Us Alive: Ranking Sheet

In a recent survey **Dun's Review** lists the most perilous products or activities in the United States, based on annual death statistics. Below, in no particular order, are listed fifteen of these death-causing hazards. Your task is to rank them in order of dangerousness according to the number of deaths caused each year. Place by the number 1 the most dangerous, by the number 2 the next most dangerous, and so forth.

1. _____ swimming

2. _____ railroads

3. _____ police work

4. _____ home appliances

5. _____ alcohol

6. _____ nuclear power

7. _____ smoking

8. _____ motor vehicles

9. _____ pesticides

10. _____ handguns

11. _____ bicycles

12. _____ firefighting

13. _____ mountain climbing

14. _____ vaccinations

15. _____ surgery

Complex Problem Solving / Decision Making

Task: Rank items from most important to least important and write out a rationale as to why you ranked the items as you did.

Goal Structures:
1. Individualistic: Individual ranking and rationale without interacting with others.
2. Cooperative:
   a. One ranking and rationale from the group.
   b. Every member must agree on the ranking and rationale.
   c. Every member must be able to explain the rationale for the ranking.

Criteria For Success: 0 - 20   Excellent

                         21 -30   Good

                         31-40   Poor

                         41+   Terrible

Individual Accountability:
1. One member will be randomly selected to explain group's ranking and rationale.
2. Each member will explain group's ranking and rationale to a member of another group.

Expected Behaviors:
1. Everyone participates.
2. Summarize and synthesize
3. Ask others for facts and reasoning.
4. Do not change your mind unless you are logically persuaded.

Intergroup Cooperation: When finished, share ranking, information, and reasoning with a nearby group.

Guides For Monitoring

Your primary responsibility while monitoring is to watch, listen, and think about what you see. You decide when and if to intervene. Monitoring is the time to find out what your students do and do not understand and how skillful they are in working together. Things to look for may include:

Did heads come together in the group?

Is everyone in the group contributing verbally?

What happens in the group after someone shares an idea? Are they paraphrased? Are they supported?

What strategies are groups using to accomplish the task?

Who are my really skillful students?

Who needs to improve on social skills? Which skills?

Effective monitoring of cooperative learning groups is your real teaching time. It is your best time with your students. Do not neglect it! You may have given the whole group instruction and directions, now you will get feedback on what students know, oversee the learning, and know to do any reteaching or elaboration that is necessary. You now change from direct giver of information to learning and group skills coach. Get your whistle, put on your track shoes, and get ready. You will want to see that students share ideas and strategies, give positive peer pressure coupled with peer support, and do a great deal of oral elaborating.

As soon as you have given the cooperative group assignment, start watching the students and moving around the room. On the first round, look for obvious problems.

Round One: Check To Make Sure Students Are Working Together

1. Are group members seated close together (knee to knee, eye to eye)? If not, help them move their chairs together. If students are left as loners because of absent group members, chose a group for them to join for the day and help them get included and welcomed by the members.

2. Are groups on the right page? Doing the right assignment? Doing it the way you asked? If not, clarify and get them on the right track.

3. Have previously absent students been welcomed back and brought up to date? Welcome them, make sure group members have welcomed them, and then have the groups go over what the absentees missed so they can get caught up and do appropriate make-up work.

4. Are there students with obvious problems or concerns who need extra attention? Bleary eyes or sullen looks often denote difficult days for students--a pat on the shoulder or a positive greeting by you and group members can go a long way toward putting them into a working mood or at least making their day more tolerable.

5. If students were asked to bring work to the group, do they have it? Ask to see such work and deal appropriately with students who did not meet their group responsibilities. This may range from excusing the lapse if the excuse is valid, asking the group to problem solve positive ways to help a student meet his or her responsibilities (peer pressure with peer support), and/or removing the student from the group to do the required work while the group proceeds without him or her.

Round Two: Check On How Well Students Are Doing The Work

1. How does the work of group members look? Give feedback on the work so far, do any clarifying or reteaching that is needed, and praise good efforts or accomplishments. Such statements as "Better check number two again," "You have three right so far," or "Excellent work on the first paragraph," help students get accurate practice and immediate feedback on their work.

2. Is every student orally explaining? Because this is so important for learning, watch for and encourage every student to explain the work. Make sure groups are including everyone in the explaining and help them structure it if it is lacking. "Listen to David," or "Have you asked Edye?" might get this going.

3. Can individual students explain the work or answers? Start quizzing individual members of the group by randomly selecting one student to explain the work so far while the other students encourage but do not answer. If the student can answer, the group gets praise. If the student can not answer, give the group more time and recheck the student later.

4. Do you have a student for whom knowing all the answers is an unrealistic demand right now? If so, pick one or two questions you will ask that student and alert the

group by saying, "I will ask Roger to explain the answer to number one today--get him ready." Next week ask harder questions. Eventually, require the same amount and level of work. After the group has had ample time to prepare the student, go back and ask the student to explain. Praise the group for correct answers.

5. How well are individual students doing? Watch how individual students learn and how they interact with others. Take notes on positive behaviors to share with the class and with parents. Take notes on behaviors you want to change as the year progresses so you can plan for the skill teaching and processing.

6. How well are students doing the assignment? Do students need reteaching or more practice? Are they ready for individual work? Are they ready to more on to new material? Evaluate the learning pace and adjust accordingly. Also, you can adjust assignments for individuals. Students who do not need extra practice can be given challenge work. Students who can not do all the assignment can have it adjusted to an appropriate level.

7. How well are students cooperating? Praise skillful behaviors. Remind students of your expectations. Stay until they demonstrate the appropriate behaviors. Then praise their efforts. Describe what you saw to help groups gain awareness of their skillful or unskillful behaviors. Role playing sometimes helps students gain an awareness of their skillful and unskillful behaviors. Sometimes changing seating (putting a reluctant student in the middle) or roles (making a dominant student the encourager) helps. You may also wish to ask the group to suggest ideas for improving.

Remember to turn problems in working together effectively back to the group to solve. Help the group members define the problem carefully, have them think of several possible solutions, then have them pick one to try. Be aware that peer pressure coupled with peer support is a strong tool for handling problem students. Getting group members to say, "We want you to help us; how can we help you do that?" to a reluctant learner is powerful, although change may not be immediate. Your job is to encourage the group to persist and let the members know you support their efforts.

You may wish to take students with severe behavior problems aside, listen privately to their problems, have them describe what they are doing, have them look at how it is helping or not helping, and help them plan to improve their behaviors. Practice with them to prepare their return to the group. Coach the group members on helpful ways of responding. Be certain that you and group members encourage and acknowledge even small improvements.

Round Three: Formally Observe, Give Feedback, And Process

1. Do I have time for formal observation? Choose an observation sheet, pick a group, and gather specific data on several group skills as "contributing ideas" and "asks for facts and reasoning." If you are teaching a skill or have assigned some specific behaviors to a group, these can go on the observation sheet. Observe a group for five minutes, then interrupt and give positive feedback or give the group feedback during processing time later in the period. Keep the observation sheets so you can document progress (useful for parent conferences!).

2. Are groups finishing the work and have nothing to do? As groups finish, check over their work and quiz individual members. If their work is not satisfactory, have them revise it. When the work is satisfactory, give an extension activity related to the assignment (write a new problem and solve it; invent a new ending; think of another example), have them help other groups, or have them process extensively. Just letting them talk quietly for a short time is sometimes appropriate here because it can build group cohesiveness.

When the groups have finished the work, monitoring is over. Bring the lesson to a close by going over answers or summarizing the learning. Report the effective use of cooperative skills you saw while you monitored. Have group members give each other positive feedback, process their group's effectiveness, make plans for improving, and thank each other for the help.

Ideas For Monitoring And Intervening

Check For	Response Ideas
Members seated closely together	Good seating or draw your chairs closer together
Group has needed materials and are on right page.	Good, you are all ready or get what you need--I will watch.
Students who are assigned jobs are doing them.	Good! You're doing your jobs. Who is supposed to do what?
Groups have started the task.	Good! You've started. Let me see you get started. Do you need any help?
Good cooperative skills	Good encouraging! Good group! Keep up the good work!
Lack of cooperative skills	What skills would help here? Look at the behavior chart; what should you be doing?
Need to prompt cooperative skill use	Who can encourage Edye? Repeat in your own words what Edye just said.
Need to prompt academic work	You need more extensive answers. Let me explain how to do this again.
Individual accountability	Roger, show me how to do #1. David, explain why the group decided on this answer.
Reluctant students involved	I'm going to ask Helen to explain #1. Get her ready and I will be back.
Oral rehearsal occurs	Have each member explain until each one can explain the answers.
Promote skill monitoring	Observe your group. During processing, tell members their positive actions.
Intervene to process	Your group is working so well. What behaviors are helping you?
Intergroup cooperation	Each of you go to another group and share your answer to #4.
Intervene for special problems	Helen, you are the first to answer every time. Now listen and affirm others' answrs.
Groups that have finished	Your work looks good. Now do the activity written on the board.

Intervening In Cooperative Learning Groups

While you monitor and intervene in cooperative learning groups you may wish to use the following structure:

O = Observe.
IDQ = Intervene, by sharing data and/or by asking a question.
SP = Have students process and plan how they will take care of issue.
BTW - Tell students to go back to work

Ideas For Monitoring / Intervening / Processing

Five Minute Walk

1. Select social skill(s) to be observed.
2. Construct observation sheet.
3. Plan route through the classroom.
4. Gather data on every book.
5. Feedback the data to the groups and/or to the class as a whole.
6. Chart / graph the results.

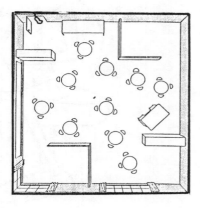

Mystery Person

1. State that you are focusing on one student -- the mystery person.
2. Observe without showing who you are observing.
3. Give report to the class without naming the person.
4. Ask students to guess who the mystery person is.

Chapter 7

Structuring Colleagial Support Groups

Table Of Contents

The Cooperative School

Schools are not buildings, curriculums, and machines. **Schools are relationships and interactions among people.** How the interpersonal interaction is structured determines how effective schools are. There are three ways that school relationships may be sstructured: competitively, individualistically, and cooperatively. School effectiveness depends on the interpersonal interactions being oriented toward cooperatively achieving the goals of the school. Schools must be cooperative places. The **cooperative school** consists of cooperative learning within the classroom and cooperative efforts within the staff. **To qualify as a cooperative school, cooperation must dominate both student and faculty life.** Within the classroom cooperative learning should be used the majority of the time. Within the school, colleagial support groups, task forces or committees, and ad-hoc decision-making groups should meet regularly and frequently. For a full discussion of how to create a cooperative school, see Johnson and Johnson (1989b).

Effective Colleagial Learning

For things we have to learn before we can do them, we learn by doing them.

Aristotle

To lead your school you need to challenge the status quo of competitive-individualistic learning and staff relations, inspire a new vision of cooperative learning and cooperation among staff members, empower staff members by organizing them into cooperative teams, lead by example by using cooperative strategies and procedures, and encourage staff members to persevere until they have gained considerable expertise in using cooperative learning. **The most important aspect of leadership is empowering your staff by organizing them into cooperative teams**. And of the three types of teams, the most important are colleagial support groups in which teachers help and assist each other to improve their teaching competence. All staff efforts within schools should be aimed directly or indirectly at educating students. There is no doubt that teachers teach better when they experience support from their peers.

It is time that the school became a modern organization. In the real world, most of the important work is done by cooperative teams rather than by individuals. For example, the development of most computer systems requires highly interactive groups of knowledgeable workers. Similarly, the number of people coauthoring scientific papers has increased dramatically in recent years. In 1986, 75 people co-authored a paper with evidence related to the location of the gene for Duchenne muscular dystrophy. Instead of requiring teachers to engage in quiet and solitary performance in individual classrooms, teachers should be organized into cooperative teams with an emphasis on seeking and accepting help and assistance from peers, soliciting constructive criticism, and negotiating by articulating their needs, discerning what others need, and discovering mutually beneficial outcomes. Modernizing the school requires that teachers work in cooperative teams as most other adults in our society do.

When teachers are isolated and alienated from their peers, they will also tend to be alienated from their work and, therefore, not likely to commit a great deal of psychological energy to their jobs or commit themselves to grow professionally by attaining increased expertise.

Colleagial support groups begin when two or more teachers to meet together and talk about their efforts to implement cooperative learning. There can be little doubt that teachers' main source of inspiration and creativity is other teachers. When teachers are asked to identify their primary source of innovative ideas about teaching and their primary source of support and assistance, their response is usually "other teachers." In a competitive / individualistic school, learning from colleagues is often informal and takes place through chance meetings in the hallway or teachers' lounge. In a cooperative school, learning from colleagues is formally structured by organizing teachers into colleagial support groups.

Being An Effective Colleague

Traditionally, teachers have not been skilled in working effectively with adult peers. Blake and Mouton (1974) found that teachers and administrators lacked teamwork skills and were too ready to resolve differences by voting or by following the "offical leader." They observed that educators were far less competent in working in small problem-solving groups than were industrial personnel. And they found that educators described themselves as being more oriented toward compromising quality of work for harmonious relationships, exerting minimal effort to get their job done, and being more oriented toward keeping good relationships than toward achieving the school's goals. Blumberg, May, and Perry (1974) found that teachers were ill- equipped behaviorally to function as part of a faculty, as they lacked the skills and attitudes needed for effective group problem-solving.

The lack of competence in being a constructive colleague, however, is not primarily the fault of teachers. The organizational structure of the school traditionally has discouraged collegiality among teachers and severely limited their opportunities to cooperate with each other. Schools are **loosely coupled** organizations in which teachers and administrators function far more independently than interdependently, with little or no supervision, enagaging in actions that do not determine or affect what others do, and engage in actions that seem isolated from their consequences (Johnson, 1979). Teachers have been systematically isolated from one another during most of the school day. And that isolation has resulted in teachers experiencing an amorphous and diffuse competition with their peers.

Colleagial Support Groups

Willi Unsoeld, a famous mountaineer and philosopher, once said to a group of mountain climbers, *"Pull together...in the mountains you must depend on each other for survival."* Teaching has a lot in common with mountain climbing.

A climbing team has a minimum of two members attached to each other by a rope (called a life line). There are two roles in a climbing team: climber and belayer. You never climb unless you are securely attached to your belayer and the belayer is securely attached to an anchor. The belayer ensures that you have a safe anchor so that he or she can catch you if you fall. The climber conceptually plans a path up the "first leg" of the cliff, advances along that path, puts in pitons, slips in the rope, and continues to advance until the first leg of the climb is completed. The pitons help the belayer catch the climber if the climber falls and they mark the path up the cliff. The rope, called the "life-line," goes from the belayer through the pitons up to the climber. When the climber has completed the first leg of the climb, the climber becomes the belayer and the belayer becomes the climber. The original belayer advances up the route marked out by the original climber until the first leg is completed, and then leap-frogs by becoming the lead climber for the second leg of the climb. This leap-frog procedure is repeated until the summit is reached.

The similarities of mountain climbing to teaching are:

1. Both are based on a commitment to accomplish something. While a climber may state that it is important to climb a mountain because "it is there," a teacher may state that it is important to teach each student because "he or she is there."

2. Both climbing and teaching involve risking failure. In teaching, failure is risked whenever the teacher tries out and attempts to perfect a new strategy and procedure.

3. It takes two people to make a climb. While it is possible for one person to hike through the mountains, if you want to scale the peaks, you need a partner. The same is true of teaching. To scale the heights, you need a belayer, a supportive colleague, who will catch you if you fall.

4. You climb with your eyes and your brain. Climbing is first and foremost a conceptual activitiy. You pick out your route and then advance. Teaching is also a conceptual activitiy that is thought through in advance and then executed.

5. Reciprocal leadership and followership is needed in climbing. To be a good climber, you must have two sets of competencies. You must be able to **lead** (finding and marking a path up the cliff so that others may easily follow you) and **belay** (providing a secure anchor for those who are climbing). You must mark out a new trail for a period of time and then provide a secure anchor for others to follow, catch up, and mark out a new trail. Then you follow their path until you have caught up to them, leap frog, and mark out a new path for them to follow. There is an ebb and flow of leading and supporting in mountain climbing. The same is true for teaching. Working with colleagues, you develop some expertise in cooperative learning, share it, provide support for their initial use of cooperative learning, and then learn new aspects of using cooperative learning from them in turn.

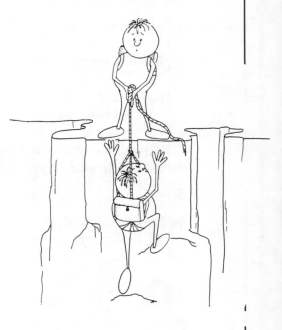

6. Both climbing and teaching involve trust. You have to be trustworthy in providing support. If your partner falls, you have to be able to catch him. When you are the climber, you have to be trusting of your partner to provide a secure anchor. It is your confidence in your belayer that gives you the courage to risk a difficult climb.

7. Climbers spend a lot of time hanging by their fingers and toes to a cliff, feeling scared, and thinking, "What is the use, I will never make it." Many teachers have similar feelings when facing their classes. When the fear gets too great, a climber becomes "gripped" or "frozen," unable to advance and unable to retreat. A climber in this state has to be rescued by partners.

The success of the school depends on the success teachers have in educating students. The success of teachers in educating students depends on (a) how committed teachers are to continually increasing their instructional expertise and (b) the amount of physical and psychological energy teachers give to their work. The commitment of physical and psychological energy to achieve the goal of improving one's instructional expertise is heavily influenced by the degree to which colleagues are supportive and encouraging. **There is no doubt that teachers teach better when they experience support from their peers.** In most schools, however, such support is hard to achieve. As a result, most teachers feel harried, isolated, and alienated. Yet there is a deep human need to work collaboratively and intimately with supportive people. Colleagial support group meetings provide teachers with the opportunity to share ideas, support each other's efforts to use cooperative learning, and encourage each other.

In the school, the colleagial support group is the climbing team. **A colleagial support group** consists of two to five teachers who have the goal of improving each other's instructional expertise and ensuring each other's professional growth. Colleagial support groups should be small and members should be heterogeneous. **Colleagial support groups are first and foremost safe places where:**

1. Members like to be.

2. There is support, caring, concern, laughter, camaraderie, and celebration.

3. The primary goal of improving each other's competence in using cooperative learning is never obscured.

The purpose of this colleagial support group is to work jointly to improve continuously each other's expertise in using cooperative learning procedures or, in other words, to:

1. Provide the help, assistance, support, and encouragement each member needs to gain as high a level of expertise in using cooperative learning procedures as possible.

2. Serve as an informal support group for sharing, letting off steam, and discussing problems connected with implementing cooperative learning procedures.

3. Serve as a base for teachers experienced in the use of cooperative learning procedures to teach other teachers how to structure and manage lessons cooperatively.

4. Create a setting in which camaraderie and shared success occur and are celebrated.

Colleagial support groups succeed when they are carefully structured to ensure active participation by members and concrete products (such as lesson plans) that members can actually use. The structure must clearly point members toward increasing each other's expertise in implementing cooperative learning to prevent meetings from degenerating into gripe sessions, destructive criticism of each other, amateur therapy, or sensitivity training. Members need to believe they sink or swim together, ensure considerable face-to-face discussion and assistance takes place, hold each other accountable to implement cooperative learning in between meetings, learn and use the interpersonal and small group skills required to make meetings productive, and periodically initiate a discussion of how effective the colleagial support group is in carrying out its mission. Task-oriented discussion, planning, and problem solving, as well as empathy and mutual support, should dominate the meetings.

The three key activities of a colleagial support group are (Little, 1981):

1. Frequent professional discussions of cooperative learning in which information is shared, successes are celebrated, and problems connected with implementation are solved.

2. Coplanning, codesigning, copreparing, and coevaluating curriculum materials relevant to implementing cooperative learning in the classrooms of the members.

3. Coteaching and reciprocal observations of each other teaching lessons structured cooperatively and jointly processing those observations.

Professional Discussions

What teachers need most of all professionally is opportunties to talk to each other about teaching. Within the colleagial support groups there must be frequent, continuous, increasingly concrete and precise talk about the use of cooperative learning procedures. Through such discussion members build a concrete, precise, and coherent shared language that can describe the complexity of using cooperative learning procedures, distinguish one practice and its virtues from another, and integrate cooperative learning procedures into other teaching practices and strategies that they are already using. Through such discussions, teachers will exchange successful procedures and materials. They will focus on solving specific problems members may be having in perfecting their use of cooperative learning strategies. Most of all, teachers' comprehension and deeper-level understanding of the nature of cooperative learning will be enhanced by explaining how they are implementing it to their colleagues.

Joint Planning and Curriculum Design

Well begun is half done.

Aristotle

Members of professional support groups should frequently plan, design, prepare, and evaluate lesson plans together. This results in teachers sharing the burden of developing materials needed to conduct cooperative lessons, generating emerging understanding of cooperative learning strategies, making realistic standards for students and colleagues, and providing the machinery for each other to implement cooperative learning procedures. Teachers should leave each meeting of their colleagial support group with something concrete that helps them implement cooperative learning. The process of planning a lesson together, each conducting it, and then processing it afterwards is often constructive. This cycle of **coplanning, parallel teaching, coprocessing** may be followed by one of **coplanning, coteaching, coprocessing**.

The discussions and coplanning that takes place within colleagial support groups ensures that teachers clarify their understanding of what cooperative learning is and creates a support and accountability system to ensure that they try it out. The next steps in increasing expertise are to assess the consequences of using cooperative learning, reflecting on how well the lesson went, and teaching another cooperative lesson in a modified way. All of these steps benefit from the input and feedback from supportive colleagues. The more colleagues are involved in your teaching, the more valuable the help and assistance they can provide.

Reciprocal Observations

Members of professional support groups should frequently observe each other teaching lessons structured cooperatively and then provide each other with useful feedback. This observation and feedback provide members with shared experiences to discuss and refer to. The observation and feedback, furthermore, have to be reciprocal. **Teachers especially need to treat each other with the deference that shows they recognize that anyone can have good and bad days and that the mistakes they note in a colleague may be the same mistakes that they will make tomorrow.**

We have found a number of important guidelines which we have teachers follow when they are observing the teaching other members of their professional support group. These guidelines include:

1. Realize that you can learn from every other member of the group, regardless of their experience and personal characteristics.

2. Make sure observation and feedback is reciprocal.

3. Ask the person you're observing what he/she would like you to focus your attention on. This may include specific students the teacher may wish observed, specific aspects of structuring interdependence or accountability, or some other aspect of cooperative learning.

4. Focus feedback and comments on what has taken place, not on personal competence.

5. Don't confuse a teacher's personal worth with her/his current level of competence in using cooperative learning procedures.

6. Be concrete and practical in your discussions about how effectively members are using cooperative learning procedures.

7. Above all, communicate respect for each other's overall teaching competence. We all have professional strengths and weaknesses. Recognize and respect those strengths in each other.

There are a number of ways to arrange time and opportunity for observing. The principal can take one teacher's class. If each building administrator taught one period a day, about one-fourth of the teachers would be released for a period each week. Two classes can be combined to view a movie or participate in an instructional activity, freeing one teacher. A class of students can be sent to the computer-lab or library and given research projects to complete. Volunteer aides or student teachers can be recruited to cover classes while teachers work together.

Working collaboratively with others brings with it camaraderie, friendship, warmth, satisfaction, and feelings of success. These are all to be enjoyed.

Helpful Norms

There are a number of helpful norms for professional support groups that will help them function effectively. These norms include:

1. I don't have to be perfect and neither do you!

2. It takes time to master cooperative learning procedures to a routine use level.

3. I'm here to improve my competence in using cooperative learning procedures.

4. You can criticize my implementation of cooperative learning procedures without me taking it personally.

5. I am secure enough to give you feedback about your implementation of cooperative learning procedures.

Structuring Colleagial Support Groups

Take care of each other. Share your energies with the group. No one must feel alone, cut off, for that is when you do not make it."

Willi Unsoeld

There are a number of steps that principals need to go through in structuring and managing colleagial support groups aimed at implementing cooperative learning procedures in the classroom. These steps include:

1. Schedule an "awareness" session in which all staff members are informed of the nature and power of cooperative learning.

2. Publicly announce your support for the use of cooperative learning procedures.

3. Specify the "key players" in your school and diagnose their level of commitment to implementing cooperative learning.

4. Recruit and select competent teachers to participate in the colleagial support groups.

5. Study the nature of cooperative learning.

6. Highlight the goal interdependence among members of a colleagial support group.

7. Negotiate a contract among the members of the colleagial support groups and a contract between the groups and you, if appropriate.

8. Convene and structure the first few meetings of the colleagial support group until members are able to structure them by themselves.

9. Provide the resources and incentives needed for the colleagial support groups to function.

10. Observe other members frequently.

11. Celebrate members' successes in implementing cooperative learning.

12. Ensure that the colleagial support groups discuss how well they function and maintain good relationships among members.

13. Build yourself in as a member not out as a consultant.

14. Keep a long-term, developmental perspective and protect the colleagial support groups from other pressures.

Table 7:1

Difference Between CSG's and Traditional Teaming

Colleagial Support Groups	Traditional Teams
Clear Positive Interdependence Is Structured Among Teachers	Teachers Are Told To Work Together
Frequent Face-To-Face Interaction	Teachers Often Work Independently
High Individual Accountability	No Individual Accountability
All Members Share Leadership Responsibilities	A Team Leader Is Assigned
Teachers Are Trained To Use Interpersonal And Small Group Skills	No Skill Training Is Provided
Teachers Process Group Effectiveness	No Group Processing

15. Be inclusive and include teachers who become interested, not exclusive.

Each of these steps will be discussed in the following sections.

Awareness Session

All members of a school staff need to participate in an awareness session on what cooperative learning is and why it should be implemented. Those teachers who do not use cooperative learning initially will then understand what their colleagues are doing and why. And when cooperative learning comes up in professional conversations and faculty meetings, all staff members will have the same definition and conception of what cooperative learning is.

Announcing Your Support

Forming of teacher colleagial support groups, aimed at improving competencies in using cooperative learning procedures, begins with the "cooperative learning leaders" announcing their support for teachers using cooperative learning strategies. This should take place in staff meetings, PTA meetings, and school newsletters. Such announcements should be frequent and cooperative learning should be described concretely in terms of life in school. The teachers who are using cooperative learning procedures should be visibly and publicly praised. The message that should be given is, "It is proper to structure learning cooperatively and therefore the staff should strive to do so." During the year, give updates on new research or describe new procedures to implement cooperative learning. Describe how cooperative learning agrees with district and school goals. Tolerate and absorb any initial failures of teachers learning how to structure lessons cooperatively. School displays and bulletin boards (as well as banners in the hallways) can be used to promote cooperative learning. An example is an elementary school in which the principal placed a large

banner opposite the main door to the school stating, "In this school we help each other learn." It is important that supervisors or principals do not kill cooperative learning by skepticism or neglect.

Specifying "Key Players" and Their Commitment

Consider the members of the school staff and administration. Who are the people whose support is necessary for a long-term, multi-year effort to implement cooperative learning to be launched and maintained in your school? These are the "key players." Identify the key players, rate their level of commitment to implementing cooperative learning, and the level of commitment you need them to have. Then plan how you will increase their commitment to the level needed.

Recruiting And Selecting Members

In selecting teachers to organize into a colleagial support group, look for teachers who are interested in trying cooperative learning, who will follow through and actually use cooperative learning, and who are your friends or at least teachers you would enjoy working with. Choose staff members who are motivated to use cooperative learning, who are committed enough to persist until the group is successful, and who are supportive, caring, and interpersonally skilled. Individuals who teach next door or across the hall from each other and who are already supporting each other's teaching efforts or are friends are often the best ones to start with.

Teachers can be recruited or selected to participate in colleagial support groups in a number of ways. You will want to look for members who are open, sensitive, supportive, and colleagially competent. Disgruntled, nonconstructive teachers tend to ruin colleagial support groups. Their criticism is rarely productive and they often lack wisdom in choosing battle-grounds. Alienated teachers may also be disruptive and demoralizing. And incompetent teachers who are struggling to survive are unprepared to begin colleagial growth until they gain basic control and self-confidence. In other words, **the members should be hand-picked to make sure the colleagial support groups are successful.** Specific methods of recruiting and selecting members may include:

1. Listening and participating in on teachers' conversations to find out who might be interested in perfecting their skills in using cooperative learning procedures.

2. Bringing teachers who like using cooperative learning procedures together.

3. Recruiting grade level groups that already informally or formally serve as colleagial support groups.

4. Recruiting teachers who are good friends with each other and who will welcome the opportunity to work more closely with each other.

5. Recruiting teachers who have the same preparation period.

When recruiting colleagial support group members, approach your staff members very carefully (to establish a collaborative relationship). This is a touchy task as it is easy to drive teachers away. Be sure to present the possibility of working together to improve your own use of cooperative procedures as well as theirs. Never say "It is easy" or "Anyone can do it!" Never say, "Have I got a good idea for you! Here is how we are going to change the way you teach!" Instead, ask for help in implementing cooperative learning in the school, use a soft approach of indicating an open door, make the cooperative (not expert-novice) relationship clear, and be clear about the purpose of providing support and assistance in helping each other increase expertise in implementing cooperative learning. Be sure to be realistic about the length of time it will take to gain some expertise in using cooperative learning procedures and the amount of work it will take.

Once you have picked two or more teachers and approached them about working together on implementing cooperative learning, they must know how to proceed. In essence, they must know how to help each other develop expertise in implementing cooperative learning.

Studying the Nature of Cooperative Learning

When you have established the membership of a colleagial support group, you will find it helpful to review the nature of cooperative learning for the members. Methods are:

1. Recommend a training course or workshop they can participate in.

2. Arrange for them to observe colleagues who are experienced in using cooperative learning procedures.

3. Provide **Circles Of Learning** or **Cooperation in the Classroom** for members to read.

4. Have consultants or experienced teachers present an awareness session for all the staff in the school.

5. Have the group meet with a district specialist in cooperative learning.

The heart of cooperative learning is the five basic elements. Simply placing teachers in small groups does not mean that they will commit themselves to each other's professional growth. Proximity may result in competition to see who is best and in high levels of evaluation apprehension and fear. Cooperative relationships among teachers or administrators have to be structured just as carefully as does cooperative learning in the classroom. This means that the five essential elements of cooperative relationships have to be carefully structured within colleagial support groups:

1. **Positive interdependence:** Each member must perceive that it is "sink or swim together."

2. **Face-to-face promotive interaction:** Each member must orally discuss what he or she is learning and promote colleagues' productivity.

3. **Personal responsibility/individual accountability:** Each member must feel personally responsible and accountable for contributing his or her fair share of the work.

© Johnson & Johnson

The emphasis on mutual responsibility for achievement sets up the cooperative relationship.

WE SINK OR SWIM TOGETHER.

4. **Social skills:** Each member must master the basic leadership, communication, decision-making, trust-building, and conflict-management skills necessary for a cooperative group to function effectively.

5. **Group processing:** Each member must periodically reflect on how well the group is functioning and analyze how the interaction among group members can become more productive.

After reviewing the nature of cooperative learning, the level of expertise of each member of the colleagial support group should be assessed. Note the amount of training each member has and discuss the next training course he or she should next attend.

A critical aspect of effective colleagial support groups is how they manage conflict among members. When teachers disagree with each other, a set of specific controversy and conflict-management skills are required to ensure that creative insights and more positive relationships result. These procedures and skills are detailed elsewhere (Johnson, Johnson, & Smith, 1986; Johnson & Johnson, 1987).

Highlighting Goal Interdependence

If a man does not know to which port he is sailing, no wind is favorable.

Seneca

The goal of a colleagial support group is to work jointly to improve continuously each other's competence in using cooperative learning procedures or, in other words, to teach each other how to better use cooperative learning strategies. Members of a colleagial support group must believe that they need each other and in order to complete the group's task, they "sink or swim together." Ways of creating the perception of positive interdependence are mutual goals, joint rewards, shared materials and information, a division of labor, and a group-space in which to meet and work. Review the chapter on positive interdependence in **Cooperation In The Classroom** and plan how to use at least four of the methods of structuring positive interdependence in planning colleagial support group meetings.

Leaders challenge the status quo of competitive / individualistic teaching and create a mutual vision of cooperative classrooms. By highlighting the mutual goals teachers are striving to achieve and creating a belief that "we sink or swim together," the leader provides meaning, significance, and heroism to teaching. In a General Motors plant a number of years ago the manager put up signs all over the walls saying "Beat Japan" and the like. The manager even enticed some Hell's Angels types into singing "God Bless America" at a plant rally. When there is meaning to what one does, ordinary people exert extraordinary effort. These are methods businesses use to highlight the mutual goals of the employees. Schools need to do likewise. Banners can proclaim that it is a cooperative school in which students help each other learn and teachers help each other provide quality instruction. All individuals need to be working towards meaningful goals. Teachers are willing to commit psychological and physical energy to a cause they perceive to be (in some sense) great. The leader becomes the "keeper of the dream" who inspires staff members to commit effort to quality teaching. It is the cooperative goals that highlight the meaning to what staff members are doing.

Negotiate the Contract

When teachers become part of a colleagial support group they accept certain mutual responsibilities. These include:

1. Attend and actively participate in the meetings of the colleagial support group.

2. Use cooperative learning procedures regularly and frequently in their classes.

3. Help, assist, encourage, and support other members' use of cooperative learning.

These responsibilities need to be made into a contract that is eventually formalized and will serve as a basis for discussing how well the colleagial support group is functioning. The responsibilities of the "cooperative learning leaders" in structuring and managing the colleagial support group need to be clear in order to legitimize their involvement in the group.

Structuring the Initial Meetings

The activities of the colleagial support group are aimed at helping all members master, refine, adapt, and experiment with cooperative learning procedures. Discussing their implementation efforts, jointly planning lessons and jointly designing curriculum materials,

Contract

and reciprocally observing each other's implementation efforts are the major activities of the group.

The "cooperative learning leader" should schedule and convene the **first meeting of the colleagial support group** and ensure that it covers the following agenda items:

1. Your support of their efforts in implementing cooperative learning procedures.

2. When the regular meeting time will be. The meeting has to last at least 50 to 60 minutes. Breakfast clubs, which meet once a week for breakfast before school begins are popular.

3. The purposes of meetings (discussion of implementation efforts, joint planning of lessons and materials, and reciprocal observation).

4. An assessment of the resources they need in order to meet regularly and engage in these activities. Potential resources are discussed in the next section.

5. Plans to make each meeting both productive and fun. With that in mind you might ask who is going to be in charge of the refreshments for the next meeting (a cooperative effort is recommended).

6. Specific plans for:

    a. When the next meeting will be.

    b. What cooperatively structured lessons they will teach before the next meeting.

    c. What the agenda for the next meeting will be (one item will be to discuss how well their cooperatively structured lessons went).

7. Agree on a tentative contract among members and between the group and yourself.

A sample agenda for the second meeting is:

1. Welcome everyone and have a "warm-up," such as a handout on the types of positive interdependence that may be used in cooperatively structured lessons.

2. Discuss their use of cooperative learning procedures:

   a. Lessons taught during the past week.

   b. Their successes--what were the things they liked best.

   c. Any problems that surfaced during the lessons.

3. Discuss the problems at some length and generate a number of alternative strategies for solving each, so that each member may select from a menu of alternative solutions rather than having to implement any one solution.

4. Jointly plan a lesson that they will all teach during the following week.

5. Plan the agenda and menu for the next meeting.

A sample agenda for the third meeting may be:

1. Warm up by handing out a list of ways of ensuring individual accountability in cooperatively structured lessons.

2. Discussing how well the lesson they taught went, identifying positive aspects and problems that arose.

3. Discuss the problems and generate a number of solutions that might be implemented. Revise the lesson to solve any problems.

4. Plan for as many of the members as possible to observe each other teach a lesson structured cooperatively during the following week. Make specific contracts as to what the observer should focus on. An outline of the teacher's role in cooperative learning situations may be helpful.

5. Set agenda and menu for the following week.

The sample agenda for the fourth meeting is as follows:

1. Warm up by handing out material on teaching students the social skills they need to work collaboratively.

2. Discuss how well the observations went and what the members observed. The roles for constructive feedback should be reviewed (see Johnson, 1990). The basic com-

ponents of cooperative learning situations should also be reviewed. Your role is to ensure that all feedback is constructive and helpful.

3. Plan for the next round of observations.

4. Set the agenda and the menu for the next meeting.

These sample agendas are only aimed at outlining what might happen in the initial meetings of the colleagial support groups. You will need to revise these meeting agendas to better meet the needs of your teachers.

Providing Resources and Incentives

Teachers' perceptions of their interdependence may be considerably enhanced if you offer joint incentives for being an effective colleagial support group. A maxim developed within the business/industrial sector of our society states, "If two individuals get paid for working as a pair, it is amazing how much interest they take in helping one another succeed!" Incentives can be classified as tangible, interpersonal, and personal. Some examples of incentives teachers find valuable are:

1. The opportunity to present an inservice session on cooperative learning procedures to the other members of the staff or to the staff of another school.

2. The opportunity to apply for summer salaries to revise curriculum for cooperatively structured lessons.

3. Visible public praise for their efforts in implementing cooperative learning procedures.

4. Written recognition of their efforts which goes into their individual files.

5. The opportunity to observe teachers in other schools implementing cooperative learning procedures.

To be effective, a colleagial support group will need a variety of resources that only supervisors and principals can provide. Needed resources include:

1. Released time during working hours to meet.

2. A small fund for materials and expenses in implementing cooperative learning.

3. Released time to observe each other teach cooperative lessons.

4. Released time to visit the classrooms of teachers in other schools who are experienced in using cooperative learning procedures.

5. Materials on cooperative learning, such as research updates, helpful hints, sample lesson plans, books, and so forth.

6. Time and resources to help them get started and to help them maintain high interest and involvement in implementing cooperative learning procedures in their classrooms.

7. Emotional support and encouragement to continue their efforts. Always remember that pressure (however subtle) on teachers to implement cooperative learning procedures in their classrooms must be coupled with tangible and visible support from you.

Observe Frequently

Leaders spend their time "where the action is." This means getting out of your office and into classrooms. This visible leadership is called "management by walking around" (Peters & Waterman, 1982). Leaders should visit classrooms frequently, observing instruction in action. Members of colleagial support groups should visit each other's classes frequently, observing cooperative learning in action. The visits do not always have to be long. Besides the structured reciprocal observations members should engage in drop-ins. A **drop-in** is simply an unannounced visit in a clasroomto spend a few minutes observing. The observer may jot down a few notes to highlight something positive observed and then give it to the teacher as a form of feedback during the next colleagial support group meeting.

Celebrating Successes

An essential aspect of providing leadership to colleagial support groups is to observe members using cooperative learning frequently enough that their successes can be celebrated. **A sense of accomplishment complements a sense of purpose.** Both must be nurtured. There is a tremendous power in regular and positive peer feedback. Colleagial support groups need to be designed to produce lots of success in implementing cooperative

Table 7:2

Recognizing And Celebrating Cooperative Learning Successes

Errors	Accuracies
Implementation Is A Mystery	Implementation Is Visible
Tell The Principal	"Good News" Swapped Among Colleagues
Recognition From Principal Only	Peer Respect And Recognition
Top Few Superstars Recognized	Recognition Of Almost Everyone
Reward For Anything	Valuable Action Must Be Completed For Reward

groups and celebrate it when it occurs. Make use of nonmonetary, interpersonal incentives. Emphasize interpersonal recognition rather than formal evaluation. In essence:

1. Seek out successful implementations of cooperative learning and honor them with all sorts of positive recognition and reinforcement.

2. Seek out opportunities for "good news" swapping among colleagues. Peer respect and recognition are powerful motivators.

In recognizing and celebrating the success of colleagial support group members in implementing cooperative learning, there are a set of errors that may be made and a set of accuracies.

There is nothing more motivating than having colleagues cheering one on and jointly celebrating one's successes. The more effective the school, the more positive peer confirmation is utilized. Create some hoopla within your colleagial support groups and school. Celebrate often!

Discussing How Well the Colleagial Support Groups Function

One area in which most teacher colleagial support groups need considerable help and encouragement is in discussing how well their meetings are contributing to achieving the group's goals and to maintaining effective working relationships among members. This means that you will need to take some initiative in ensuring that one teacher periodically systematically observes a meeting and time is spent on processing how well the group is functioning. After the teachers become experienced in helping their student groups discuss their group functioning, the teachers' abilities to discuss the functioning of their own meetings should increase. But even the most experienced teachers may avoid discussing the functioning of meetings unless the supervisors or principals structure it.

Building Yourself In As a Member

You should be part of each colleagial support group in your jurisdiction. Build yourself in not out! Do not be lonely! Members of a colleagial support group will enjoy considerable success, feel a sense of accomplishment, like each other, see each other as supportive and accepting, and have a sense of camaraderie that significantly increases the quality of their colleagial lives. You should be part of these feelings!

Protecting and Nurturing

When teachers become serious about implementing cooperative learning procedures in their classrooms supervisors and principals will have to do a number of things to protect and nurture the teachers' efforts. Some examples are:

1. There will inevitably be initial failures and problems. Students may be unhappy about the change in the "system," students will be unskilled in working collaboratively, materials may be inappropriate, and what a teacher may define as cooperative learning may not be what you define as cooperative learning. You will have to allow for these initial problems and communicate strongly to your teachers that such initial "start-up costs" are to be expected and accepted. Do not require your teachers to be perfect during the first week they try structuring lessons cooperatively!

2. There will be other innovations within your jurisdiction that will compete for teachers' attention and energy. Part of your responsibilities are to find commonalties of interest and intent among presumably opposing innovations. Encourage your teachers to integrate cooperative learning with other instructional strategies they use or are trying out. But at all costs avoid the cycle of making cooperative learning the focus for a few months or a year and then springing another innovation on your teachers. The "try it and then drop it for the next fad" cycle is especially destructive to quality teaching. Make sure that your teachers recognize that your and their commitment to cooperative learning has to span a number of years.

3. Translate what cooperative learning is so that diverse groups of teachers can understand its importance and usefulness.

4. Deflect, soften, and negate resistance to implementing cooperative learning within your staff. If some teachers believe "I tried that once and it did not work," protect the teachers who are willing to become involved in implementing cooperative learning in their classrooms from demoralizing conversations and criticism from such colleagues.

5. Within any staff there may be destructive competition among teachers as to who is best. Part of your responsibilities are to defuse such "win-lose" dynamics and encourage mutual respect, support, and assistance among your teachers.

6. Within any colleagial support group there will come a time when one member has hurt the feelings of another member or when conflicts arise that disrupt the cohesiveness and productivity of the group. Your task at that point is to ensure that hurt feelings become repaired and that conflicts are constructively resolved. For specific procedures for doing so, see Johnson and Johnson (1987).

7. Most teachers are concerned that, if a parent complains about their use of cooperative learning procedures, they will receive strong support from their principal and supervisors. Give it. If the parents of the students are concerned and involved in their children's education, they may be curious or even skeptical at any modification of teaching procedures. Be ready to explain why a teacher is using cooperative learning procedures and that it is with your full support and approval.

8. Have the courage to see your teachers through the process of learning how to use cooperative learning procedures effectively.

Think Developmentally

Mastering cooperative learning procedures so that they are used routinely takes time. For most teachers it does not happen in a few weeks or even in a few months. Most teachers work hard for two to three years gaining a thorough understanding of cooperative learning and a solid expertise in using it. You should always think in terms of development, not in radically changing everything the teacher is doing immediately. Have the teacher start with one area, perfect his or her procedures for implementing cooperative learning, and then expand to a second area. Plan developmentally for a two or three year process with heavy emphasis on supporting and maintaining interest. While doing so, you will need to communicate to other staff members that cooperative learning is not this year's fad. A long-term, multi-year emphasis on implementing cooperative learning is required and

leaders must protect implementation efforts from being deemphasized to make way for new fads.

Be Inclusive, Not Exclusive

As your success in reaching out to and working with teachers is recognized, teachers will begin asking you to work with them next. Be open to such invitations. When you do not have time to meet all the requests, pair each new teacher with an experienced veteran whom you have trained. Keep your colleagial support groups small. Each time a teacher you are working with achieves some expertise in implementing cooperative learning, pair him or her with a teacher just expressing an interest in doing so. This matchmaking will allow the teacher with newly gained expertise to solidify what they have learned by teaching it to another person. Give guidance as to how to reach out effectively. Keep in contact with the teachers you have worked with and regularly provide support and assistance. Finally, periodically lead a celebration of the success they are having in implementing cooperative learning. **Both a sense of purpose and accomplishment should be nurtured among the teachers you train.**

Points To Remember

1. For your teachers to gain sufficient expertise that they can use cooperative learning routinely without considerable thought and planning will take them two to three years.

2. From working with you and from any training programs they participate in, your teachers will need (a) a clear conceptual model of what "good" cooperative learning is and (b) to be empowered and assisted to practice and practice and practice structuring lessons and units cooperatively.

3. One difficulty in convincing teachers to adopt a new instructional practice is in their fears about the responses it will elicit from students. "When students say x, what will I say back?" is a critical barrier. In order to reduce their fears, your teachers will need to see each other (and you) teach. It is through seeing other teachers respond to students' questions and actions that an understanding of how to do so is achieved. Just as ball-players need to see other people play in order to form a frame-of-reference as to how good they are and where they need to improve, teachers

need to compare their implementations of cooperative learning with those of others.

4. The more relaxed and playful teachers are in observing each other in guided practice sessions the better, as the same learning mood will transfer to post-training practice.

A District Strategy

General procedures "cooperative learning leaders" may use in institutionalizing cooperative learning within their school district are as follows:

1. Give a general awareness inservice session to an entire school and ask for volunteers to become a school-based colleagial support group to work systematically on improving their skills in using cooperative learning procedures.

2. Give the basic training in cooperative learning, using this book to ensure that all the critical aspects are covered systematically.

3. Work with each teacher individually:

   a. Teach a cooperatively structured lesson in his or her classroom.

   b. Co-plan a cooperatively structured lesson which is then jointly taught.

   c. Co-plan a lesson that the teacher teaches while you observe.

Through repeated classroom visits each teacher should be trained one-on-one. Some basic rules for working with an individual teacher are:

   a. All lessons are prepared together.

   b. The teacher is the expert on his or her classroom while you are the expert on cooperative learning.

   c. When you are in the teacher's classroom, the teacher owns the lesson. It is the teacher's lesson, not yours.

d. Each time you meet with a teacher have some new helpful strategy, activity, or set of materials that is tailored to the teacher's subject area or to a specific problem student in the teacher's classroom. This builds a personal as well as a colleagial aspect to the help and assistance in implementing cooperative learning procedures.

4. Network the teachers you are training into colleagial support groups. These groups may meet with and without you.

5. As an additional maintenance procedure, each month send out a newsletter on "How to Help Students Work in Groups." The newsletter contains lesson plans and classroom activities that teachers can try out and/or discuss in the meetings of their colleagial support groups.

6. Meet regularly with curriculum directors, talk to parent groups, attend the principals' cabinet meetings, trouble-shoot for your teachers, coordinate collaboration among support group members, and generally spend your days in schools and classrooms.

7. Be genuinely enthusiastic about the use of cooperative learning procedures. Build personal and supportive relationships with the teachers you work with, and show ingenuity in discovering ways to help teachers use cooperative learning procedures.

Summary: Colleagial Support Groups

To lead your school you need to challenge the status quo of competitive / individualistic learning and staff relations, inspire a new vision of cooperative learning in the classroom and cooperation among staff members, empower staff members by organizing them into cooperative teams, lead by example by using cooperative strategies and procedures, and encourage staff members to persevere until they have gained considerable expertise in using cooperative learning. The intent of such leadership is to improve the quality of instruction and learning within the school. Empowering teachers to teach better is the number one priority of leadership. This means that colleagial support groups are the most important staff cooperative team structured within the school. Gaining expertise requires a cooperative context in which colleagues whom one trusts are committed to one's professional growth and willing to provide assistance, support, and encouragement to further it.

Professional competence is not achieved in isolation from one's peers. When teacher colleagial support groups are structured cooperatively (as opposed to competitively or individualistically) to improve the expertise of all members, productivity will tend to increase as members do in fact gain increased expertise, committed and positive relationships will tend to develop among teachers, social support among staff members will tend to increase, and professional self-esteem will tend to be enhanced. These conclusions are supported by at least 133 studies that have been conducted over the past 90 years. These results apply, however, only when the teacher colleagial support groups have carefully structured positive interdependence, face-to-face promotive interaction, personal responsibility, and periodic group processing. In addition, the teachers must possess the required leadership, communication, trust-building, decision-making, and conflict-management skills.

Colleagial support groups need to be safe places where (1) members like to be, (2) there is support, caring, concern, laughter, and camaraderie, and (3) the primary goal of improving each other's expertise in implementing cooperative learning is never obscured.

Teacher colleagial support groups cannot survive in isolation. If the classroom and the overall district are structured competitively, the cooperation among teachers needed for teachers to learn from each other will not be sustained. A consistent and coherent organizational structure is established when teachers use cooperative learning in the classroom, administrators organize their faculty into colleagial support groups, and the superintendent organizes the district's administrators into colleagial support groups. The long-term support and assistance necessary for teachers to learn from each other over their entire careers may then be sustained.

Implementation Assignment 7

1. List the steps you have taken during this course to provide yourself with collegial support as you implement cooperative learning groups.

2. List five things you could do to strengthen your collegial support group.

3. Do three of these things this week. Bring your lists and a report of the results of your efforts to class to share.

4. Take the phone numbers of your base group. Call them periodically and provide encouragement and support for their efforts to implement cooperation learning.

⟨ Cooperative Learning Contract ⟩

Major Learnings	Implementation Plans

Date _____ Date of Progress Report Meeting _____

Participant's Signature _____

Signatures of Other Group Members _____ _____

_____ _____ _____

⊶❰ Cooperative Learning Progress Report ❱⊷

NAME _____   SCHOOL _____

AGE LEVEL _____   SUBJECT _____

DAY AND DATE	DESCRIPTION OF TASKS and ACTIVITIES PERFORMED	SUCCESSES EXPERIENCED	PROBLEMS ENCOUNTERED

Description of critical or interesting incidents:

7:31

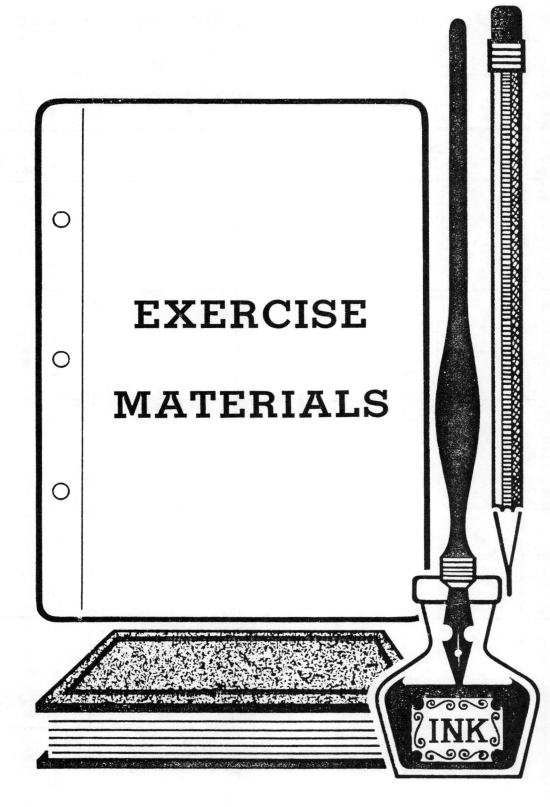

EXERCISE

MATERIALS

Reaching Out to Build A Support System

1. Select another teacher to work with who is a friend, who has an interest in cooperative learning, who tends to be supportive, or who you believe you can work with easily.

   The name of the teacher selected is _____

2. Generate a list of rules/guidelines for initiating contact:

   a._____

   b._____

   c._____

   d._____

   e._____

Possible rules include:

   a. Being enthusiastic (but not a zealot).

   b. Communicate research support.

   c. Ask for help to fulfill the requirements of the course.

   d. Say: "You would be terrific at this."

   e. Relate it to their concerns and needs.

   f. Connect it with material they are familiar with.

It is important not to drive colleagues away from cooperative learning by the way you present it or by pressuring them to use it. It is also important not to give the impression that using cooperative learning procedures is "easy" or that "anyone can do it."

3. Invite your colleague to observe you teach a cooperatively structured lesson. This will entail:

   a. Meeting before the lesson to brief your colleague on the nature of cooperative learning and what you would like him or her to observe.

   b. Conducting the lesson while your colleague observes using an observation sheet.

   c. Meeting after the lesson to process how well the lesson went.

4. Develop an orientation sheet so that your colleague will know what you are trying to do and what to watch for. This observation sheet might include:

   a. A definition of cooperative learning.

   b. Objectives of the lesson.

   c. The way in which positive interdependence is structured.

   d. The decisions (group size, assigning students to groups, and so forth) made before cooperative learning begins.

   e. What you would like your colleague to observe. The observing teacher's role must be clearly defined.

   f. Reviewing how to use the observation sheet.

   g. Precuing the processing of the lesson.

5. Develop a procedure for processing the results of your colleague's observing. The goal of this session is to persuade your colleague to become part of a professional support group to facilitate the implementation of cooperative learning. Things to include in the procedure are:

   a. The cooperative goal of discussing how best to implement cooperative learning procedures.

   b. A description of the results of your colleague's observation.

    c. A way to make your colleague feel appreciated for the time and effort he or she has contributed.

    d. A discussion of the possibility of meeting regularly to continue working on implementing cooperative learning.

Give a copy of the article, **Cooperative Learning: Ignored but Powerful**, and perhaps a lesson plan to your colleague.

6. Role play helping a colleague plan a cooperative lesson through the following procedure:

    a. Assign one person to be the veteran who is helping, one person to be the new person who is learning how to structure lessons cooperatively, and an observer to watch the interaction.

    b. Work through a real lesson using the assigned roles and the lesson planning sheet:

        1. The new teacher asks as many difficult questions as possible.

        2. The veteran works on building a collaborative relationship.

        3. The observer collects positive strategies, insights, and key interactions.

As a triad, write down ten pieces of advice to teachers who are helping colleagues get started implementing cooperative learning groups.

7. Plan for reciprocal observations:

    a. Review the goals for observing each other teach cooperative lessons.

    b. Go through the observation sheet category by category making sure that each of you are comfortable with using the observation sheet.

    c. Develop a set of rules or guidelines for processing data with another teacher (start with observations about students and work your way to observations about the teaching).

Chapter 8

Where You Go From Here

Table Of Contents

Types Of Cooperative Learning

Now that you have mastered the use of formal cooperative learning groups, there are a number of steps you might consider. The first is to expand your use of cooperative learning to include three types of cooperative learning (Johnson, Johnson, & Holubec, 1988b): **formal cooperative learning groups, informal cooperative learning groups,** and **cooperative base groups**.

Formal Cooperative Learning Groups

Formal cooperative learning groups may last for several minutes to several class sessions to complete a specific task or assignment (such as solving a set of problems, completing a unit, writing a report or theme, conducting an experiment, and reading and comprehending a story, play, chapter, or book). This book has focused on formal cooperative learning groups. Any course requirement or assignment may be reformulated to be cooperative rather than competitive or individualistic through the use of formal cooperative learning groups. **Gaining expertise in using formal cooperative learning groups provides the foundation for gaining expertise in using informal and base groups.**

Informal Cooperative Learning Groups

Informal cooperative learning groups are temporary, ad hoc groups that last for only one discussion or one class period. Their **purposes** are to focus student attention on the material to be learned, create an expectation set and mood conducive to learning, help organize in advance the material to be covered in a class session, ensure that students cognitively process the material being taught, and provide closure to an instructional session. They may be used at any time, but are especially useful during a lecture or direct teaching. The length of time students can attend to a lecture before their minds drift away is estimated to be from 12 to 15 minutes.

During direct teaching the instructional challenge for the teacher is to ensure that students do the intellectual work of organizing material, explaining it, summarizing it, and integrating it into existing conceptual networks. This may be achieved by having students do the advance organizing, cognitive process what they are learning, and provide closure to the lesson. Breaking up lectures with short cooperative processing times will give you less lecture time, but will enhance what is learned and build relationships among the students in your class. It will help counter what is proclaimed as the main problem of lectures: "The information passes from the notes of the teacher to the notes of the student without passing through the mind of either one."

The following procedure may help to plan a lecture that keeps students actively engaged intellectually. It entails having **focused discussions** before and after a lecture (i.e., bookends) and interspersing **turn-to-your-partner** discussions throughout the lecture.

1. **Focused Discussion 1**: Plan your lecture around a series of questions that the lecture answers. Prepare the questions on an overhead transparency or write them on the board so that students can see them. Students will discuss the questions in pairs. The discussion task is aimed at promoting **advance organizing** of what the students know about the topic to be presented and creates an **expectation set** and a learning mood conductive to learning.

2. **Turn-To-Your-Partner Discussions**: Divide the lecture into 10 to 15 minute segments. Plan a short discussion task to be given to pairs of students after each segment. The task needs to be short enough that students can complete it within three or four minutes. Its purpose is to ensure that students are actively thinking about the material being presented. **It is important that students are randomly called on to share their answers after each discussion task.** Such **individual accountability** ensures that the pairs take the tasks seriously and check each other to ensure that both are prepared to answer. Each discussion task should have four components: **formulate** an answer to the question being asked, **share** your answer with your partner, **listen** carefully to his or her answer, and to **create** a new answer that is superior to each member's initial formulation through the processes of association, building on each other's thoughts, and synthesizing. Students will need to gain some experience with this procedure to become skilled in doing it within a short period of time.

3. **Focused Discussion 2**: Give students an ending discussion task to provide closure to the lecture. Usually students are given five or six minutes to summarize and discuss the material covered in the lecture. The discussion should result in students integrating what they have just learned into existing conceptual frameworks. The task may also point students toward what the homework will cover or what will be presented in the next class session.

Until students become familiar and experienced with the procedure, **process** it regularly to help them increase their skill and speed in completing short discussion tasks.

The informal cooperative learning group is not only effective for getting students actively involved in processing what they are learning, it also provides time for you to gather your wits, reorganize your notes, take a deep breath, and move around the class listening to what students are saying. Listening to student discussions provides you with "windows" into your students' levels of reasoning and gives you direction and insight into how the concepts you are teaching are being grasped by your students.

Base Groups

Base groups are long-term, heterogeneous cooperative learning groups with stable membership. **The primary responsibility of members is to provide each other with the support, encouragement, and assistance they need to make academic progress.** The base group verifies that each member is completing the assignments and progressing satisfactorily through the academic program. Base groups may be given the task of letting absent group members know what went on in the class when they miss a session and bring them up to date. The use of base groups tends to improve attendance, personalize the work required and the school experience, and improve the quality and quantity of learning. The base group is the source of permanent and caring peer relationships within which students are committed to and support each other's educational success.

Base groups last for at least a semester or year and preferably for several years. The larger the class and the more complex the subject matter, the more important it is to have base groups. Learning for your groupmates is a powerful motivator. Receiving social support and being held accountable for appropriate behavior by peers who care about you and have a long-term commitment to your success and well-being is an important aspect of growing up and progressing through school.

It is important that some of the relationships built within cooperative learning groups are permanent. School has to be more than a series of "ship-board romances" that last for only a semester or year. In elementary, junior-high, high-schools, and colleges students should be assigned to permanent base groups. The base groups should then be assigned to most classes so that members spend much of the day together and regularly complete cooperative learning tasks. Doing so can create permanent caring and committed relationships that will provide students with the support, help, encouragement, and assistance they need to make academic progress and develop cognitively and socially in healthy ways.

When used in combination, these formal, informal, and base cooperative learning groups provide an overall structure to classroom life. The use of informal and base groups are described in depth in:

Johnson, D. W., Johnson, R., & Holubec, E. (1988). **Advanced cooperative learning**. Edina, MN: Interaction Book Company.

Teaching Students' Social Skills

The second step in adding to your expertise in using cooperative learning is to teach students additional social skills. There are many sources of further social skills to be taught to students, including **Advanced Cooperative Learning** (Johnson, Johnson, & Holubec, 1988b), **Reaching Out** (Johnson, 1990), and **Joining Together** (Johnson & F. Johnson, 1991).

Integrated Use Of All Three Goal Structures

The third step in increasing your expertise in using cooperative learning is to use all three goal structures within an integrated way. While the dominant goal structure within any classroom should be cooperation (which ideally would be used about 60 - 70 percent of the time), competitive and individualistic efforts are useful supplements. Competition may be used as a fun change-of-pace during an instructional unit that is predominantly structured cooperatively and individualistic learning is often productive when the information learned is subsequently used in a cooperative activity. The integrated use of cooperative, competitive, and individualistic learning is described in depth with in Johnson and Johnson (1991) and Johnson, Johnson, and Holubec (1988b).

Utilizing Creative Conflict

The fifth step is to promote the creative use of conflict within the classroom and school. Teachers are peacemakers. Much of their time is spent dealing with conflicts among students, between students and staff, between staff and parents, or even among staff members. Conflicts are inevitable whenever committed people work together to achieve mutual goals. Whether the conflicts are constructive influences that promote greater productivity and closer personal relationships, or destructive influences that create divisiveness and ineffectiveness, depends on how they are managed.

Conflicts are constructively managed through a five step procedure (Johnson & Johnson, 1987). **The first step is creating a cooperative context.** In order for long-term mutual interests to be recognized and valued, individuals have to perceive their interdependence and be invested in each other's well being. **The second step is structuring academic controversies.** In order to maximize student achievement, critical thinking, and higher-level reasoning, students need to engage in intellectual conflicts. Within structured controversies, students work with a learning partner in examining an academic issue, preparing a pro or con position, advocating their position to an opposing pair, criticizing the opposing position, reversing perspectives, and synthesizing the best arguments on both sides to derive a conclusion. The use of academic controversy is a very powerful instructional procedure that will move cooperative learning groups to new heights of productivity and higher-level learning.

The third step is teaching students how to negotiate and the fourth step is teaching students how to mediate. Students first try to negotiate their conflicts and, if that fails, ask a mediator for help. Finally, when mediation fails, **the teacher or principal arbitrates the conflict.** This is a last resort because it typically involves deciding who is right and wrong, leaving at least one student angry toward the arbitrator.

The procedures for using this five-step process of utilizing constructive conflict to improve instruction may be found in:

Johnson, D. W., & Johnson, R. (1987). **Creative conflict**. Edina, MN: Interaction Book Company.

Empowering Staff Through Cooperative Teams

What is good for students is even better for staff. A cooperative school is one in which cooperative learning dominates the classroom and cooperative teams dominate staff efforts. It is social support from and accountability to valued peers that motivates committed efforts to succeed. Empowering individuals through cooperative teamwork is done in three ways: (1) **colleagial support groups** (to increase teachers' instructional expertise and success), (2) **task forces** (to plan and implement solutions to school-wide issues and problems such as curriculum adoptions and lunchroom behavior), and (3) **ad hoc decision-making groups** (to use during faculty meetings to involve all staff members in important school decisions). How to structure and use these three types of cooperative teams may be found in:

Johnson, D. W., Johnson, R. (1989). **Leading the cooperative school**. Edina, MN: Interaction Book Company.

Looking Forward

At the end of this book you are at a new beginning. Years of experience in using cooperative learning in your classroom are needed to gain expertise in its use. While you are using cooperative learning there is much more to learn about its use. The addition of informal cooperative learning activities and long-term permanent base groups will increase the power and effectiveness of cooperation in your classroom. Teaching students more and more sophisticated social skills will improve how well they work together to maximize their learning. Supplementing the use of cooperative learning with appropriate competitions and individualistic assignments will further enrich the quality of learning within your classroom. Structuring academic controversies within your cooperative learning groups will move students to higher levels of reasoning and thinking while providing a considerable increase in energy and fun. Teaching students how to negotiate their differences and mediate each other's conflicts will accelerate their skills in managing conflicts within cooperative learning groups. Finally, moving cooperation up to the school and district levels by structuring staff p73 into cooperative teams will create a congruent organizational structure within which both faculty and students will thrive.

References

Aronson, E. (1978). **The jigsaw classroom**. Beverly Hills, CA: Sage Publications.

Belonging (16 mm film/videotape) (1980). Edina, MN: Interaction Book Company.

Berman, P., & McLaughlin, M. (1978). **Federal programs supporting educational change, Vol. VIII: Implementing and sustaining innovations.** Santa Monica, CA: Rand Corporation.

Blake, R., & Moulton, J. (1961). Comprehension of own and outgroup positions under intergroup competition. **Journal of Conflict Resolution, 5**, 304-310.

Bower, S. (1960). **Early identification of emotionally handicapped children in school.** Springfield, IL: Thomas.

Campbell, J. (1965). **The children's crusader: Colonel Francis W. Parker.** PhD dissertation, Teachers College, Columbia University.

Circles of Learning (16mm film/videotape)(1983). Edina, MN: Interaction Book Co.

Cartwright, D., & Zander, A. (Eds.) (1968). **Group dynamics.** New York: Harper & Row.

Cohen, E. (1986). **Designing groupwork.** New York: Teachers College Press.

Crawford, J., & Haaland, G. (1972). Predecisional information seeking and subsequent conformity in the social influence process. **Journal of Personality and Social Psychology, 23**, 112-119.

Deutsch, M. (1949). An experimental study of the effects of cooperation and competition upon group processes. **Human Relations, 2**, 199-232.

Deutsch, M. (1962). Cooperation and trust: Some theoretical notes. In M.R. Jones (Ed.), **Nebraska symposium on motivation** (pp. 275-319). Lincoln, NE: University of Nebraska Press.

Deutsch, M. (1973). **The resolution of conflict**. New Haven, Conn.: Yale University Press.

Deutsch, M. (1975). Equity, equality, and need: What determines which values will be used as the basis for distributive justice. **Journal of Social Issues, 31,** 137-149.

Deutsch, M. (1979). A critical review of equity theory: An alternative perspective on the social psychology of justice. **International Journal of Group Tensions, 9,** 20-49.

DeVries, D., & Edwards, K. (1973). Learning games and student teams: Their effects on classroom process. **American Journal of Educational Research, 10,** 307-318.

DeVries, D., Slavin, R., Fennessey, G., Edwards, K., & Lombardo, M. (1980). **Teams-games-tournament.** Englewood Cliffs, NJ: Educational Technology.

Dishon, D., & O'Leary, P. (1981). Teaching students to work in groups: Cooperative learning in the classroom. In P. Roy (Ed.), **Structuring cooperative learning experiences in the classroom: The 1982 handbook.** Edina, MN: Interaction Book Company.

Dishon, D., & O'Leary, P. (1984). **A guidebook for cooperative learning.** Holmes Beach, FL: Learning Publications.

Gibbs, J. (1987). **Tribes.** Santa Rosa, CA: Center Source Publications.

Glasser, W. (1986). **Control theory in the classroom.** New York: Harper & Row.

Gronlund, N. (1959). **Sociometry in the classroom.** New York: Harper.

Hartup, W. (1976). Peer interaction and the behavioral development of the individual child. In E. Schloper and R. Reicher (Eds.), **Psychopathology and child development.** New York: Plenum.

Hartup, W., Glazer, J., & Charlesworth, R. (1967). Peer reinforcement and sociometric status. **Child Development, 38,** 1017-1024.

Horowitz, F. (1962). The relationship of anxiety, self-concept, and sociometric status among 4th, 5th, and 6th grade children. **Journal of Abnormal and Social Psychology, 65,** 212-214.

Johnson, D. W. (1970). **Social psychology of education.** Edina, MN: Interaction Book Co.

Johnson, D. W. (1971). Role reversal: A summary and review of the research, **International Journal of Group Tensions, 1**, 318-334.

Johnson, D. W. (1974). Communication and the inducement of cooperative behavior in conflicts. **Speech Monographs, 41**, 64-78.

Johnson, D. W. (1975a). Affective perspective-taking and cooperative predisposition. **Develpmental Psychology, 11**, 869-870.

Johnson, D. W. (1975b). Cooperativeness and social perspective taking. **Journal of Personality and Social Psychology, 31**, 241-244.

Johnson, D. W. (1979). **Educational psychology**. Englewood Cliffs, NJ: Prentice-Hall.

Johnson, D. W. (1980a). Constructive peer relationships, social development, and cooperative learning experiences: Implications for the prevention of drug abuse. **Journal of Drug Education, 10**, 7-24.

Johnson, D. W. (1980b). Group processes: Influences of student-student interactions on school outcomes. In J. McMillan (Ed.), **Social psychology of school learning**. New York: Academic Press.

Johnson, D. W. (1981). Student-student interaction: The neglected variable in education. **Educational Researcher, 10**, 5-10.

Johnson, D. W. (1990). **Reaching out: Interpersonal effectiveness and self-actualization** (4th ed). Englewood Cliffs, NJ: Prentice-Hall, Inc.

Johnson, D. W. (1991). **Human relations and your career: A guide to interpersonal skills** (3rd ed.) Englewood Cliffs, NJ: Prentice-Hall.

Johnson, D. W., & Ahlgren, A. (1976). Relationship between students' attitudes about cooperative learning and competition and attitudes toward schooling. **Journal of Educational Psychology, 68**, 29-102.

Johnson, D. W., & Johnson, F. (1991). **Joining together: Group theory and group skills** (4th ed.). Englewood Cliff, NJ: Prentice-Hall, Inc.

Johnson, D. W., & Johnson, R. (1974). Instructional goal structure: Cooperative, competitive, or individualistic. **Review of Educational Research, 44**, 213-240.

Johnson, D. W., & Johnson, R. (Eds.) (1978). Social interdependence within instruction. **Journal of Research and Development in Education, 12**(1).

Johnson, D. W., & Johnson, R. (1978). Cooperative, competitive, and individualistic learning. **Journal of Research and Development in Education, 12**, 3-15.

Johnson, D. W., & Johnson, R. (1979). Conflict in the classroom: Controversy and learning. **Review of Educational Research, 49**, 51-70.

Johnson, D. W., & Johnson, R. (1980). Integrating handicapped students into the mainstream. **Exceptional Children, 46**, 89- 98.

Johnson, D. W., & Johnson, R. (1982). Healthy peer relationships: A necessity not a luxury. In P. Roy (Ed.), **Structuring cooperative learning: The 1982 handbook**. Edina, MN: Interaction Book Company.

Johnson, D. W., & Johnson, R. (1983). The socialization and achievement crisis: Are cooperative learning experiences the solution? In L. Bickman (Ed.), **Applied social psychology annual 4**. Beverly Hills, CA: Sage Publishing.

Johnson, D. W., & Johnson, R. (Eds.) (1984). **Structuring cooperative learning: The 1984 handbook of lesson plans for teachers**. Edina, MN: Interaction Book Company.

Johnson, D. W., & Johnson, R. (1985a). Mainstreaming hearing-impaired students: The effect of effort and interpersonal attraction. **Journal of Psychology, 119**, 31-44.

Johnson, D. W., & Johnson, R. (1985b). The internal dynamics of cooperative learning groups. In R. Slavin, S. Sharan, S. Kagan, R. Hertz-Lazarowitz, C. Webb, & R. Schmuck (Eds.). **Learning to cooperate, cooperating to learn.** New York: Plenum Press.

Johnson, D. W., & Johnson, R. (1986). Impact of classroom organization and instructional methods on the effectiveness of mainstreaming. In C. Meisel (Ed.), **Mainstreaming handicapped children.** Hillsdale, NJ: Lawrence Erlbaum.

Johnson, D. W., & Johnson, R. (1987a/1991). **Learning together and alone: Cooperative, competitive, and individualistic learning** (3rd ed.). Englewood Cliffs, NJ: Prentice-Hall.

Johnson, D. W., & Johnson, R. (1987b). **Creative conflict**. Edina, MN: Interaction Book.

Johnson, D. W., & Johnson, R. (1987c). Research shows the benefits of adult cooperation. **Educational Leadership, 45**(3), 27-30.

Johnson, D. W., & Johnson, R. (1988). Critical thinking through structured controversy. **Educational Leadership**, May, 58-64.

Johnson, D. W., & Johnson, R. (1989a). **Cooperation and competition: Theory and research**. Edina, MN: Interaction Book Company.

Johnson, D. W., & Johnson, R. (1989b). **Leading the cooperative school**. Edina, MN: Interaction Book Company.

Johnson, D. W., & Johnson, R., & Anderson, D. (1978). Relationship between student cooperative, competitive, and individualistic attitudes toward schooling. **Journal of Psychology, 100**, 183-199.

Johnson, D. W., Johnson, R., & Holubec, E. (1987). **Structuring cooperative learning: The 1987 handbook of lessons plans for teachers**. Edina, MN: Interaction Book Company.

Johnson, D. W., Johnson, R., & Holubec, E. (1988). **Advanced cooperative learning.** Edina, MN: Interaction Book Company.

Johnson, D. W., Johnson, R., & Holubec, E. (1990). **Circles of learning: Cooperation in the classroom** (Revised edition). Edina, MN: Interaction Book Company.

Johnson, D. W., Johnson, R., & Maruyama, G. (1983). Interdependence and interpersonal attraction among heterogeneous individuals: A theoretical formulation and a meta-analysis of the research. **Review of Educational Research, 53**, 5-54.

Johnson, D. W., Johnson, R., & Smith, K. (1986). Academic conflict among students: Controversy and learning. In R. Feldman, (Ed.). **Social psychological applications to education**. Cambridge University Press.

Johnson, D. W., & Matross, R. (1977). The interpersonal influence of the psychotherapist. In A. Gurman and A. Razin (Eds.), **The effective therapist: A handbook**. Elmsford, NY: Pergamon Press.

Johnson, D. W., Maruyama, G., Johnson, R., Nelson, D., & Skon, L. (1981). Effects of cooperative, competitive, and individualistic goal structures on achievement: A meta-analysis. **Psychological Bulletin, 89**, 47-62.

Johnson, D. W., & Norem-Hebeisen, A. (1977). Attitudes toward interdependence among persons and psychological health. **Psychological Reports, 40**, 834-850.

Johnson, R., & Johnson, D. W. (1985). **Warm-ups, grouping strategies, and group activities**. Edina, MN: Interaction Book Company.

Kagan, S. (1988). **Cooperative learning**. San Juan Capistrano, CA: Resources for Teachers.

Kohn, A. (1986). **No contest**. Boston: Houghton Mifflin.

Laughlin, P., & McGlynn, R. (1967). Cooperative versus competitive concept as attainment as a function of sex and stimulus display. **Journal of Personality and Social Psychology, 7**, 398-402.

Lawrence, G. (1974). **Patterns of effective inservice education: A state of the art summary of research on materials and procedures for changing teacher behaviors in inservice education**. Tallahassee: Florida State Department of Education.

Lippitt, R., & Gold, M. (1959). Classroom social structure as a mental health problem. **Journal of Social Issues, 15**, 40-58.

Little, J. (1981). **School success and staff development in urban desegregated schools**. Paper presented at the American Educational Research Association Convention, Los Angeles, CA: April, 1981.

Lorber, N. (1966). Inadequate social acceptance and disruptive classroom behavior. **Journal of Educational Research, 59**, 350-362.

Male, M., Johnson, R., Johnson, D., & Anderson, M. (1988). **Cooperative learning and computers: An activity guide for teachers**. Santa Cruz, CA: Ed. Apple-cations.

Mayer, A. (1903). Uber einzel-und gesamtleistung des schulkindes. **Archiv fur die Gesamte Psychologie, 1**, 276-416.

McLaughin, M., & Marsh, D. (1978). Staff development and school change. **Teachers College Record, 80**, 69-94.

McKeachie, W., Pintrich, P., Lin, Y., & Smith, D. (1986). **Teaching and learning in the college classroom.** Ann Arbor, MI: University of Michigan.

Mensh, I., & Glidewell, J. (1958). Children's perceptions of relationships among their family and friends. **Journal of Experimental Education, 27**, 23-39.

Montagu, A. (1965). **The human revolution**. New York: World Publishing Company.

Napier, R., & Gerschenfeld, M. (1981). **Groups: Theory and experience**. Boston: Houghton-Mifflin.

Orlick, T. (1982). **Cooperative sports and games book**. New York: Pantheon.

Pepitone, E. (1980). **Children in cooperation and competition**. Lexington, MA: Lexington Books.

Rhoades, J., & McCabe, M. (1985). **Simple cooperation**. Willits, CA: ITA.

Sarason, I., & Potter, E. (1983). **Self-monitoring, cognitive processes, and performance.** Seattle: University of Washington, mimeographed report.

Schmuck, R. (1963). Some relationships of peer liking patterns in the classroom to pupil attitudes and achievement. **School Review, 71**, 337-359.

Schmuck, R. (1966). Some aspects of classroom social climate. **Psychology in the School, 3**, 59-65.

Schmuck, R., & Schmuck, P. (1983). **Group processes in the classroom**. Dubuque, Iowa: Wm. C. Brown.

Schniedewind, N., & Davidson, E. (1987). **Cooperative learning, cooperative lives**. Dubuque, Iowa: Wm. C. Brown.

Sharan, S. (1980). Cooperative learning in small groups. **Review of Educational Research, 50**, 241-271.

Sharan, S., & Sharan, Y. (1976). **Small-group teaching**. Englewood Cliffs, N.J.: Educational Technology Publications.

Slavin, R. (1983). **Cooperative learning**. New York: Longman.

Slavin, R. (1986). **Using student team learning**. Baltimore, MD: Center for Research on Elementary & Middle Schools, Johns Hopkins University.

Slavin, R., Sharan, S., Kagan, S., Lazarowitz, R., Webb, C., & Schmuck, R. (Eds.). (1985). **Learning to cooperate, cooperating to learn**. New York: Plenum.

Tjosvold, D. (1986). **Working together to get things done.** Lexington, MA: D. C. Heath.

Tjosvold, D., & Johnson, D. W. (1983). **Productive conflict management**. New York: Irvington.

Triplett, N. (1897). The dynamogenic factors in pacemaking and competition. **American Journal of Psychology, 9**, 507-533.

Turk, S., & Sarason, I. (1983). **Test anxiety and causal attributions.** Seattle: University of Washington, unpublished report.

Van Egmond, E. (1960). **Social interrelationship skills and effective utilization of intelligence in the classroom**. Doctoral dissertation, University of Minnesota.

Wheeler, R., & Ryan, R. (1973). Effects of cooperative and competitive classroom environments on the attitudes and achievement of elementary school students engaged in social studies inquiry activities. **Journal of Educational Psychology, 65**, 402-407.

Winget, P. (Ed.). (1987). **Integrating the core curriculum through cooperative learning: Lesson plans for teachers**. Sacramento, CA: California State Department of Education.